The Tarskian Turn

The Tarskian Turn

Deflationism and Axiomatic Truth

Leon Horsten

The MIT Press
Cambridge, Massachusetts
London, England

© 2011 Massachusetts Institute of Technology

All rights reserved. No part of this book may be reproduced in any form by any electronic or mechanical means (including photocopying, recording, or information storage and retrieval) without permission in writing from the publisher.

For information about special quantity discounts, please email special_sales@mitpress.mit.edu

This book was set in Syntax and Times Roman by Westchester Book Group. Printed and bound in the United States of America.

Library of Congress Cataloging-in-Publication Data

Horsten, Leon.
The Tarskian turn : deflationism and axiomatic truth / Leon Horsten.
  p. cm
Includes bibliographical references and index.
ISBN 978-0-262-01586-8 (hardcover : alk. paper)
1. Truth—Deflationary theory.   I. Title.
BD171.H65   2011
121—dc22

                                          2010049672

10 9 8 7 6 5 4 3 2 1

To Steding

Contents

Preface   xi

1   **About This Book**   1
    1.1   What Is It About?   1
    1.2   What Is It Not About?   5
    1.3   For Whom Is It Intended?   6
    1.4   How Is It Structured?   7
    1.5   Note on Technicality and Notation   8

2   **Axiomatic Theories of Truth**   11
    2.1   Pilate's Question   11
    2.2   Essence and Function   14
    2.3   Tarski's Distress   19
    2.4   The Framework   22
    2.5   Soundness and Strength   24

3   **On the Shoulders of Giants**   27
    3.1   Introduction   27
    3.2   Coding in the Language of Peano Arithmetic   28
    3.3   The Diagonal Lemma   29
    3.4   Metatheorems   31
        3.4.1   The First Incompleteness Theorem   31
        3.4.2   The Second Incompleteness Theorem   32
        3.4.3   The Completeness Theorem   34
        3.4.4   The Undefinability Theorem   35
    3.5   More Strengthenings   36
        3.5.1   The Extended Diagonal Lemma   36
        3.5.2   The Naive Theory of Truth   37
        3.5.3   The Paradox of the Knower   39
    3.6   Bounded Truth Predicates   41
        3.6.1   Complexity Classes of Arithmetical Formulae   41
        3.6.2   True Equations   42
        3.6.3   Defining Bounded Truth Predicates   43
    3.7   Simplify, Simplify   44

4 The Disquotational Theory   47
- 4.1 Tarski on Defining Truth   47
- 4.2 The Disquotational Theory of Truth   49
- 4.3 The Soundness of the Disquotational Theory   51
- 4.4 Climbing Tarski's Ladder   53
- 4.5 The Uniformity of the Concept of Truth   55
- 4.6 Contextual Theories of Truth   56

5 Deflationism   59
- 5.1 The Unbearable Lightness of Truth   59
- 5.2 Commitments of Deflationist Theories   60
  - 5.2.1 The Meaning of the Concept of Truth   61
  - 5.2.2 The Function of the Concept of Truth   63
  - 5.2.3 Truth as a Logico-Linguistic Notion   65
- 5.3 Foreign Tongues   66

6 The Compositional Theory   69
- 6.1 Clouds on the Horizon   69
- 6.2 The Compositional Theory of Truth   71
- 6.3 Truth and Satisfaction   73
- 6.4 The Power of Truth   74

7 Conservativeness and Deflationism   79
- 7.1 Defining Conservativeness   79
- 7.2 Conservative Over What?   81
  - 7.2.1 Conservativeness Over Logic   81
  - 7.2.2 Conservativeness Over Arithmetic   82
  - 7.2.3 Conservativeness Over Empirical Science and Metaphysics   85
- 7.3 Truth and Epistemology   86
- 7.4 Truth and Meaning   91
- 7.5 Deflating Arithmetical Nonconservativeness   92
- 7.6 Substantiality and Irreducibility   94
  - 7.6.1 Reducibility and Interpretability   94
  - 7.6.2 A Conservative but Noninterpretable Truth Theory   95
  - 7.6.3 Disquotationalism Revisited   97
- 7.7 A Serious Game   99

8 Maximizing Classical Compositionality   103
- 8.1 Typed and Untyped Theories   103
- 8.2 The Friedman–Sheard Theory   104
- 8.3 The Revision Theory of Truth   105
- 8.4 Probing the Friedman–Sheard Theory   107
- 8.5 Is the Friedman–Sheard Theory Sound?   111
- 8.6 A Somewhat Frivolous Game   113
  - 8.6.1 Subsystems of Second-Order Arithmetic   113
  - 8.6.2 The Strength of *FS*   114
  - 8.6.3 The Weakness of *FS*   115

9 Kripke's Theory Axiomatized 117
- 9.1 Kripke's Semantical Theory of Truth 117
  - 9.1.1 Constructing Models for Self-Referential Truth 117
  - 9.1.2 Properties and Variations 120
- 9.2 Kripke–Feferman 124
- 9.3 The Inner Logic of *KF* 126
- 9.4 A Conservative Type-Free Theory 130
- 9.5 Partial Kripke–Feferman 132
  - 9.5.1 Restricted Conditionalization 132
  - 9.5.2 Partial Arithmetic and Determinate Truths 133
  - 9.5.3 The Truth Rules 134
- 9.6 Analysis and Evaluation 135
  - 9.6.1 Naturalness 135
  - 9.6.2 Methodology 136
  - 9.6.3 Soundness 137
  - 9.6.4 Strength 138

10 Truth and Philosophy 141
- 10.1 Strong Theories of Truth 141
- 10.2 Inferential Deflationism 143
  - 10.2.1 Truth and Logical Notions 143
  - 10.2.2 Silence 144
  - 10.2.3 A Concept Without an Essence 146
- 10.3 How Truth Rules Are Used 148
  - 10.3.1 Truth in the Foundations of Mathematics 148
  - 10.3.2 Truth in Philosophy 150
- 10.4 A Last Look at Deflationism 150

Bibliography 153
Glossary 159
Author Index 161
Subject Index 163

Preface

Deflationism is a doctrine about the role of the concept of truth in philosophy as a whole. This makes the doctrine relevant to analytic philosophers from all subdisciplines of philosophy.

Deflationism about truth comes in many varieties. These are usually articulated against the background of formal, axiomatic theories of truth. Yet in the philosophical literature, these background theories are often not made completely explicit. This is unfortunate because many philosophical debates concerning deflationism are intimately related to formal aspects of these axiomatic truth theories.

Axiomatic truth theories also come in a wide variety. They have been thoroughly analyzed over the years in a particular branch of mathematical logic called proof theory. But the logical literature on axiomatic theories of truth is rather specialized. It leads a scattered existence in the logical and philosophical journals. Yet the essential results of the analysis of axiomatic truth theories can be explained in elementary terms and thus made accessible to the average analytical philosopher. To do this is one of the aims of the present monograph.

It should then be left to philosophers to determine, on philosophical grounds, which of the axiomatic theories of truth are the more attractive ones, and whether they can be interpreted in a deflationist way. Eventually, this should enable philosophers of all subdisciplines of philosophy to determine which role the concept of truth plays in their field. With this book, I hope to make a small contribution to that enterprise.

In sum, this book tries to bridge the gap between the philosophical and logical literature about the concept of truth. It is about getting philosophers and logicians who are interested in the concept of truth to talk to instead of past each other. Some sections in this book are based on material that I have published as articles, with or without co-authors. In particular, section 7.3 is based on [Horsten 2010], section 9.5 is based on [Halbach & Horsten 2006], and section 10.2 is based on [Horsten 2009].

I wish to express my gratitude to many of my colleagues and students. In writing this book, I have drawn extensively from work that Volker Halbach and I have carried out in recent years, and from my recollections of discussions that we have had about this book's subject matter. I owe Volker an enormous debt: It was an honor and a privilege to collaborate with him on axiomatic theories of truth and deflationism. Nevertheless, I assume full responsibility for the material in this book. In particular, I do not claim that Volker agrees with the position of inferential deflationism that I elaborate on and defend toward the end of this book. The other members of the Luxemburger Zirkel, Hannes Leitgeb and Philip Welch, have concentrated more on semantical theories of truth. I am much indebted to them, too, for many discussions on aspects of truth and deflationism, and for providing such a wonderful environment for thinking about truth. In addition, I am grateful to Jeff Ketland, Michael Sheard, Igor Douven, Martin Fischer, and Karl-Georg Niebergall for stimulating discussions on this book's subject matter. Henri Galinon, Jon Sneyers, Rafal Urbaniak, Lieven Decock, Øystein Linnebo, and Anthony Everett carefully read through earlier versions of the manuscript. Thanks also to anonymous referees for providing useful comments and suggestions, and to Philip Laughlin and Marc Lowenthal of MIT Press for their efficiency and encouragement.

To conclude, I am much indebted to my students in Leuven and in Bristol, to whom I have had the privilege to teach on the subjects covered in this book.

Bristol, February 2011

1 About This Book

1.1 What Is It About?

Horwich's book *Truth* first appeared in 1990. It established deflationism about truth as a central subject of philosophical investigation. In the first decade after the appearance of this book, deflationism was mostly associated with an axiomatic theory of truth that is known as the disquotational theory. This theory has its origins in Tarski's work: It is the earliest axiomatic theory of truth that meets minimal adequacy conditions.

In recent years, the attention of philosophers is gradually shifting to stronger axiomatic theories of truth. There is a growing consensus that truth theories stronger than the disquotational theory are needed for the uses to which the concept of truth is put in ordinary language, philosophy, and science.

A debate about the question of whether these stronger axiomatic theories are compatible with the main tenets of deflationism is currently in its formative stages. So far this discussion has been rather murky. There are several reasons for this. First, there is disagreement about what deflationism about truth is committed to. Second, it is less than clear which axiomatic theories of truth are philosophically attractive for the deflationist and which are not. Third, there is no unanimity about how strong truth theories need to be for performing the functions that the concept of truth needs to fulfill. This book aims to clarify these issues, and thereby to contribute to the question of whether the theories of truth that we need can be interpreted in a deflationary manner. A new philosophical theory of truth that provides a deflationary interpretation of our best axiomatic theory of truth is proposed and defended against possible objections.

My objective is to present the central concerns, questions, theories, and arguments perspicuously and concisely, and not to get carried too far into argumentative exchanges that somehow involve intangibles.

Here are some of the questions that are given only scant attention in this book:

1. Is truth a property?

2. Of what is truth a property: sentences, theories, utterances, assertions, judgements, propositions, etc.?

My answers are "yes," and "sentences," respectively. There is an extensive body of literature devoted to these questions. Some of the classical articles on these matters are reprinted in (Blackburn & Simmons 1999, Part III). A cursory reading of this literature reveals that my answers to the two questions agree with many contemporary philosophers' answers to these questions.

On the first question, I have little to say. It lives in a sphere where the air is almost too thin to breathe. My reason for taking truth to be a property is simple. The truth predicate has an extension—the collection of all true sentences—and this collection does not, unlike the "extension" of the expression "exists," consist of everything or even of all sentences. This does not entail that the property of truth is metaphysically deep or that there is a nature of truth to be discovered in reality. Truth may be a metaphysically uninteresting property; it is a property nonetheless.[1] Note that this reason for taking truth to be a property can be adapted to a view that takes propositions or utterances to be the truth-bearers.

On the second question, I have two remarks to offer. First, under certain conditions, one might be prepared to compromise for all that is said in this book. For instance, one *might* be willing to take truth to be a property of propositions, as long as propositions are structured in the way that sentences are. However, every such proposal must be carefully evaluated because it may introduce problems of its own. Some argue, for instance, that because the notion of proposition presupposes the notion of truth, it should not be used to explicate the notion of truth—on pain of circularity.

Second, it must be admitted that, strictly speaking, utterances are better candidates for being truth-bearers than sentences. This is because one sentence can be used to express a truth in one context and a falsehood in another. Take, for instance, the following short conversation between Bertie Wooster and Bingo Little [Wodehouse 1930, p. 15]:

Bingo: [...] if your aunt supposed I was a pal of yours, she would naturally sack me on the spot.

Bertie: Why?

Bingo: Why? Be reasonable, Bertie. If you were your aunt, and you knew the sort of chap you were, would you let a fellow you knew to be your best pal tutor your son?

---

[1]. Arguments against the thesis that truth is a property can be found in [Grover 2001].

A generous dose of pragmatic enrichment is needed to answer Bingo's retorical question truthfully. When uttered by Bingo when addressing Bertie, the answer is undoubtedly "no," as even Bertie is ready to admit. But when uttered by you, addressing your best friend, the answer may very well be "yes." Nonetheless, I take sentences to be the truth-bearers. Here is why. When abstraction is made of contextual reference-fixings, disambiguations, and so on, what are left are, for all intents and purposes, "eternal" sentences about the world. We are concerned with theories of truth for such sentences. If we want to extend such theories to theories of truth for utterances, more work has to be done. But even if truth must ultimately be seen as a property of utterances, it is reasonable to expect that in developing a theory of truth for eternal sentences, we are off to a good start.

This book is about the relation between formal theories of truth and deflationism about truth. Deflationism is a view that takes the notion of truth to be a light and insubstantial notion. This is a truly philosophical view that can be and has been made more precise in multiple ways. Crucial in making the deflationary intuition precise is the way in which this philosophical view is related to formal or logical aspects of the notion of truth.

In analogy with the division between the syntactic and semantic view in the philosophy of science, theories of truth and the paradoxes can be divided roughly into two classes. On the one hand, there are *semantical* theories of truth, which are primarily interested in describing one or more models for languages that contain a truth predicate. On the other hand, there are *axiomatic* (or syntactic) theories of truth, which are primarily interested in explicating basic logical principles governing the concept of truth. It is argued that if we want a theory of truth for a natural language such as English, we ultimately have to opt for an axiomatic theory of truth, although semantical theories of truth can be, and often are, of great heuristic value. For this reason, we are more concerned with axiomatic than with semantical theories of truth.

Because we prefer axiomatic truth theories over semantical ones, this book is about the relation between *axiomatic* truth theories and deflationism. Every deflationist theory presupposes at least a quasi-formal theory of truth. Not so long ago, virtually the only axiomatic theory of truth that was discussed consisted of a collection of sentences of the form

ϕ if and only if it is true that ϕ,

which are known as *Tarski-biconditionals*. Today, many discussions of deflationism still proceed against the background of this theory. But in recent decades, a number of other natural axiomatic theories of truth have come to the fore in the logical literature. Most of them are proof-theoretically stronger than (natural) consistent collections of Tarski-biconditionals: They prove more sentences. So a philosophical question arises: Which of these axiomatic theories should a deflationist about truth adopt?

Despite its importance, this question has not received the attention it deserves in the literature. We see that the plausibility of a deflationist theory of truth depends in part on the plausibility of the axiomatic theory of truth on which it is built. For one thing, it is argued that the attractiveness of Horwich's minimalist theory of truth is diminished by the fact that he takes the meaning of the concept of truth to be exhausted by the Tarski-biconditionals. If a plausible version of deflationism is to be found, it must be based on one of the best axiomatic theories of truth that are available today. These are deductively significantly stronger than the traditional axiomatic truth theories that consist solely of Tarski-biconditionals.

The question of whether our best axiomatic theories of truth are compatible with deflationism at all cannot be prejudged at the outset. Indeed, we see that the most influential versions of deflationism about truth do not harmonize with the best axiomatic theories of truth that are available today. Some authors infer from this that deflationism is simply misguided. But this is a rash conclusion. Instead, I argue that the insubstantiality of truth has been misunderstood in the literature. In the later chapters of this book, I develop and argue for a new kind of deflationism, which I call *inferential deflationism*. According to inferential deflationism, truth is a concept without a nature or an essence. This is betrayed by the fact that there are no unrestricted logical laws that govern the concept of truth. Inferential deflationism concerning the concept of truth is a philosophical position, so it cannot be literally entailed by any formal truth theory. Nonetheless, this form of deflationism is seen to flow naturally from some of our best contemporary axiomatic theories of truth.

One of the goals of this book is to provide lessons for philosophers interested in deflationism and for logicians interested in the concept of truth. Therefore, these writings are semi-philosophical and semi-technical nature. Technicality cannot be altogether avoided in the subject under investigation. One of the first lessons of proof theory is that the details of a formal system are important. Changing one apparently minute detail in a formal system can transform it from a weak theory to a strong theory, or vice versa. Therefore, the details of the truth theories behind deflationist positions should be made explicit. Philosophers have tended to neglect to do this. But if one wants to address the question of whether a given truth theory can be interpreted in a deflationary way, one needs to know whether it is weak or strong, and in which ways it is weak or strong. So the details of the system do matter!

About This Book

A certain degree of recognition of the importance of precision and detail in philosophical debates about truth has been forthcoming in recent years [Williamson 2006, p. 179]:

> One clear lesson [of technical work by philosophical and mathematical logicians] is that claims about truth need to be formulated with extreme precision, not out of pedantry but because in practice correct general claims about truth often turn out to differ so subtly from provably incorrect claims that arguing in impressionistic terms is a hopelessly unreliable method.

Williamson is surely right about this. But when the logicians have done their business, it is the philosopher's job to interpret the formal truth-theoretical results that have been reached. This book intends to help bridge the gap between the logical and philosophical literature on truth. The goal is to make the essentials of existing logical knowledge about axiomatic theories of truth as accessible as possible to philosophers, and to explicate how they are related to the philosophical discussion about deflationism.

1.2 What Is It Not About?

The present book is not intended as a comprehensive critical discussion of all contemporary varieties of deflationism of truth. There are simply too many such deflationist positions around to do them justice in the span of a monograph. The philosophical literature on deflationism about truth is too extensive to be comprehensively covered here. Also, relatively little is said about the relation between the theory of truth and the theory of meaning. This is a subject in its own right, and a vast one at that.

The liar paradox puts pressure on classical logic. Aside from logic, so little is needed to generate the liar paradox that one wonders whether the laws of classical logic are unrestrictedly valid after all. So it comes as no surprise that many theories of truth have been formulated in an environment of nonclassical logic.

Within such environments, a distinction between two classes of theories can be made. The first kind of nonclassicality stays close to classical logic. It shares with classical logic the assumption that there are no more than two mutually exclusive truth values: *true* and *false*. But contrary to classical logic, it maintains that some sentences fail to have a truth value. Perhaps the liar sentence is a good candidate for being a sentence without a truth value. The logical calculus of sentences that do have truth values are just like classical logic. But the classical setting has to be extended to accommodate sentences that lack a truth value. The second kind of nonclassicality denies that there are only two truth values and/or denies that truth values are mutually exclusive. Thus, some multivalued logics will claim that some sentences are "half true," and dialetheist logicians will claim that some sentences are both true and false at the same time.

In this book, we hold onto classical logic as much as we possibly can. Bending but not breaking is our device. In response to the semantical paradoxes, we are willing to entertain—albeit grudgingly—the possibility that some sentences lack a truth value. But we are not concerned with theories which claim that sentences can have more than one truth value at the same time or a sentence can have an intermediate truth value. This means that theories of truth based on paraconsistent logic or fuzzy logic or combinations thereof will not be dealt with here.

As adumbrated earlier, we also are not concerned with semantical theories of truth. It is argued that semantical theories of truth can never pass the ultimate adequacy test. They can at best be of heuristic value: as stepping stones to an axiomatic theory of truth. For this reason, certain prominent semantical theories of truth are not treated in depth in this book. Kripke's semantical theory of truth is discussed because it has inspired promising axiomatic theories of truth. Indeed, the version of deflationism that is defended is inspired by an axiomatisation of Kripke's theory of truth. The revision theory of truth is also discussed in this book because it is closely connected to certain influential axiomatic truth theories.

1.3 For Whom Is It Intended?

The present book is intended for anyone interested in the debate about the relation between philosophical and formal theories of truth. It can be used as a textbook on this subject for senior undergraduate and beginning graduate students in philosophy. It is intended to be relevant for all students and teachers of analytic philosophy regardless of which area of philosophy carries their preference (epistemology, philosophy of language, moral philosophy, metaphysics, etc.).

No specific prior philosophical knowledge is presupposed. That being said, it is useful for the reader to have general background knowledge in analytic philosophy—but that almost goes without saying. In particular, it is useful, albeit not required, for the reader to be familiar with the distinction between substantial and deflationist views of truth. A decent introduction to this debate is [Kirkham 1995], and a good collection of articles about deflationism is [Armour-Garb & Beall 2005].

It is beneficial if the reader has taken an intermediate logic course. Too many philosophy students are required to go through introductory and intermediate courses of logic but graduate without being convinced that, in particular, the more advanced logic course was of essential importance in their philosophical education. One of the objectives of the present monograph is to show what intermediate and advanced logic courses in philosophy departments are really good for.

It would be helpful if the reader has gone through some standard detailed proof of Gödel's completeness and incompleteness theorems. In particular, knowledge of Gödel's proof of the first incompleteness theorem facilitates a deeper understanding of this book than can otherwise be obtained. Even though, historically, Tarski's ground-breaking work on truth was carried out independently from Gödel's work on the incompleteness theorems, Tarski's results are best explained as applications of Gödel's proof techniques. If the reader already possesses ample knowledge of the incompleteness and undefinability results, she can safely skip chapter 3. In chapter 3, the technical results used in the remainder of the book are stated and explained. But most of them are not proved in detail there. Good expositions of the proofs of the incompleteness and undefinability theorems can be found in [Goldstern & Judah 1998] and [Boolos & Jeffrey 1989].

Aside from this, some basic set theory is presupposed in the later chapters of this book. [Enderton 1977] is a good source for obtaining even more than the set theoretical background needed for reading them. Elementary knowledge of transfinite ordinals and cardinalities is especially helpful. In particular, on several occasions, use is made of *Cantor's theorem*, which states that no set, finite or infinite, stands in a one-to-one correspondence with its power set, which is the set of all its subsets.

1.4 How Is It Structured?

There is a pattern of alteration between logical and philosophical chapters. We start with a chapter on the *Dämmerung* of "substantial" theories of truth. This is followed by a technical chapter in which the background of Tarski's results on truth is reviewed. Subsequently, Tarski's disquotational theory is discussed. The deflationist view of truth, which is often closely associated with the disquotational theory, is then critically scrutinized. It is argued that, even according to deflationism, a truth theory that is stronger than the disquotational theory is needed. A first such theory is found in the compositional theory of truth, which also traces back to Tarski. It turns out that the compositional theory allows us to prove mathematical facts that go beyond what the background mathematical theory can prove on its own. In that sense, the compositional theory is said to be "non conservative." The question of whether this is compatible with the tenets of deflationism is probed. In this context, attention is also given to the wider question of what role the concept of truth can legitimately play in the empirical sciences and in subdisciplines of philosophy.

Then we resume our ascent on the ladder toward stronger truth theories. Above the compositional theory, the path forks. When we try to construct strong theories of truth that explain how the truth predicate behaves with respect to sentences that contain occurrences of the truth predicate, tough choices have to be made. Either we hold onto classical logic and try to construct a classical truth theory that is as strong as possible. This leads us to the Friedman–Sheard theory. Or we abandon classical logic in favor of truth value gaps and try to strengthen the truth theory along this path. This leads to the Kripke–Feferman theory and variants of it. Both of these classical and partial theories of truth are theories of *reflexive truth*: They allow us to prove truth-iterations ("It is true that it is true that so-and-so"). To conclude, a new version of deflationism, called *inferential deflationism*, is articulated. It is argued that this way of viewing the concept of truth is naturally suggested by the correct axiomatization of Kripke's theory of truth. In the final chapter, we also reflect on the minimal strength of truth theories that is needed to reconstruct philosophical arguments in which the concept of truth plays a role.

Not reading the chapters in the indicated order might prove awkward and difficult: Later chapters tend to presuppose and build on what is said in earlier ones. But there is a natural stopping point for the weary intellectual traveller. A reader who simply wants to acquire insight into the relation between most existing versions of deflationism and the axiomatic theories with which they ally themselves can stop after chapter 7, which deals with the subject of conservativeness. What comes afterward is a bit more advanced. However, it is my expectation that as the debate on deflationism moves forward over the coming years, the material in the later chapters will turn out to become more and more essential for understanding what is going on.

1.5 Note on Technicality and Notation

A sustained and determined attempt has been made to keep the technicality of this book down to the essential minimum. But I must admit that, in my opinion, the essential minimum contains a bit more than some of the experts on deflationism think it does.

In this book, I try to bridge the gap that divides philosophers and logicians who think about truth. This requires striking a happy balance between the need for logical precision, on the one hand, and the need not to go beyond the level of precision and technicality that is absolutely required for addressing the philosophical questions that lie at the heart of the investigation, on the other hand. I labor under no illusion that I have succeeded in this task to everyone's satisfaction. There are bound to be philosophers who will find many discussions in the book needlessly and distractingly technical, whereas many a logician will lament the sloppiness with which certain logical issues are treated—and in the back of their minds the question will form: "*Can* he work out the details?"

One of the things that impede communication between philosophers and philosophical logicians on the subject of truth is simply gödel coding. Doing the coding correctly is difficult. In addition to that, formulae involving gödel coding are hard to interpret: They do not wear their intended interpretation on their sleeves.

The course that is followed is the following. In chapter 3, in which the metamathematical background results are reviewed, we are careful to express all formulae correctly. But at the end of chapter 3, we drop gödel coding completely. This results in a whole array of ungrammatical formulae throughout the remainder of the book. But the ungrammatical formulae have clear advantages that more than compensate for their being ungrammatical. First, they *do* wear their intended interpretation on their sleeves—they are just not spelled correctly. Second, the logically educated reader can, if she so desires, correct any ungrammatical sentences so as to proudly produce a correct, virtually unreadable formula. If, as a philosophical logician, one tries to give a logical analysis of an axiomatic truth theory, one can hardly forsake the gödel coding. But if one looks as a philosopher at formal truth theories and their formal properties, the gödel coding is something one can do without.

Aside from some standard mathematical symbols, fairly widely used logical notation is used throughout this book. Standard symbols are used for the logical connectives: $\wedge$ (and), $\vee$ (or), $\neg$ (not), $\rightarrow$ (material implication), $\leftrightarrow$ (material equivalence), $\exists$ (existential quantifier), $\forall$ (universal quantifier), $\Box$ (necessity), $\Diamond$ (possibility), K (knowledge). The symbol $=:$ stands for equality by definition. Lowercase Greek letters are used for formulae and sentences, whereas capital Greek letters are used for sets of formulae and sentences. Capital roman letters (such as S, S') and abbreviations (such as DT for the *Disquotational Theory*) are used for theories (i.e., computably axiomatisable sets of sentences). $\vdash$ stands for the classical logical derivability relation; a subscript on the $\vdash$-relation (as in $\vdash_S$) indicates derivability in a particular theory. $\models$ stands for the classical semantic consequence relation; a subscript on the $\models$-relation (as in $\models_S$) indicates a nonclassical semantical modeling relation. $\mathbb{N}$ stands for the natural numbers structure. Calligraphic letters (such as $\mathcal{L}_{PA}$) (the language of Peano arithmetic) are used for formal languages; Gothic-type letters (such as $\mathfrak{M}$) are used for models. In the first chapters, where the gödel coding is still used, we use $\ulcorner \ldots \urcorner$ for referring to gödel codes, and we use overlining ($\overline{n}$) to refer to standard numerals. Additional specific details about notation are explained as we go along. After the bibliography, the reader finds a glossary of logical notation that is used throughout the book. The beginning of the subject index contains a list of abbreviations of formal theories, axioms, and rules.

The final sections of some of the chapters in this book are a bit more technical than the rest. A thorough understanding of them presupposes some familiarity with certain basic concepts of proof theory. More on the elements of proof theory that are needed for a thorough understanding of these sections is contained in [Franzen 2004]. The reader can, if she so chooses, skip these sections without missing too much.

I do not present the proofs of all the theorems that we encounter. Especially for the more difficult proofs, the reader is referred to the specialized literature.

2 Axiomatic Theories of Truth

In this chapter, contemporary theories of truth will first be distinguished from more traditional, substantial truth theories. Subsequently, a distinction is drawn, within contemporary theories, between semantic and axiomatic approaches. It will be argued that the axiomatic approach ought to be preferred over the semantic approach. Thus we will acquire a strong motivation for embarking on a search for adequate axiomatic theories of truth.

2.1 Pilate's Question

What is truth? (John 18:38)

The philosophical debate about truth was dominated until recently by deep and substantial theories of truth. No attempt is made here to do justice to the complexity of these theories. We content ourselves here with briefly rehearsing the central tenets of some of the most influential deep theories of truth. This provides the contrasting background against which deflationist views about truth are formulated.

The correspondence theory of truth   This is one of the oldest deep theories of truth. Some trace it all the way back to the work of Aristotle. However, Aristotle's remarks on the matter seem too cryptic to label him with much confidence as the first card-carrying correspondence theorist. The correspondence theory does find a fairly clear expression in the work of Thomas Aquinas, who writes [Aquinas 1981, I^a, Q.16]:

Further, Isaac says in his book *On Definitions* that truth is the equation of thought and thing. Now just as the intellect with regard to complex things can be equated to things, so also with regard to simple things; and this is true also of sense apprehending a thing as it is.

Modern correspondence theorists no longer take things to correspond to true propositions; they consider *facts* to be the *truthmakers* of propositions:[1]

A proposition is true if and only if it corresponds with a fact that makes it true.

The coherence theory of truth   The roots of the coherence theory of truth can be traced back to certain versions of German idealism. The coherence theory takes the primary truth-bearers to be theoretical wholes rather than propositions. Its central idea is:

A theory is true if and only if it is coherent.

A modern-day expression of the coherence theory of truth can be found in the works of Nicholas Rescher.[2]

Peirce's anti-realist theory   Peirce expresses his anti-realist view by equating truth with

"[t]he opinion which is fated to be ultimately agreed by all who investigate" [Peirce 1978, 5.407].

Thus, according to the pragmatic theory of truth, there is an intimate connection between truth and knowledge. In a nutshell:

A hypothesis is true if and only if it is known in the ideal limit.

The pragmatic theory   William James succinctly expresses the core of the pragmatic view [James 1907, p. 59]:

The essential thing is the process of being guided. Any idea that helps us to *deal*, whether practically or intellectually, with either the reality or its belongings, that doesn't entangle our progress in frustrations, that *fits*, in fact, and adapts our life to the reality's whole setting, will agree sufficiently to meet the requirement. It will hold true of that reality.

So according to the pragmatic theory of truth, there is an intimate connection between truth and usefulness. In a nutshell:

A theory is true if and only if it is practical.

There are prima facie objections to most of these theories. They may or may not in the end be decisive, but they are reasonable concerns.

---

1. For more about present-day truthmaker theories, see [Armstrong 2004] and [Beebee & Dodd 2005].
2. See [Rescher 1982].

The coherence theory of truth at first sight seems too liberal: It is hard to see why there can be only one systematic whole that is coherent. Indeed, it seems that there can be more than one such systematic wholes, which, while being internally coherent, contradict each other, and thus cannot all be true. Therefore, coherence appears to be a necessary condition for truth, but not a sufficient one.

Peirce's anti-realist theory of truth is a verificationist theory. Truth is judged to be an epistemic notion. But truth is not a wholly epistemic notion, it seems. Whether a judgment is true depends solely on the meaning of the words out of which the judgment is composed and the way things are. Especially this last factor is independent of the evidence that we may be able to obtain for or against the judgment.

The pragmatic theory of truth is unsatisfactory because usefulness is a *relative* notion. One theory can be useful for group A while being thoroughly impractical for group B. This would seem to make the theory both true and false, but no single theory can be both true and false. We can modify the view and say that truth as such does not exist; only truth for X exists. But prima facie this is implausible because in ordinary language we do not commonly use truth as a relativized notion.

The correspondence theory of truth is not so easy to take a pot shot at. What must be dismissed offhand are (what should surely be) caricatures of the correspondence theory. According to one caricature of the correspondence theory, truth is "out there in the world," "radically objective." The correspondence theory of truth is not committed to such statements. Truth surely is in part of our own making. Truth of a sentence depends in part on the meanings of its words, and meaning assignments are human acts.

The principal difficulty of the correspondence theory of truth is its vagueness. The correspondence theory of truth is too vague really to be called a theory until more information is given about what is meant by the term "correspondence" and by the term "fact." And it turns out to be a fiendishly difficult task to render the correspondence theory informative without burdening it with a heavy ontology by invoking "facts." In particular, while positive and perhaps even negative atomic facts may be unproblematic, it seems excessive to commit oneself to the existence of logically complex facts such as disjunctive facts, for example.

In fact, all substantial theories of truth suffer from a lack of formal precision. In the spirit of the can-do attitude that we have seen advocated by Williamson earlier on, it must surely be considered a worthwhile task for future philosophical work to articulate versions of existing substantial truth theories with the explicitness and precision that they deserve.

The cry for precision and exactness has until now largely fallen on deaf ears.[3] But philosophers have long been aware of the philosophical objections against the deep theories of truth that we have just considered. Defenses have been mounted against these charges, and these defenses have subsequently been critically examined. Thus, a lively debate concerning the nature of truth has been carried on for centuries, and a merry time was had by all.

2.2 Essence and Function

Although it has been around for ages, the *liar paradox* does not figure prominently in the debate between these theories. It was regarded as merely an intellectual puzzle, a brain twister that does not teach us anything substantial about the nature of truth. But as Quine once put it [Quine 1961, p. 18]:

Of all the ways of paradox, perhaps the quaintest is their capacity on occasion to turn out to be so very much less frivolous than they look.

However, it took a radical change to put the semantic paradoxes in center stage.

To understand this radical change, it is useful to move back in time to the seventeenth century and recall how Galilei and Newton transformed our thinking about the concept of force. On the nature of force, Galilei writes [Galilei 1638, p. 160]:

The present does not seem to be the proper time to investigate the cause of the acceleration of natural motion concerning which various opinions have been expressed by various philosophers, some explaining it by attraction to the center, others by repulsion between the very small parts of the body, while still others attribute it to a certain stress in the surrounding medium which closes in behind the falling body and drives it from one of its positions to another. Now, all these fantasies, and others too, ought to be examined; but it is not really worth while. At present it is the purpose of our Author merely to investigate and to demonstrate some of the properties of accelerated motion (whatever the cause of this acceleration may be).

And Newton agrees with him [Newton 1687, p. 546]:

Hitherto we have explained the phenomena of the heavens and of our sea by the power of gravity, but we have not yet assigned the cause of this power [...] But hitherto I have not been able to discover the cause of those properties of gravity from phenomena, and I frame no hypotheses; for whatever is not deduced from the phenomena is to be called an hypothesis; and hypotheses, whether metaphysical or physical, whether of occult qualities or mechanical, have no place in experimental philosophy. In this philosophy particular propositions are inferred from the phenomena, and afterwards

---

3. An attempt to formulate a precise version of Peirce's theory of truth is made in [Douven et al. 2010].

rendered general by induction. Thus it was that the impenetrability, the mobility and impulsive force of bodies, and the laws of motion and of gravitation, were discovered. And to us it is enough that gravity does really exist, and act according to the laws which we have explained, and abundantly serves to account for all the motions of the celestial bodies, and of our sea.

Now we move forward in history to the years 1934–1935 and redirect our attention to theories of truth. Heidegger gave his lecture Vom Wesen der Wahrheit, which was later published as [Heidegger 1943]. And Tarski published his article Der Wahrheitsbegriff in den formalisierten Sprachen [Tarski 1935].

Heidegger aimed to develop a radically new conception of truth. In particular, he argued that in the philosophical tradition, truth had not been investigated in its proper setting. He thought, for instance, that Thomas Aquinas made a monumental mistake when he took the investigation of the nature of truth to be part of metaphysics. Heidegger argued that the proper setting for the investigation of truth is the theory of Being [Heidegger 1943, p. 28]:

Das Wesen der Wahrheit is der Wahrheit des Wesens.[4]

Heidegger was right that the importance of the proper setting of the subject of truth can hardly be overemphasized, and the philosophical tradition has indeed made mistakes here. But his professed aim and his criticism on the traditional philosophical way of thinking about truth notwithstanding, Heidegger's lecture is very much a product of that philosophical tradition. After all, he inquires into the being of truth, which is not the same as but clearly related to the traditional question concerning the nature of truth. It is Tarski's theory that is fundamentally different from and incomparable with all that came before. This is not to say that Tarski's work came completely out of the blue. His work has clearly distinguishable antecedents, such as [Ramsey 1927]. But Tarski was the first person to generate a fully articulated *theory* of truth that is different from the theories that came before.

Tarski's article The concept of truth in formalized languages (1935) is a momentous achievement. In it we find the same kind of radical shift as we find in Galilei and Newton with respect to the concept of force. In a sense, Tarski's move can be seen as an emancipation of truth theory from traditional philosophy.

In the 1920s, truth was regarded in scientific circles as a suspect notion: It seemed to reek of a metaphysical past. Tarski was unimpressed by truth's bad reputation. But he no longer posed what one may call *Pilate's question*: "*What* is truth?" (or "What is the *essence* of truth?"). Instead, Tarski posed the

---

4. "The being of truth is the truth of being." [my translation]

questions: "How is truth used?", "How does truth function?", and "How can its functioning be described?" Pilate's question was mused over for centuries and centuries. One feels that in the process, only painfully slow progress was made. In the meantime, simple instances of the Tarskian question were not systematically answered by deep theories of truth. For instance, such theories do not unequivocally speak to the question: "If A is true and B is true, does it then follow that $A \wedge B$ is also true?" But in Tarski's work, real progress on such questions has been made (as we see later).

Does this amount to the Wittgensteinian dictum that "meaning is use" [Wittgeustein 1950]? No. If a slogan is called for at this place, it should read something like "meaning is theory."[5] A scientific theory is an extension of common sense. For a long time, philosophy was thought to be different from the sciences in this respect. But this is not so. Even the theory of truth is an extension of common sense. Tarski developed a *theory* of truth that describes the functioning of the concept of truth, which puts truth to use. Traditional theories of truth, by contrast, entail little about the use of the concept of truth, just as Aristotle's theory of motion does not make precise predictions about the velocity of falling bodies.

Tarski was not as self-conscious about the radical shift as Galilei was in his time.[6] At one point, Tarski claimed that his theory of truth is a variant of the correspondence theory [Tarski 1969]. Defenders of the correspondence theory tend to find Tarski's theory as it stands an insufficiently *substantial* account of correspondence. But there is no need to go into that debate at this moment: The radical shift is there regardless.

All this has not in the least deterred philosophers from continuing to develop and discuss the old truth theories (correspondence, pragmatic, Peircean, coherence, etc.) in the old philosophical style right up to the present, in the same way as scores of scholastic philosophers of nature continued for centuries after Galilei's death to develop variants of Aristotelian theories of force. But where are present-day *philosophical* theories of force to be found? The moral of the story is that if philosophers want the scientists to let them hang onto the notion of truth for a while, if they want their work to be relevant in the area of theories of truth, then they have to change their ways.

If it is hopeless to give a substantial definition of truth, then we must try to write down axioms that describe the functioning of the notion of truth as closely as possible—we must try to find the analogues for truth of Newton's laws of force.

---

5. The later Wittgenstein was notoriously skeptical about theories in philosophy.
6. In section 2.3 we see why.

The proper setting for a theory of force turned out to be mathematical analysis. In Frege's view, the proper setting for a theory of truth turns out to be formal logic [Frege 1918, p. 30]:

Wie das Wort "schön" der Ästhetik und "gut" de Ethik, so weist "wahr" der Logik die Richtung. Zwar haben alle Wissenschaften Wahrheit als Ziel; aber die Logik beschäftigt sich noch in ganz anderer Weise mit ihr. Sie verhält sich zur Wahrheit etwa so wie die Physik zur Schwäre oder zur Wärme. Wahrheiten zu entdecken ist die Aufgabe aller Wissenschaften: der Logik kommt es zu, die Gesetze des Wahrseins zu erkennen.[7]

The function of truth is to be found in our reasoning practices: It facilitates expressing thoughts and inferring conclusions. So we have a new proposal concerning the proper setting for the investigation of the notion of truth: logic. As always, the proof of the pudding is in the eating. Whether a given setting is appropriate for the investigation of truth is measured by its fruitfulness.

As we see later, Frege was not *quite* right.[8] The province of the investigation of the concept of truth lies on the crossroads between logic and linguistics. It seems that Frege did not clearly discern that the concept of truth is intimately related to the theory of syntax. He did not realize that a theory of truth requires a theory of syntax in the background.

There is no alternative to rolling up one's sleeves and getting down to business. The immediate and most natural suggestion for an axiomatic theory of truth consists in the following axiom schema:

Sentence "ϕ" is true if and only if ϕ.

The instances of this schema are called the (unrestricted) *Tarski-biconditionals*.[9]

This axiom scheme is motivated by what may be called the *disquotational intuition*, which can be described as follows. Suppose that you are willing to hypothetically assume or outright assert that ϕ. Then you had better also be willing to hypothetically assume or outright assert that ϕ is true. And, conversely, suppose that you are willing to hypothetically assume or outright assert that ϕ is true. Then you had better also be willing to hypothetically assume or outright assert that ϕ. Not to have these dispositions would be irrational.

At first blush, this intuition appears to justify only the rules of inference corresponding to the Tarksi-biconditionals, and not the Tarski-biconditionals

---

7. "Just as 'beautiful' points the ways for aesthetics and 'good' for ethics, so does the word like 'true' for logic. All sciences have truth as their goal; but logic is also concerned with it in a quite different way: logic has much the same relation to truth as physics has to weight or heat. To discover truths is the task of all sciences; it falls to logic to discover the laws of truth." [my translation]

8. Compare chapter 5, section 5.2.3.

9. This is not Tarski's own formulation. Tarski was using so-called structural-descriptive names of sentences instead of quotation marks. Compare infra, section 4.1.

themselves, which are axioms instead of inference rules. But the standard rejoinder to this objection is to refer to the *deduction theorem*, which says that a sentence ψ is derivable in classical predicate logic from a sentence ϕ if and only if the sentence $\phi \to \psi$ is a theorem of classical predicate logic. The deduction theorem entails that, at least within classical predicate logic, a rule of inference from ϕ to ψ is truth-preserving if and only if the axiom scheme $\phi \to \psi$ is provable. Thus, even if our intuition only directly supports a rule of inference, it seems that it indirectly also supports the Tarski-biconditionals. We shall see in chapter eight that if one works in a nonclassical logic, the deduction theorem may fail, in which case this line of reasoning does not go through without further ado.

Some contemporary philosophers deny that the Tarski-biconditionals bring out a fundamental property of the concept of truth. Patterson, for example, writes [Patterson 2002, p. 13]:

[…] for an inflationist, not only is there more to be said about truth, but *such biconditionals say nothing important about what truth is at all.*

Such philosophers do not think it to be an adequacy condition for good truth theories that they derive many Tarski-biconditionals. After all, what do the Tarski-biconditionals have to do with "the essence of the property of truth"? But if the ordinary use of the concept of truth is going to be our guidance for constructing a truth theory, then such views should be regarded as rearguard action. This is exactly what we will do.

At this point, the liar paradox steps forward and occupies its rightful place. Consider the liar sentence L, which says of itself that it is not true. The "naive" axiom scheme, which we have just proposed, tells us that L is true if and only if L. But L if and only if L is not true—for this is what L says of itself. So L is true if and only if L is not true: A short truth table calculation convinces us that we have lapsed into inconsistency.

The liar sentence refers to itself, and one might suspect that self-reference is ultimately incoherent. So it is not immediately clear how compelling this argument against the naive theory of truth really is. But Gödel has *shown* that self-reference is coherent. He articulated a mathematically precise way in which in a sufficiently expressive language sentences can talk about themselves (via coding). Tarski showed how in such a self-referential language, the argumentation of the liar paradox can be carried out—this is Tarski's *theorem* on the undefinability of truth.[10] So we *must* do better. It turns out that it is hard to

---

10. Compare infra, section 3.4.4.

do well. Formulating a satisfactory list of axioms for the notion of truth is a fiendishly difficult task.

God is in the details, they say, and the Devil is, too. We will see how through working out the details of a formal theory of truth the contours of philosophical conceptions of the notion of truth can emerge. And we will see that weaknesses of philosophical views of the notion of truth can be exposed by spelling out their core with formal precision. For several deflationist conceptions of truth, this is what has begun to happen in recent decades. One would expect of substantial theories of truth that they also work out the details of their own views in formal detail. Unfortunately, this has not happened until now.

In the nineteenth century, Newton's forces were put to work for us: The steam engine was invented. It is scarcely imaginable how the Industrial Revolution could have occurred in the Western world without being preceded by the Scientific Revolution of the early seventeenth century. Perhaps the concept of truth can in a somewhat analogous fashion be put to work for us. It will probably not be of much help in constructing a new type of bulldozer. But we shall see that, surprisingly, it gives us extra power in mathematics, the queen of sciences.

2.3 Tarski's Distress

I argue that truth is a logico-linguistic notion. Like all other logico-linguistic concepts, truth is most naturally investigated in formal settings, in the context of other logical notions. We see that the linguistic building blocks with which sentences, the bearers of truth, are constructed can be taken to be the natural numbers. Therefore, a logico-mathematical framework such as Peano arithmetic will turn out to be suitable for investigating truth. We attempt to analyze truth in this formal context, and the resulting definitions, axioms, and theorems should be regarded as logico-linguistic truths about truth.

Tarski rehabilitated truth as a respectable notion in his seminal article, The concept of truth in formalized languages [Tarski 1935]. In this article, he gave a *definition* of truth for a formal language in purely logical and mathematical terms. We have seen how substantial theories of truth likewise attempt to *define* truth. At the same time, I have claimed in the previous section that Tarski was the first one to ask a different question: *How does truth function?* Are these two enterprises then not in conflict with each other? Not really. Tarski never attempted to define truth for mathematical English as a whole. Instead, he defined truth for fragments of (mathematical) English that do not themselves contain the truth predicate. Most important, he imposed an adequacy condition on any definition of truth: A definition of truth for a fragment of English should imply all the sentences of the form

"It is true that ϕ if and only if ϕ"

for ϕ being any sentence of the fragment in question. This is a condition that concerns the use that is made of the truth predicate in English. Incidentally, it may have been his aim to define truth for fragments of English that obscured to Tarski the fact that his theory of truth was fundamentally different from the theories that came before.

It is well known that Tarski also invented the logical notion of a *model* for a formal language and explained what it means for a sentence of a formal language to be *true in a model*. Giving a model for a formal language can be seen as giving a *semantic* theory of truth for that formal language.

Some of the most popular contemporary semantic theories of truth and the semantic paradoxes are Kripke's theory of truth and the revision theory of truth ([Kripke 1975], [Gupta & Belnap 1993]). These theories describe or define a class of models for languages with a truth predicate. There is an important difference between contemporary semantic theories of truth and Tarski's semantic theory of truth. Contemporary semantic theories attempt to describe interesting models or classes of models for formal languages that contain a (unique) truth predicate, whereas Tarski was in the first place interested in constructing models for formal languages that do not themselves contain the truth predicate.

The most influential present-day philosophical theories of the role of truth are varieties of deflationism. Contemporary deflationists do not attempt to define truth. Most of them also do not rely on particular "interesting" or "intended" models for languages that contain a truth predicate. Instead, they can be seen as philosophical interpretations of *axiomatic theories of truth*. Axiomatic theories of truth are simply formal theories that contain basic laws of truth. One can of course try to construct interesting models, which make these basic truth laws true. But that is another, and for the deflationist secondary, matter.

Whence the preference of many contemporary deflationists for axiomatic theories of truth instead of definitions or models for truth?

First, in the next chapter we see how Tarski demonstrated that in general a sufficiently expressive formal language cannot contain its own definition of truth. Yet, ideally, we want a definition of truth for *our* language: English. But it appears that English is the most encompassing language that we have. So it is unclear, to say the least, in which language a definition of truth should be stated. If we go the definitional way, then we enter a regress. This does not exclude that a definition of truth for English as we now speak and write it can be given in some future extension of English. But that does not help us at present.

Second, there is a close connection between attempting to define truth for a language with a truth predicate and giving a semantic theory of truth for a language with a truth predicate. Semantic theories of truth describe a class of models for a language with a truth predicate, but they single out one or more individual models as somehow preferred. These models are presented as candidates for being the intended interpretation of a simplified version of English. These intended models can only be given in words. One can "give" a model only by describing it. This description can be seen as a definition of truth. We see in detail in the next chapter how Tarski has taught us that this description will on pain of contradiction have to be given in a more encompassing framework than the language for which the models are intended. So again the question arises as to how the semantics for this more encompassing language is to be expressed. In summary, if we go the model-theoretic way, then we enter a regress. This is regarded by some as a devastating objection to the model-theoretic approach to the concept of truth.

The problem is that philosophers have universalist ambitions for theories of truth. They are not satisfied with anything less than a truth theory for a language that includes the language in which the truth theory is expressed. The definitional and semantic approaches simply cannot satisfy this demand.

The axiomatic approach does not suffer from the regress problem: An axiomatic truth theory at least partially gives the meaning of the truth predicate of the language in which it is stated. This is why the axiomatic approach should be preferred. Yet semantic theories and definitions of truth have turned out to contain the great heuristic value. We see that some of the most interesting axiomatic theories of truth have been obtained as attempts to axiomatize (in the sense of "describe") semantic theories of truth.

Another problem for the model-theoretic approach has been stressed by McGee [McGee 1991, pp. 92, 105].[11] On the model-theoretic approach, we seek to construct a nice model for a formal language that includes the truth predicate. Such a nice model should emulate (in a simplified fashion) our informal interpretation of English. But the domain of discourse of English does not form a set for the simple reason that every set is included in it. Such is the lesson of Russell's paradox. But by the definition of the notion of a model, its domain must form a set. Many of the mathematical results concerning models crucially depend on their domain forming a set. So we are confronted with a sense in which models are radically unlike an interpreted informal language such as English. Some say that even in English we cannot quantify over everything. They say that we cannot help restricting our quantifiers to some set-sized domain. But it is not easy to make sense of this. If they are right, then when

---

11. This problem is also stressed in [Field 2008, chapter 27].

these philosophers say that we cannot quantify over everything, their universal quantifier does not range over everything but only over some set. But that means that these philosophers have not succeeded in expressing the position they wanted to express.

In combination, the previous considerations provide good reasons to at least give the axiomatic approach a try. Tarski was already clearly aware of the fact that the axiomatic way is one possible approach to theories of truth. However, it was a road that he did not think worth traveling. In particular, he suspected that any (consistent) collection of axioms of truth would have an "arbitrary and accidental" character [Tarski 1936, pp. 405–406]. I disagree with Tarski. I try to convince the reader that when an axiomatic theory is motivated by a particularly interesting model or class of models, Tarski's distress can be alleviated to a considerable extent.

2.4 The Framework

Gödel's first incompleteness theorem says that for every computably enumerable consistent extension T of Peano arithmetic, sentences can be found that are independent of T. This particular fact is not important for theories of truth; but the technique that Gödel developed for proving it is.

For concreteness, let us focus on Peano arithmetic. As is well known, the independent sentence that is produced by Gödel's technique "says" of itself that it is not provable in Peano arithmetic. This means that the language of Peano arithmetic must be able to do two things:

1. Express the notion of being a theorem of Peano arithmetic,
2. Refer to itself.

More generally, it can be shown that the language of Peano arithmetic can express the notion of being a theorem of any formal system. A formula ϕ is a theorem of a formal system T if there is a finite list of formulae that constitutes a proof of ϕ. Each formula in the list is either an axiom of T or is obtained from previous lines by rules of inference of T. All of this (finite list of sentences, being an axiom, being obtained from previous lines by a specific rule of inference) can be expressed in the language of Peano arithmetic. Thus, a notion of formal provability can be articulated in Peano arithmetic, which exactly mirrors our notion of provability in a system.

The notion of being a theorem in a formal system is a (sophisticated) "linguistic" notion, rather than a mathematical notion. So it is surprising that it can be expressed in the language of Peano arithmetic. After all, Peano arithmetic is a mathematical and not a linguistic theory; its language intends to talk about the natural numbers, not about sentences in formal languages.

The key, of course, is coding. The language of Peano arithmetic can code syntactic notions concerning formal languages in an elegant way. Peano arithmetic can also prove facts about these syntactic notions (relative to a coding scheme). After all, formulae of formal systems are just finite strings constructed from a finite alphabet. So in the final analysis, a syntactic theory concerning a language is just a bit of finite combinatorics. It is no real surprise that Peano arithmetic can do finite combinatorics!

It makes little difference, at least in extensional contexts, whether the truth bearers are propositions or sentences (or assertions). Even if the bearers of truth are taken to be propositions rather than sentences, propositions are structured rather in the way that sentences are. That means that the coding machinery of Peano arithmetic still applies, whereby Peano arithmetic is still the ideal setting for investigating truth.

So we assume that Peano arithmetic is in the background throughout this book. We are interested in it primarily as a theory of syntax. Here the connection with the concept of truth emerges. For truth is also a property of sentences: Some sentences are true, whereas others are false. Whether a sentence is a theorem is determined just by the existence of a linguistic object called a proof, which is a finite sequence of finite strings of symbols. Whether a sentence is true depends on its *interpretation*. In other words, in contrast to theoremhood, for instance, truth is a semantic notion. Nevertheless, every reasonable formal system should be sound: It should prove only truths. So clearly there is a deep connection.

In the investigation of the notion of truth, the liar paradox occupies a central role. But a key feature of the liar sentence is *self-reference*. This is another reason that Peano arithmetic is the ideal setting for studying truth: The language of Peano arithmetic allows us to construct sentences that (relative to a coding scheme) refer to themselves, and Peano arithmetic can reason about such sentences.

It is important to keep firmly in mind that for our purposes Peano arithmetic serves first and foremost as a way to talk and reason about syntax. We are not interested in the natural numbers *per se*. As our background theory, we also *could* have used a theory that *directly* describes the structure of expressions.[12] Our reasons for opting for Peano arithmetic instead are twofold. First, in the literature on theories of truth and the semantic paradox, it is standard practice to take Peano arithmetic as a background theory. One of the aims of this book

---

12. This idea was worked out in detail in [Quine 1946] and [Smullyan 1957].

is to function as an inroad to the logico-philosophical literature on truth. Second, theories about expressions simply are not as simple and elegant as Peano arithmetic. Perhaps this is in the end just a matter of familiarity. After all, we have all been exposed to arithmetic since we were slips of boys and girls. This can hardly be said for the theory of concatenation of finite strings of symbols.

The formal language in which the axiomatic theories of truth are formulated consists of the language of first-order arithmetic plus one (or several) truth predicate(s). But we are interested in *our* concept of truth. The natural habitat of our concept of truth is a *natural language* (English, say), not a formal language in which only arithmetical and truth facts can be expressed.

It is true that natural language is much more sophisticated and complicated than the toy language that we use here. But by using a toy language, we abstract away from all complications of natural language that are irrelevant for our purposes. It is *hoped* that the subtleties of the structure of natural language that are relevant for the investigation of truth are not artificially ignored by working in a restricted setting.

2.5 Soundness and Strength

Axiomatic theories of truth should be *sound*. They should prove only sentences that we instinctively and immediately accept or, after reflective consideration, can come to see to be correct.

Against the convictions of many dialetheist logicians, it is maintained that inconsistency is a sure sign of unsoundness. I am unwilling to admit that theories that prove sentences of the form $\phi \wedge \neg \phi$ can be sound. In particular, I do not have much sympathy with the view that the liar sentence and its negation are both true.[13] I am unable to imagine what it would be like for such a situation to be the case. Because epistemic impossibility is a fairly reliable (albeit not infallible) indicator of metaphysical impossibility, I regard it impossible for contradictions to be true.[14]

I may be wrong about all this, so I do not want to suggest that inconsistent theories of truth do not merit investigation. They do, and indeed they are intensively studied. So intensively, in fact, that the innocent bystander might walk off with the impression that there is little of interest to be said about consistent theories of truth. I want to counter this impression.

---

13. For an exchange of views about the viability of the view that the liar sentence is both true and false, see [Field 2005] and [Priest 2005].

14. If the reader wants a second opinion on these matters, [Priest & Beall 2004] contains a number of articles that are sympathetic to the possibility of true contradictions.

Inconsistent truth theories are usually presented in a semantic way.[15] Not much energy has hitherto been invested in fully *axiomatizing* inconsistent truth theories and analyzing the resulting formal systems. This constitutes a more practical reason for not discussing inconsistent truth theories in this book.

Being consistent is not enough. We also see that consistent truth theories, which at first sight look promising, can fail to meet the soundness requirement. In general, exactly when a truth theory crosses the border between soundness and unsoundness turns out to be a philosophically delicate and subtle question.

Throughout most of this monograph, it is maintained that classical logic is sound. But toward the end of the book, we also give serious consideration to axiomatic truth theories that are formulated in partial logic. I find it easier to imagine what it is like for a sentence to lack a truth value than to imagine what it is like for a sentence to be both true and false. So I am willing, albeit grudgingly, to entertain the possibility that certain sentences (such as the liar sentence) lack a truth value.

In this connection, it is worth remembering that, in sharp contradistinction with the thesis that some sentences are both truth and false, the thesis that certain sentences lack a truth value has independent support. According to influential theories of vagueness, certain sentences containing vague predicates lack a truth value.[16] According to influential semantic theories of presuppositions, sentences with unfulfilled presuppositions lack a truth value.[17] According to influential theories of conditionals sentences, indicative conditionals do not have truth conditions.[18]

Due to the incompleteness phenomenon, axiomatic truth theories can in some sense not reasonably be expected to be complete. There will always be true Gödel-like sentences that the theory cannot prove to be true.

But *modulo* gödelian incompleteness, we should have, until further notice, the highest expectations of our theories of truth. There seems at present to be no reason that we cannot ideally expect our theory to be *truth-theoretically complete* (i.e., to prove all basic laws of the concept of truth). At least truth theories should aspire to come as close to truth-theoretic completeness as possible.[19]

---

15. The *locus classicus* is [Priest 1987].
16. A seminal article in this area is [Fine 1975].
17. See for instance [Strawson 1950].
18. See [Bennett 2003].
19. I use the term "completeness" for theories of truth in a sense that is related to the use of this term in [Tarski 1935, p. 257] and [Ketland 1999, section 5]. Volker Halbach has rightly emphasized (in conversation) that it would be helpful if the notions of truth-theoretic completeness and basic truth law could be made more precise.

This is extremely important for the assessment of deflationism. If one adopts a theory of truth that is truth-theoretically incomplete and one shows how it can be given a deflationist interpretation meeting certain requirements, then one has not shown much. For there is then a possibility that more truth-theoretically complete systems cannot be given such a deflationist interpretation.

The axiomatic truth theories that one would naively construct are susceptible to the argument of the liar paradox. They are inconsistent and therefore clearly fail to meet the soundness requirement.

For this reason, we have to weaken our axioms. We see that Tarski's definitions suggest axioms for truth, which are not only consistent but appear to be clearly sound. Unfortunately, they turn out to be truth-theoretically incomplete. Hence, stronger axiomatic theories of truth have been developed. A history unfolds of trying to develop ever stronger axiomatic theories of truth without transgressing the boundaries of intuitive soundness for the intended interpretation.

We see later that, although arithmetical completeness is unattainable due to the incompleteness theorems, natural proof-theoretic measures of mathematical strength exist. Unfortunately, we have at present no natural proof-theoretic measures of truth-theoretic strength. We see that some truth theories are mathematically surprisingly strong. But mathematical strength of a truth theory need not be a reliable indicator for its truth-theoretic strength.[20]

It is at present in general easier to argue for truth-theoretic weakness of a theory than for truth-theoretic strength: one can point to principles of truth that intuitively should be provable but that the theory in question cannot prove. So our policy shall be to accord truth theories the benefit of doubt as long as it is possible. Until examples of intuitively acceptable truth principles have been unearthed, which a given truth theory cannot prove, it will be considered truth-theoretically strong.

In this book, I only discuss some of the main axiomatic theories of truth and their relation to deflationism. Indeed, I want to restrict myself to truth theories that have a distinct and direct philosophical relevance. Those who are interested in a more in-depth proof-theoretical investigation of axiomatic truth theories are referred to [Cantini 1996]. Those who want not only an in-depth logical investigation of a large collection of axiomatic truth theories but also an extensive discussion of their philosophical significance are referred to [Halbach 2010].

---

20. We return to this point in chapter eight.

3 On the Shoulders of Giants

Our first results concerning axiomatic truth theories are of a negative nature. Gödel proved that no sufficiently strong, consistent mathematical theory proves its own consistency. Using Gödel's techniques, Tarski's theorem can be proved. This theorem says that no sufficiently expressive language can define its own truth predicate. Tarski's theorem on the undefinability of truth in turn has negative consequences for axiomatic theories of truth. It implies that no consistent truth theory implies all the Tarski-biconditionals.

3.1 Introduction

Tarski's theorem on the undefinability of truth is the starting point of contemporary axiomatic theories of truth. Versions of Tarski's theorem are reviewed in this chapter. This leads us to the realization that "naive" attempts to construct an axiomatic theory of truth fail miserably. We also review other metatheorems that are put to use in the chapters to come: Gödel's two incompleteness theorems and Gödel's completeness theorem. In addition, it is indicated how in the language of Peano arithmetic truth definitions for arithmetical sentences of bounded complexity can be articulated.

I do not present all details of the proofs in this chapter. For the details, the reader is referred to the literature. A good source for many of these proofs is [Goldstern & Judah 1998, chapter 4].

There exist weaker and stronger versions of both Gödel's two incompleteness theorems and Tarski's undefinability theorem. Detailed proofs of the weaker versions of these metatheorems are really not hard to give. So it is misleading to speak of *the* incompleteness theorem and of *the* undefinability theorem: Several incompleteness and undefinability theorems can be distinguished. It is better to speak, in the spirit of Goldstern and Judah, of the incompleteness *phenomenon* and of the undefinability *phenomenon*.

Once one has gone through the proofs of the weaker versions of the metatheorems, it becomes plausible that the stronger versions also hold. But if one insists on the details of these stronger versions, then more (somewhat tedious) work needs to be done. Those who do want to walk the extra mile are referred to [Boolos & Jeffrey 1989, chapters 15 and 16].

3.2 Coding in the Language of Peano Arithmetic

For a while we are sticklers for notation. This is just to refresh the reader's mind about how it is done according to the rules of the art. Then from chapter 4 onward, in the interest of readability, we abandon all notational scruples and express ourselves in a carefree, non-well-formed manner. But by then it should be clear how our non-well-formed stammering can be transformed into coherent speech.

We first revisit the first-order *language* $\mathcal{L}_{PA}$ *of Peano arithmetic*.

The *logical vocabulary* of $\mathcal{L}_{PA}$ contains the propositional operators of conjunction ($\wedge$) and negation ($\neg$). Disjunction, material implication, and material equivalence are defined (in the metalanguage) in terms of $\neg$ and $\wedge$ in the usual manner. Furthermore, $\mathcal{L}_{PA}$ contains the universal quantifier $\forall$. The existential quantifier is again defined in terms of $\forall$ and $\neg$ in the usual manner. Furthermore, $\mathcal{L}_{PA}$ contains an infinite stock of variables x_i for $i \in \mathbb{N}$ and the identity relation $=$.

The *mathematical vocabulary* of $\mathcal{L}_{PA}$ consists of a successor function symbol s, a zero constant 0, and function symbols $+$ and $\times$ for addition and multiplication.

Using the successor function symbol and the zero constant, we can build *standard numerals* for natural numbers. For each number $n \in \mathbb{N}$, the standard numeral for n consists of the zero constant prefixed by n copies of the successor symbol. The standard numeral for n is denoted as $\overline{n}$.

Next, the elements of the vocabulary of $\mathcal{L}_{PA}$ are algorithmically assigned unique numerical codes (*gödel codes* or *gödel numbers*) according to some coding scheme. We need not go into the details of this coding scheme here, but, for definiteness, let us say that we adopt the coding scheme of [Goldstern and Judah 1998, p. 209]. Then, given some further conventions, this coding scheme can be extended to terms, formulae, sentences of $\mathcal{L}_{PA}$. If e is a simple or complex expression of $\mathcal{L}_{PA}$, then we denote its gödel number as $\ulcorner e \urcorner$.[1]

---

1. The idea of coding the structure of a language using natural numbers can be traced back to Leibniz. But Gödel was the first to work out accurately and in detail how this project should be executed.

In the language of Peano arithmetic, some standard axiomatization of classical first-order logic and the Peano axioms can be expressed. I take it that the reader is familiar with the principles of first-order logic.[2] The nonlogical axioms of Peano arithmetic are:

1. $\neg \exists x : s(x) = 0$
2. $\forall x \exists y : s(x) = y$
3. $\forall x \forall y : s(x) = s(y) \rightarrow x = y$
4. $\forall x : x + 0 = x$
5. $\forall x \forall y : s(x + y) = x + s(y)$
6. $\forall x : x \times 0 = 0$
7. $\forall x \forall y : x \times s(y) = (x \times y) + x$
8. $[\phi(0) \wedge \forall x (\phi(x) \rightarrow \phi(s(x)))] \rightarrow \forall x \phi(x)$ for all $\phi(x) \in \mathcal{L}_{PA}$

The last of these axioms is thus an *axiom scheme* (i.e., an infinite collection of axioms). This scheme is called the principle of *mathematical induction*. The closure of all these axioms under first-order logic is called *Peano arithmetic* (*PA*). Not to worry. We are not in the business of proving theorems *in PA* in this book!

It can be shown that relative to the coding conventions elementary syntactical categories and operations can be defined in $\mathcal{L}_{PA}$. There exists a formula *term*(x) of $\mathcal{L}_{PA}$, which is true of all and only the gödel numbers of terms of $\mathcal{L}_{PA}$. There exists a formula *formula*$_{PA}(x)$, which is true of all and only the gödel numbers of formulae of $\mathcal{L}_{PA}$. There exists a formula *negation*(x, y), which holds of a pair of gödel numbers e, f of formulae of $\mathcal{L}_{PA}$ if and only if e is the gödel number of the negation of the formula of which f is the gödel number. Similarly, the relation between a conjunction and its conjuncts, and so on, can be expressed in $\mathcal{L}_{PA}$. Finally, there exists a formula *Bew*$_{PA}(x)$, which is true of all and only the gödel numbers of theorems of Peano arithmetic.[3] *Bew*$_{PA}(x)$ is a long and complicated formula of the language of $\mathcal{L}_{PA}$. We are not concerned here with the way in which it is constructed.

3.3 The Diagonal Lemma

Consider the function d, which takes as input the code of a *formula* $\phi(x)$ of $\mathcal{L}_{PA}$ with one free variable x and returns as output the *sentence* of $\mathcal{L}_{PA}$, which is

---

2. An axiomatization of predicate logic can be found in [Goldstern & Judah 1998, chapter 1, section 1.4].

3. *Bew* stands for the German word *beweisbar* (provable).

the result of substituting for x the standard numeral for the gödel code of $\phi(x)$, that is, $\phi(\overline{\ulcorner \phi(x) \urcorner})$. This function is called the *diagonal function*. Again, there will be a formula $diag(x, y)$ of $\mathcal{L}_{PA}$, which expresses the relation between (the code of) a formula of $\mathcal{L}_{PA}$ and the (code of the) sentence, which results from applying the diagonal function to this formula.

The expressibility of the diagonal function is the key element in the *diagonal lemma*, from which the incompleteness and undefinability theorems flow [Goldstern & Judah 1998, pp. 219–220]:

Theorem 1 (Diagonal Lemma) *For each formula $\phi(x) \in \mathcal{L}_{PA}$, there is a sentence $\lambda \in \mathcal{L}_{PA}$ such that λ is true in the standard model of the natural numbers if and only if $\phi(\overline{\ulcorner \lambda \urcorner})$ is true.*

Proof *Consider the sentence*

$$\psi(x) =: formula_{PA}(x) \wedge \exists y (diag(x, y) \wedge \phi(y))$$

We have seen that for any formula ξ, $diag(\overline{\ulcorner \xi \urcorner}, y)$ is true just in case y is the code of the diagonalization of ξ. So for any formula ξ, $\psi(\overline{\ulcorner \xi \urcorner})$ is true just in case $\phi(\overline{\ulcorner d(\xi) \urcorner})$ is true. This holds in particular for $\xi =: \psi$, so we get:

$$\psi(\overline{\ulcorner \psi \urcorner}) \leftrightarrow \phi(\overline{\ulcorner d(\psi) \urcorner})$$

Then $\psi(\overline{\ulcorner \psi \urcorner})$, i.e., $d(\psi)$, is the sentence we are looking for. ∎

Although literally speaking it only speaks about the natural numbers, this sentence λ can be taken, relative to the coding conventions, to say of itself that it has the property ϕ.

To see that the diagonal lemma is true (in the standard model of the natural numbers), we did not need to prove anything in any formal system. But the diagonal lemma can be strengthened: The equivalence mentioned in the theorem can be proved in *PA*.

Theorem 2 (Strengthened Diagonal Lemma) *For each formula $\phi(x) \in \mathcal{L}_{PA}$, there is a sentence $\lambda \in \mathcal{L}_{PA}$ such that*

$$PA \vdash \lambda \leftrightarrow \phi(\overline{\ulcorner \lambda \urcorner}).$$

Already in the light of the (weak) diagonal lemma, one suspects that the strengthened diagonal lemma holds. But to *show* that it holds, one has to do some tedious spadework: One has to prove things in *PA*. I need scarcely mention that we have no intention of walking the extra mile in this book. But the reader interested in the details can find them in [Boolos & Jeffrey 1989, chapter 14].

3.4 Metatheorems

We now see how important metatheorems concerning provability, logical consequence, and truth follow from the diagonal lemma.

3.4.1 The First Incompleteness Theorem

In 1931, Gödel proved that there are arithmetical sentences that are neither provable nor refutable in Peano arithmetic. Such sentences are said to be *independent* from *PA*. This is the content of Gödel's famous *first incompleteness theorem*:

Theorem 3 *There is an arithmetical sentence that is independent of PA.*

Proof *We apply the diagonal lemma to the formula $\phi(x) =: \neg Bew_{PA}(x)$. This gives us a sentence σ, which is true if and only if σ is not a theorem of PA. Suppose, for a reductio, σ is not true. Then σ is a theorem of PA. But PA proves only true statements. So σ is true. Contradiction. So we reject the supposition and conclude categorically that σ is true. But then it is not a theorem of PA. So we have a true arithmetical sentence, which is not a theorem of PA. But if it is true, then its negation is not provable in PA. So σ is undecidable in PA.* ∎

The sentence σ in this proof is the famous *gödel sentence* for Peano arithmetic. It is not difficult to see that σ is in fact an arithmetical truth. For suppose, for a reductio ad absurdum, that $\neg\sigma$. Then, by the diagonal property, σ is provable in *PA*. But *PA* only proves true sentences. Therefore σ, which contradicts our hypothesis. So our hypothesis $\neg\sigma$ has to be rejected (i.e., σ is true).

In the proof of theorem 3, we used the fact that *PA* is *correct* or *sound* for its intended interpretation: It proves only true statements. So it would be slightly more accurate to say that we have proved:

Theorem 4 (First Incompleteness Theorem) *If PA is sound, then there is an arithmetical sentence that is independent of PA.*

If we make use of the strengthened diagonal lemma, we can prove an even stronger incompleteness theorem by weakening the assumption.[4] Let us say that for a theory S containing Peano arithmetic to be consistent means that S does not prove any absurdity, such as $0 = 1$. Then Gödel's first incompleteness theorem can be strengthened to:

---

4. Gödel originally proved an incompleteness theorem that is intermediate in strength between the two independence theorems that we discuss.

Theorem 5 *If PA is consistent, then there is a sentence that is independent of PA.*

Proof   See *[Boolos & Jeffrey 1989, chapter 15]*.   ∎

Saying that theorem 5 is *stronger* than theorem 4 entails that it is *conceivable* (albeit barely) that *PA* is consistent but unsound. In contrast, the soundness of *PA* immediately implies its consistency.

The incompleteness phenomenon reappears whenever we have a *sound* theory S extending *PA*, where a *theory* is a computably enumerable collection of sentences. The only difference in the proof is that we now have to consider the property of being unprovable in S instead of the property of being unprovable in *PA*. But it is clear that once we are able to express being a theorem of *PA* in $\mathcal{L}_{PA}$, we are also able to express being a theorem of S in $\mathcal{L}_{PA}$. So we have:

Theorem 6

1. For every arithmetically sound theory $S \supseteq PA$, there is a sentence that is independent of S.

2. For every consistent theory $S \supseteq PA$, there is a sentence that is independent of S.

This means that the incompleteness theorem is remarkably robust: There is no escaping the incompleteness phenomenon.

3.4.2 The Second Incompleteness Theorem

Gödel also proved a *second* incompleteness theorem:[5]

Theorem 7 (Second Incompleteness Theorem)   *For every consistent theory $S \supseteq PA$, S cannot prove its own consistency.*

Note that the consistency of S can be naturally articulated in the language of S, namely, as $\neg Bew_S(\ulcorner 0 = 1 \urcorner)$. Let us abbreviate $\neg Bew_S(\ulcorner 0 = 1 \urcorner)$ as $Con(S)$.[6]

The proof of this theorem is much like that of the first incompleteness theorem. One needs an application of the strengthened diagonal lemma. Moreover, one needs to show that certain properties of the proof predicate Bew_S can be proved inside S. Here, I merely outline the proof.[7]

---

5. To be precise, the following is a slightly strengthened version, due to Rosser, of the theorem that was proved by Gödel.

6. One has to be careful here. There exist "unnatural" ways of expressing consistency of S for which Gödel's second incompleteness theorem does not hold: see [Franzen 2004, chapter 12].

7. For more details, see [Boolos & Jeffrey 1989, chapter 16].

First, it must be shown that the proof predicate $Bew_{PA}(x)$ satisfies three derivability conditions:

1. $PA \vdash Bew_{PA}(\overline{\ulcorner \phi \to \psi \urcorner}) \to (Bew_{PA}(\overline{\ulcorner \phi \urcorner}) \to Bew_{PA}(\overline{\ulcorner \psi \urcorner}))$;
2. If $PA \vdash \phi$, then $PA \vdash Bew_{PA}(\overline{\ulcorner \phi \urcorner})$;
3. $PA \vdash Bew_{PA}(\overline{\ulcorner \phi \urcorner}) \to Bew_{PA}(\overline{\ulcorner Bew_{PA}(\overline{\ulcorner \phi \urcorner}) \urcorner})$.

It is not too difficult, but admittedly tedious, to show that $Bew_{PA}(x)$ satisfies these properties. As an example, I sketch how 1. is proved. We reason in PA. We assume that there is a PA-proof of $\phi \to \psi$ and a PA-proof of ϕ. These proofs are, as far as PA is concerned, finite sequences a and b of numbers, such that the code of $\phi \to \psi$ is an element of a and the code of ϕ is an element of b. It can be proved in PA that there must then exist the sequence that is the concatenation $a * b$ of a and b. Then, in PA, the even longer sequence $a * b * \langle \ulcorner \psi \urcorner \rangle$ is formed. It can easily be verified in PA that $a * b * \langle \ulcorner \psi \urcorner \rangle$ is the code of a PA-proof, the last element being obtained by modus ponens from an element of a and an element of b. Thus, PA can see that there is a code of a proof of ψ.

Using these derivability conditions, an application of the strengthened diagonal lemma shows that:

Lemma 8 *For every sentence ϕ, if $PA \vdash Bew_{PA}(\overline{\ulcorner \phi \urcorner}) \to \phi$, then $PA \vdash \phi$.*

Proof *Suppose $PA \vdash Bew_{PA}(\overline{\ulcorner \phi \urcorner}) \to \phi$. Consider the formula*

$Bew_{PA}(y) \to \phi$.

Apply the diagonal lemma to this formula in order to obtain a sentence λ such that

$PA \vdash \lambda \leftrightarrow (Bew_{PA}(\overline{\ulcorner \lambda \urcorner}) \to \phi)$.

By the second derivability condition, we obtain

$PA \vdash Bew_{PA}(\overline{\ulcorner \lambda \to (Bew_{PA}(\overline{\ulcorner \lambda \urcorner}) \to \phi) \urcorner})$.

From this we obtain by the first derivability condition that

$PA \vdash Bew_{PA}(\overline{\ulcorner \lambda \urcorner}) \to Bew_{PA}(\overline{\ulcorner Bew_{PA}(\overline{\ulcorner \lambda \urcorner}) \to \phi \urcorner})$.

Using the first derivability condition again, this transforms into

$PA \vdash Bew_{PA}(\overline{\ulcorner \lambda \urcorner}) \to (Bew_{PA}(\overline{\ulcorner Bew_{PA}(\overline{\ulcorner \lambda \urcorner}) \urcorner}) \to Bew_{PA}(\overline{\ulcorner \phi \urcorner}))$.

But the third derivability condition tells us that

$PA \vdash Bew_{PA}(\overline{\ulcorner \lambda \urcorner}) \to Bew_{PA}(\overline{\ulcorner Bew_{PA}(\overline{\ulcorner \lambda \urcorner}) \urcorner})$,

from which we obtain

$PA \vdash Bew_{PA}(\overline{\ulcorner \lambda \urcorner}) \to Bew_{PA}(\overline{\ulcorner \phi \urcorner})$.

Combining this with our initial assumption yields

$PA \vdash Bew_{PA}(\overline{\ulcorner \lambda \urcorner}) \to \phi$.

The right-to-left direction of the application of the diagonal lemma transforms this into

$PA \vdash \lambda$.

Now the second derivability condition yields

$PA \vdash Bew_{PA}(\overline{\ulcorner \lambda \urcorner})$.

Because we also had $PA \vdash Bew_{PA}(\overline{\ulcorner \lambda \urcorner}) \to \phi$, an application of modus ponens finally gives us $PA \vdash \phi$. ∎

This lemma is known as *Löb's lemma*. It yields the second incompleteness theorem as a corollary in the following way. First, instantiate ϕ by "$0 = 1$." Next, because PA does not prove that $0 = 1$, it follows that PA does not prove that $Bew_{PA}(\overline{\ulcorner 0 = 1 \urcorner}) \to 0 = 1$. This latter formula is equivalent to $\neg Bew_{PA}(\overline{\ulcorner 0 = 1 \urcorner})$, so we have our desired result.

The second incompleteness theorem has played an important role in the foundations of mathematics. But for us, the second incompleteness theorem serves as a tool for comparing the strength of axiomatic theories of truth. Suppose we have two axiomatic truth theories, S and S', of which we are convinced that they are consistent. Suppose also that we are unsure whether the two theories coincide: Perhaps one of them proves some sentence but the other doesn't. Proving that a theory proves a given sentence is sometimes rather easy, but proving that a theory does *not* prove a given sentence is often difficult. Now suppose that we find out that $S \vdash Con(S')$. Then the second incompleteness theorem allows us to conclude that there is a sense in which S is stronger than S' because S does not prove its own consistency!

3.4.3 The Completeness Theorem

To top it off and to demonstrate that he does not have a one-track mind, Gödel also proved a *completeness theorem*. It says, roughly, that for (first-order) logic, formal derivability ($\vdash$) corresponds to logical consequence ($\models$). More exactly:

Theorem 9 (Completeness Theorem) *For all sets of formulae Γ, and for all formulae ϕ:*

$\Gamma \vdash \phi \Leftrightarrow \Gamma \vDash \phi$.

In particular, this implies that the collection of theorems of first-order logic provides a *complete* list of all first-order logical truths.

We do not prove the completeness theorem in this book.[8] But we use the completeness theorem, among other things, for the following two purposes.

First, the completeness theorem can be employed to show that a formal theory is *consistent*. For the following statement is obviously equivalent to the completeness theorem:

A theory is consistent if and only if there is a model that makes it true.

This shows that as a tool for comparing formal theories, the second incompleteness theorem is even more informative than appears at first sight. For suppose again that a formal theory S proves $Con(S')$ for some theory S'. Then, by the completeness theorem, in a manner of speaking, S contains a model of S'.

Second, the completeness theorem can be used to prove that a formula ϕ is not provable in a theory S. A sentence ϕ is not derivable from theory S if and only if $S \cup \neg \phi$ is consistent. But $S \cup \{\neg \phi\}$ is consistent if and only if it has a model. Thus, to show that S does not prove ϕ, it suffices to construct a model of S that is not a model of ϕ.

3.4.4 The Undefinability Theorem

Gödel used the diagonal lemma to prove incompleteness theorems. Tarski saw that the diagonal lemma can also be used to prove *undefinability theorems*. In particular, Tarski proved that the property of being an arithmetical truth is undefinable in $\mathcal{L}_{PA}$ [Goldstern & Judah 1998, p. 220]:

Theorem 10 (Undefinability Theorem) *There is no formula $Artrue(x) \in \mathcal{L}_{PA}$ such that for all arithmetical sentences ϕ:*

$\overline{Artrue(\ulcorner \phi \urcorner)} \leftrightarrow \phi$.

Proof *The proof has the form of a reductio ad absurdum. Suppose that such a formula $Artrue(x)$ does exist. By the diagonal lemma, there must be a sentence λ that is true if and only if $\neg Artrue(\ulcorner \lambda \urcorner)$. But because $Artrue(x)$ defines arithmetical truth, we must also have $\overline{Artrue(\ulcorner \lambda \urcorner)} \leftrightarrow \lambda$. Putting these findings together, we find:*

---

8. A standard proof of the completeness theorem is given in [Goldstern & Judah 1998, chapter 2].

$\neg Artrue(\overline{\ulcorner \lambda \urcorner}) \leftrightarrow Artrue(\overline{\ulcorner \lambda \urcorner})$.

But this is a contradiction. So the supposition must be rejected. ∎

In plain English, the proof says that if there exists an arithmetical formula that defines arithmetical truth, then there exists an arithmetical sentence that says of itself that it is not an arithmetical truth. This is of course a *liar sentence*: the liar sentence is the driving force behind this proof.

As with the first incompleteness theorem, we can strengthen the undefinability theorem by making use of the strengthened diagonal lemma instead of the weaker version:

Theorem 11 (Strengthened Undefinability Theorem) *If PA is consistent, then there exists no arithmetical formula $Artrue(x)$ such that*

$$PA \vdash Artrue(\overline{\ulcorner \phi \urcorner}) \leftrightarrow \phi$$

for all $\phi \in \mathcal{L}_{PA}$.

Proof *We shall prove the contraposition. Suppose that for some arithmetical formula $Artrue(x)$, PA proves*

$Artrue(\overline{\ulcorner \phi \urcorner}) \leftrightarrow \phi$

for all $\phi \in \mathcal{L}_{PA}$. By the strengthened diagonal lemma, PA must prove

$\neg Artrue(\overline{\ulcorner \lambda \urcorner}) \leftrightarrow \lambda$

for some arithmetical λ. Putting these equivalences together, we see that PA would be inconsistent. ∎

3.5 More Strengthenings

3.5.1 The Extended Diagonal Lemma

The diagonal lemma also holds for extensions of the language of PA. Here we consider the extension of $\mathcal{L}_{PA}$ with one new primitive predicate T. We call this language $\mathcal{L}_T$: the *language of truth*. But our results apply equally to extensions of $\mathcal{L}_{PA}$ with many new primitive nonlogical symbols.

Let us conventionally assign some gödel code to the new primitive predicate T (for 'True'). Then obviously we can define, relative to the resulting extended coding scheme, the notion of being a formula of $\mathcal{L}_T$: Some arithmetical formula $formula_T(x)$ will be true of all and only the codes of formulae of $\mathcal{L}_T$.

Classical models of the extended language $\mathcal{L}_T$ will be just like models for $\mathcal{L}_{PA}$, except that we now also have to assign a set of numbers $\mathcal{E}$ as the extension of the new predicate T. Because in this book we only consider models based on the standard natural numbers, models of $\mathcal{L}_T$ can be denoted as $\mathfrak{M} =: \langle \mathbb{N}, \mathcal{E} \rangle$ for some set of natural numbers $\mathcal{E}$.

Now we can repeat the arguments we have gone through previously to conclude that the diagonal lemma also applies to the extended language $\mathcal{L}_T$:

Theorem 12 (Extended Diagonal Lemma) *For each formula $\phi(x) \in \mathcal{L}_T$, there is a sentence $\lambda \in \mathcal{L}_T$ such that λ is true in any model $\mathfrak{M}$ based on the natural numbers if and only if $\phi(\overline{\ulcorner \lambda \urcorner})$ is true in $\mathfrak{M}$.*

The reason that this holds is that when one carefully goes through the argument of the diagonal lemma, one sees that the extension of T does not play any role.

As before, we can obtain a strengthened version of the extended diagonal lemma by doing some extra work. Let PA^T be Peano arithmetic formulated in the extended language $\mathcal{L}_T$. This means that the predicate T is allowed to occur in instances of the induction scheme of PA^T. Then it can be shown that:

Theorem 13 (Strengthened Extended Diagonal Lemma) *For every formula $\phi(x) \in \mathcal{L}_T$, there is a sentence $\lambda \in \mathcal{L}_T$ such that:*

$$PA^T \vdash \lambda \leftrightarrow \phi(\overline{\ulcorner \lambda \urcorner}).$$

We now see how these theorems can be used to prove facts about the notion of truth.

3.5.2 The Naive Theory of Truth

In $\mathcal{L}_T$, infinitely many biconditional statements of the form

$$T(\overline{\ulcorner \phi \urcorner}) \leftrightarrow \phi$$

can be formulated. We have seen that statements of this form are called *Tarski-biconditionals*. These sentences play a key role in discussions of axiomatic theories of truth.

The Tarski-biconditionals seem eminently natural and plausible. As we have remarked earlier, they seem to latch on to the disquotational intuition. If you are prepared to sincerely assert, categorically or hypothetically, a sentence ϕ, then you had also better be prepared to assert (categorically or hypothetically) that ϕ is true. If you are prepared to sincerely assert, categorically or hypothetically, that ϕ is true, then you had also better be prepared to assert (categorically or hypothetically) that ϕ. This gives us an inferential version of the Tarski-biconditionals. But given the deduction theorem of first-order logic, the Tarski-biconditionals can be obtained from them.

Nevertheless, the Tarski-biconditionals cannot all be correct. The argument of the strengthened undefinability theorem can be carried over unchanged to the extended language $\mathcal{L}_T$, yielding an extended strengthened undefinability theorem:

Theorem 14 (Strengthened Extended Undefinability Theorem) *No consistent extension S of PA^T proves*

$$T(\ulcorner\phi\urcorner) \leftrightarrow \phi$$

for all $\phi \in \mathcal{L}_T$.

Proof *The proof has the form of a reductio. We use the extended strengthened diagonal lemma to produce a (liar) sentence λ such that:*

$$PA^T \vdash \lambda \leftrightarrow \neg T(\ulcorner\lambda\urcorner).$$

If the theory S in question indeed proves $T(\ulcorner\phi\urcorner) \leftrightarrow \phi$ for all $\phi \in \mathcal{L}_T$, then in particular S proves $T(\ulcorner\lambda\urcorner) \leftrightarrow \lambda$. Putting these two equivalences together, we obtain a contradiction in S:

$$S \vdash T(\ulcorner\lambda\urcorner) \leftrightarrow \neg T(\ulcorner\lambda\urcorner). \blacksquare$$

In other words, no consistent theory extending Peano arithmetic can prove all the Tarski-biconditionals. This is the liar paradox all over again. (Someone once said that paradoxes are just ill-understood theorems.) In particular, the Tarski-biconditional for the liar sentence is inconsistent. This is a strange result because we have seen how we are intuitively inclined to regard the Tarski-biconditionals as utterly unproblematic.

One might reason: If we cannot arithmetically *define* the notion of arithmetical truth, then why don't we just introduce a new predicate T and *postulate* that it defines the notion of truth? This can be done by collecting all the Tarski-biconditionals for the language $\mathcal{L}_T$ and take them as the sole axioms of our axiomatic theory of truth. This theory of truth is called the *naive theory of truth* (*NT*). But it is not so easy to escape the undefinability theorem. *NT* is rightly called naive because theorem 14 shows that it is inconsistent.

Indeed, the argument of the liar paradox can be literally carried out inside *NT*. In other words, *NT formalizes* the argument of the liar paradox. To see this, let us reason inside *NT*. An application of the extended strengthened diagonal lemma yields a liar sentence L such that

$$L \leftrightarrow \neg T(\ulcorner L \urcorner).$$

Now to arrive at a contradiction, we construct a disjunctive syllogism. $L \vee \neg L$ is an instance of the law of excluded middle. From L we obtain $\neg T(\ulcorner L \urcorner)$.

The Tarski-biconditional for L then yields $\neg L$. Contradiction. But from $\neg L$ we obtain $T(\overline{\ulcorner L \urcorner})$. The other direction of the same Tarski-biconditional then yields L. Contradiction again. So in any case we reach a contradiction.

At this point, it is sometimes argued that *NT* might nevertheless be *our* theory of truth. Perhaps the notion of truth that is used in ordinary parlance is ultimately simply incoherent. This may or may not be the case. In the final analysis, this is an empirical question.

But even if our ordinary truth concept is incoherent, it is incumbent on us as philosophers to excise this inconsistency from our ordinary use of the notion of truth and to replace our ordinary concept with a natural concept of truth that is as close as possible to our pretheoretic notion without being inconsistent. Indeed, we require more. Our theory of truth has to be sound. After all, we may want to make use of the concept of truth in our philosophical and perhaps even scientific argumentation. So in any case, we must and will do better than *NT*.

3.5.3 The Paradox of the Knower

Closer inspection of the argument of the previous theorem reveals that actually the full scheme $T(\overline{\ulcorner \phi \urcorner}) \leftrightarrow \phi$ is not used in the argumentation. The argument only uses the left-to-right direction of the Tarski-biconditionals. The right-to-left direction is only used as a rule of inference, the premise of which must be a *theorem*: This is in general weaker than a schematic conditional. After all, the Rule of Necessitation of modal logic ($\vdash \phi \Rightarrow \vdash \Box \phi$) is perfectly acceptable, but its conditional counterpart $\phi \to \Box \phi$ is not. In other words, we can sharpen Tarski's theorem a bit further [Montague 1963]:

Theorem 15 (Montague's Theorem) *There is no consistent extension S of PA^T which proves the scheme*

$$T(\overline{\ulcorner \phi \urcorner}) \to \phi$$

and is closed under the rule of inference

$$\vdash \phi \Rightarrow \vdash T(\overline{\ulcorner \phi \urcorner}).$$

Proof *By the extended strengthened diagonal lemma, there must be a sentence κ (the "knower sentence"), which is such that*

$$PA^T \vdash \kappa \leftrightarrow T\overline{\ulcorner \neg \kappa \urcorner}.$$

Now we reason in S about the knower sentence.
Suppose, for a reductio, κ. Then by the construction of the knower sentence, $T\overline{\ulcorner \neg \kappa \urcorner}$ follows. Then by the left-to-right sentence of the Tarski-biconditionals,

$\neg \kappa$ *follows. This is a contradiction, so we can reject the supposition and categorically conclude* $\neg \kappa$. *Again on the basis of the construction of* κ, *we infer* $\neg T^{\ulcorner}\neg \kappa^{\urcorner}$. *But by the inference rule* $\vdash \phi \Rightarrow \vdash T(\overline{\ulcorner \phi \urcorner})$, *we may also conclude* $T^{\ulcorner}\neg \kappa^{\urcorner}$. *Contradiction.* ∎

The left-to-right direction of the Tarski-biconditional scheme is known in the literature as the axiom of *reflexivity*. Because of its analogy with the Rule of Necessitation of modal logic (but perhaps somewhat confusingly), the inference rule $\vdash \phi \Rightarrow \vdash T(\overline{\ulcorner \phi \urcorner})$ is also known as the rule of *necessitation*. So the moral of Montague's theorem is that one cannot consistently have reflexivity and necessitation.

For the interpretation of T as truth, Montague's theorem shows that a minor weakening of *NT* is not sufficient to yield a consistent theory of truth. In other words, it would be a mistake to think of the naive theory of truth as "just barely overstepping the bounds of consistency." There is a moral in this: Even truth theories that appear at first sight to be significantly weaker than *NT* may on closer inspection turn out to be inconsistent.

Montague's theorem is also known as the *Knower Paradox* or the *Paradox of Necessity*. The reason is that just as the extended strengthened undefinability theorem is a formalization of a paradox concerning truth, Montague's theorem can be seen as a paradox concerning *informal* provability (as opposed to provability in a given formal system) or concerning necessity.

Let us look at the notion of informal provability first. Interpret the new predicate T not as truth but as the (somewhat vague) property of informal provability. For this interpretation, our intuitions do not suggest that the full Tarski-biconditionals are true. After all, it seems *prima facie* hard to say whether there are true but absolutely unprovable sentences. Nevertheless, if the left-to-right direction of the Tarski-biconditionals are taken as one's sole basic informal provability principles and the right-to-left direction of the Tarski-biconditionals are taken as one's sole rule of inference concerning informal provability, then it would appear that one has a sound (although probably incomplete) theory of informal provability. Let us call this theory the naive theory of proof (*NP*). Informal provability implies truth. In the other direction, an induction on the length of informal proofs would appear to show that we can see that *NP* only proves informally provable sentences. Yet Montague's theorem shows that *NP* is inconsistent.

This argumentation can be repeated for the interpretation of T as necessity. (On one interpretation of the word, necessity is just another word for informal provability.) This gives us a paradox for the notion of necessity. Montague's theorem thus appears to undermine modal logic and formal epistemology.[9]

Still, it is well known that ordinary modal logic is consistent and the standard systems of modal logic *do* contain reflexivity ($\Box \phi \to \phi$) and necessitation ($\vdash \phi \Rightarrow \vdash \Box \phi$). How can this be? Ordinary modal logic is consistent just because its expressive resources are restricted. In ordinary modal logic, necessity is treated as a sentential operator. This means that we are not allowed to quantify over the objects (propositions, sentences) that are deemed necessary. If we treat necessity as a predicate (of propositions or sentences), then we can apply the diagonal lemma to construct self-referential sentences. We have seen that there is nothing wrong with self-reference *per se*. No insight is gained by just sweeping the paradoxes of modality under the carpet, as is done in ordinary modal logic. Rather, we should confront them head on and come to terms with them. Nevertheless, we do not pursue this issue further in this book. We concentrate on the concept of truth instead of on these other notions.

3.6 Bounded Truth Predicates

So far this chapter only contains bad news. We end this chapter on a positive note. We show how in the language of arithmetic truth predicates can be defined for ever larger fragments of the language of first-order arithmetic.

3.6.1 Complexity Classes of Arithmetical Formulae

Every formula of the language of Peano arithmetic can be put in *prenex normal form*. This means that for every formula ϕ of the language of *PA*, there is a formula ψ of the language of *PA*, such that ϕ is logically equivalent to ψ where ψ is of the form

$$Q\vec{x}\, A(\vec{x}),$$

with $Q\vec{x}$ a string of quantifiers and $A(\vec{x})$ a quantifier-free part. In fact, $A(\vec{x})$ can be taken to consist of a disjunction of conjunctions of equations and negations of equations (i.e., the quantifier-free part can be taken to be in *disjunctive normal form*). This is a general feature of formulae of first-order predicate logic. In the case of arithmetic, we can even take the string of quantifiers to be constantly alternating. For if we have, for example, a formula of the form

---

9. Montague-like impossibility results can also be obtained for tense logic: see [Horsten & Leitgeb 2001].

$\exists x \exists y(\ldots)$, then we replace this double existential quantifier by a single existential quantifier, which ranges over numerical codes of ordered pairs $\langle x, y \rangle$. So, typically, the formula ψ will look like this:

$$\exists x \forall y \exists z \ldots (\ldots x \ldots y \ldots z \ldots)$$

Now suppose such a formula ψ is given. Then we can count the number of quantifiers. If the quantifier string begins with an existential quantifier and contains n quantifiers, then we call ψ a Σ_n-formula. If ψ begins with a universal quantifier and the string contains n quantifiers, then we call the formula a Π_n-formula. In this way, *every* arithmetical formula can be assigned to a complexity class: We call an *arbitrary* formula (not necessarily in prenex normal form) Σ_n exactly if it is equivalent to a Σ_n-formula. Similarly, we call an arbitrary formula Π_n if it is equivalent to a Π_n-formula.

3.6.2 True Equations

There is a formula $Eq(x)$ of the language of *PA* that is true exactly of the gödel numbers of atomic formulae of the language of *PA* (i.e., of the equations). We now want to show that there also exists an arithmetical formula $val^+(x)$ that holds exactly of the gödel numbers of the *true* equations of the language of *PA*.

First, we want to express in the language of arithmetic the relation $den(t, n)$, which holds exactly if t is the gödel number of a term that denotes the number n. This relation $den(t, n)$ is defined in *PA* as follows:

$$term(t) \wedge [(t = \ulcorner 0 \urcorner \wedge n = 0) \vee (\exists t' : term(t') \wedge t = \ulcorner st' \urcorner \wedge n = st')]$$

In words, this formula says that a term t denotes a number n if and only if either (1) t is the numeral "0" and n is the number 0, or (2) t is a successor numeral obtained by prefixing "s" to t': In this case, t denotes the successor of the number denoted by t'.

Now we can define $val^+(x)$ as follows:

$$val^+(x) =: \exists t \exists t' [term(t) \wedge term(t') \wedge x = \ulcorner t = t' \urcorner \wedge$$
$$\exists m \exists n (den(t, n) \wedge den(t', m) \wedge m = n)]$$

This formula says that x is an equation built from terms t and t', which denote the same natural number.

It is then easy to see how we can define an arithmetical formula $val^-(x)$, which holds exactly of the gödel numbers of true negations of arithmetical equations.

3.6.3 Defining Bounded Truth Predicates

Now we can define a formula *truecon(x)* of the language of arithmetic that holds exactly of the gödel numbers of all true conjunctions of equations and negated equations. Roughly, *truecon(x)* is expressed as: "there is a number n such that x is a conjunction of n conjuncts, and for each y, if y is a conjunct of x, then either $val^+(y)$ or $val^-(z)$ with y being the negation of z." We trust that the reader can supply the details. Using *truecon(x)*, we can define a formula *trueqfree(x)*, which holds exactly of the gödel numbers of true quantifier-free arithmetical formulae in disjunctive normal form.

Now we are ready to simultaneously define in the language of arithmetic the class of arithmetical Σ_n and Π_n truths. We do this recursively. We already have defined the class of Σ_0 ($= \Pi_0$) truths: They are defined by *trueqfree(x)*. So let us assume that the Σ_n and Π_n truths are defined and proceed to the Σ_{n+1} truths:

$true\Sigma_{n+1}(x) =: \exists y \exists z (x = \overline{\ulcorner \exists z(y) \urcorner} \wedge \exists u \exists v (Sub(y, z, u, v) \wedge true\Pi_n(v)))$.

Here $Sub(y, z, u, v)$ codes the *substitution function*: It expresses that v is obtained from y by replacing all free occurrences of z by occurrences of the standard numeral for u. So this formula says that a Σ_{n+1}-truth is a formula beginning with an existential quantifier $\exists z$ such that there is a Peano-numeral u for which the following holds: If the initial existential quantifier is erased and the numeral u is uniformly substituted for free occurrences of the variable z, then a Π_n-truth results. In a similar way, we define the class of arithmetical Π_{n+1} truths for each n by a formula $true\Pi_{n+1}(x)$ using the formula $true\Sigma_n(x)$.

By the manner in which the bounded truth predicates are constructed, we have:

Theorem 16 *For every arithmetical Σ_n sentence ϕ:*

$\mathbb{N} \models true\Sigma_n(\overline{\ulcorner \phi \urcorner}) \Leftrightarrow \mathbb{N} \models \phi$.

For every arithmetical Π_n sentence ϕ:

$\mathbb{N} \models true\Pi_n(\overline{\ulcorner \phi \urcorner}) \Leftrightarrow \mathbb{N} \models \phi$.

So even though by Tarski's theorem the collection of all arithmetical truths cannot be arithmetically defined, the truth predicate for each individual arithmetical complexity class *can* be arithmetically defined. The language of arithmetic is just not capable of contracting all these restricted arithmetical truth predicates into one single *master* truth predicate.

It should not surprise us—although we do not verify it in detail here—that the reasoning that led us to the previous theorem can be carried out in *PA*. Thus, we have the stronger:

Theorem 17

1. For every arithmetical Σ_n arithmetical sentence ϕ:

$PA \vdash true\Sigma_n(\overline{\ulcorner\phi\urcorner}) \leftrightarrow \phi$.

2. For every arithmetical Π_n arithmetical sentence ϕ:

$PA \vdash true\Pi_n(\overline{\ulcorner\phi\urcorner}) \leftrightarrow \phi$.

So the situation is as follows. We can carve up the language of arithmetic in a natural way in complexity classes. Then $\mathcal{L}_{PA}$ contains a truth predicate for each of these complexity classes of formulae. But $\mathcal{L}_T$ is unable to synthesize these partial truth predicates into one master truth predicate.

3.7 Simplify, Simplify

As announced earlier, in the interest of readability, we are going to be *very* sloppy about notation in the remainder of the book.

From now on, we are simply going to drop gödel quotes. This means that our notation is going to suggest that we treat truth as a sentential operator rather than as a predicate. Of course, we know that truth is not really an operator but a predicate. So, officially, most of the sentences containing the truth predicate are not even going to be well formed. But we trust that the reader can patch it up if she feels a desire to do so.

For instance, we are going to casually write formulae such as:

$\forall \phi \in \mathcal{L}_{PA} : T(\neg\neg\phi) \rightarrow T(\phi)$.

This is not even close to being well formed. But it is easily readable as: If a double negation of an arithmetical formula is true, then the arithmetical formula must also be true. It certainly is more easily readable than the well-formed way of expressing what is intended:

$\forall x : formula_{PA}(x) \rightarrow [\exists y \exists z (negation(y, x) \wedge negation(z, y) \wedge T(z)) \rightarrow T(x)]$

This is just a simple sentence. The reader can appreciate that if we are going to express more complicated propositions involving the notion of truth (and quantification!), the gain in readability that is obtained by sloppy notation is going to be considerable indeed.

I *promise* that I do not pass on as formulae of formal languages extending $\mathcal{L}_{PA}$ any formulae that are *not* straightforwardly "repaired," such as

$$\forall \phi \in \mathcal{L}_{PA} : T(\phi) \to \phi.$$

The reader is free to check whether I have lived up to my promise.

The important thing is that the reader should feel confident that if she is given enough time and stimulants, she can express all the notions properly, correct the sins against grammar that are committed, and prove "ordinary things" about syntactical notions in Peano arithmetic. She should have a solid, reliable *feeling* for what can and cannot be done.

4 The Disquotational Theory

Tarski wanted to define truth. He saw that truth could not be defined in the object language: It has to be done in an essentially stronger metalanguage. In his definition, Tarski assigned a pivotal role to the Tarski-biconditionals. Nowadays, many a deflationist philosopher takes a suitable class of Tarski-biconditionals as the *axioms* of her theory of truth.

4.1 Tarski on Defining Truth

Tarski's theory, as set out in [Tarski 1935], is the point of departure for most, if not all, recent publications on truth. Rather than giving a historically precise account of Tarski's account, I elaborate on those features that are most important for later developments.

Tarski's truth predicate pertains to a specific formal language, the so-called *objectlanguage*. In our case, the objectlanguage is $\mathcal{L}_{PA}$. The truth predicate does not belong to the objectlanguage. It forms part of the *metalanguage*. In the simplest case, the objectlanguage is a sublanguage of the metalanguage (i.e., all formulae of the objectlanguage are also formulae of the metalanguage). If the metalanguage does not include the objectlanguage, then a *translation* of the object- into the metalanguage is required. Whether a translation is correct depends of course on the meaning of the sentences of the objectlanguage, but—surely Pilate has asked himself this question—what is "meaning"? Thus, the need for a translation has caused much anxiety. We stick to the simple case and assume that $\mathcal{L}_{PA}$ is a sublanguage of the metalanguage.

Tarski develops his theory at first in natural language enriched by some mathematical symbols. However, Tarski is aware of the need for a precisely defined metalanguage that allows for strict formal proofs in it.

For the metalanguage, Tarski needs some rules governing the use of the expressions of the objectlanguage. Tarski assumed that we have axioms and rules, stated in the metalanguage, that allow for derivations within the metalanguage. He called the resulting theory "Metawissenschaft," which is usually translated as *metatheory*. Tarski stated some conditions that should be satisfied by the metatheory. It is a deductive system with axioms and rules, which contains the theory of the objectlanguage (if there is one) and is able to prove certain facts about expressions.

It is assumed that the metalanguage has a *name* for each sentence of the objectlanguage. However, not just any kind of name will do. It must be possible to read off the syntactic shape of the sentence from its name. For this purpose, Tarski introduced his *structural-descriptive* names. We do not discuss Tarski's original approach, but we present two examples of naming systems that comply with the requirement that one must be able to recover the shape of an expression from its name.

In natural language, the *quotational* name of a sentence satisfies the condition that the name has to reveal the structure of the sentence: The singular term

"Snow is white"

designates the sentence within the quotation marks, and thus the name displays the exact shape of the sentence.

Because the metalanguage contains the objectlanguage $\mathcal{L}_{PA}$ and therefore also all standard numerals, the metalanguage has names for all sentences of the objectlanguage. Indeed, a gödel code implicitly contains the structure of the expression that it codes.

Tarski aimed at a definition of truth. A (potential) definition of truth in the objectlanguage is given as an explicit definition of the primitive predicate symbol T in the metalanguage. It takes the following form:

$\forall x \in \mathcal{L}_{PA} : T(x) \leftrightarrow TDef(x)$,

where $TDef(x)$ is a complex formula in the metalanguage, containing one free variable x. The resulting theory is a definitional extension of the metatheory. We are sloppy and call the formula $TDef(x)$ itself a truth definition.

Of course, the sentence $\forall x \in \mathcal{L}_{PA} : T(x) \leftrightarrow TDef(x)$ is the general pattern for introducing new unary predicate predicates by an explicit definition. Thus, obviously not every choice of $TDef(x)$ is acceptable as a definition of *truth*. However, there may be different acceptable choices. What are the distinguishing features of an *adequate* definition of truth?

Tarski's answer to this question is contained in his *material adequacy condition*. Whether a definition is materially adequate depends on the metatheory. The metatheory must prove certain things about the predicate $TDef(x)$ that is supposed to define truth.

In terms of our present setup involving $\mathcal{L}_{PA}$ as objectlanguage and a metalanguage including $\mathcal{L}_{PA}$, Tarski's condition can be rephrased as follows:

Definition 18 *A definition of truth for $\mathcal{L}_{PA}$ is materially adequate if and only if $T(\phi) \leftrightarrow \phi$ is provable in the metatheory for every sentence ϕ of $\mathcal{L}_{PA}$.*

In other words, a truth definition for an objectlanguage is adequate if and only if the Tarski-biconditionals for all sentences of the objectlanguage are derivable in the metalanguage. Tarski requires for the adequacy also that the metatheory proves that only sentences (or their codes) are true. We ignore this additional restriction, which is also according to Tarski not essential.

4.2 The Disquotational Theory of Truth

From the undefinability theorems, we may conclude that trying to define the concept of truth of *our* language is a hopeless enterprise. Instead, we opt for the axiomatic approach: We take the truth predicate to express an irreducible, primitive notion. The meaning of the truth predicate is partially explicated by proposing certain laws of truth as basic principles, as axioms.

We have already encountered one axiomatic theory of truth. This was the naive theory of truth *NT*, which, aside from PA^T, contains all the Tarski-biconditionals as axioms. *NT* was seen to be inconsistent. Montague's theorem entails that *NT* is not even *close* to being acceptable.

A crude attempt to solve this problem is to collect as many of the Tarski-biconditionals as consistently possible and to declare the result to be one's preferred theory of truth. This strategy was suggested at one point by Horwich [Horwich 1998, p. 42]. Unfortunately, McGee has shown that this will not do [McGee 1992]. There are many maximal consistent but mutually incompatible collections of Tarski-biconditionals. Selecting one maximal consistent collection of Tarski-biconditionals as one's theory of truth rather than another one would already seem arbitrary. Moreover, none of these collections is computably axiomatizable. So even if we could settle on one of them in a non arbitrary way, we would not have a *theory* in the true sense of the word.

It may be more fruitful to inspect somewhat more closely the derivation of the contradiction from the axioms of *NT*. We see that the crucial axiom in the derivation of the contradiction is the Tarski-biconditional

$T(L) \leftrightarrow L$,

where L is the liar sentence. If we reflect on the construction of L, we see that it contains the truth predicate. So in the fateful Tarski-biconditional $T(L) \leftrightarrow L$, there is a subformula (namely, $T(L)$) in which an occurrence of the truth predicate occurs in the scope of the truth predicate.

This inspired Tarski to offer an immensely insightful *diagnosis* of what went wrong. He conjectured that the root of the disease lies in allowing the Tarski-biconditionals to regulate the meaning of sentences that contain the truth predicate.

If Tarski's diagnosis is correct, then one possible cure for the disease of the liar paradox is to excise from one's theory of truth, for every formula ϕ that contains occurrences of the truth predicate, the corresponding Tarski-biconditional.

What we are left with is a new axiomatic theory of truth. This theory is called the *disquotational theory* (*DT*). It contains the following axioms:

DT1 PA^T;

DT2 $T(\phi) \leftrightarrow \phi$ for all $\phi \in \mathcal{L}_{PA}$.

The sentences of the form $T(\phi) \leftrightarrow \phi$ with $\phi \in \mathcal{L}_{PA}$ are called the *restricted Tarski-biconditionals*. Thus, *DT* has as its sole truth axioms the restricted Tarski-biconditionals.

This form of disquotationalism was first defended by W. V. O. Quine [Quine 1970, chapter 1]. Now in a wider sense of the word, we may call a *disquotationalist* anyone who believes that our best theory of truth consists of some collection of Tarski-biconditionals. In this wider sense, Paul Horwich is surely the most renown present-day disquotationalist [Horwich 1998]. We have seen that at one point Horwich believed that we should settle on some maximal consistent collection of Tarski-biconditionals. However, he is currently not taking this line even though he is still a disquotationalist. Nevertheless, Horwich definitely still believes that more than just the restricted Tarski-biconditionals should be adopted as basic principles of truth [Horwich 2005, pp. 81–82]. Because Horwich has not hitherto developed his preferred formal truth theory in formal detail, we do not consider it in what follows. Instead, we will assume that *DT*, or some variant on it, is the formal truth theory of choice of the disquotationalist.

Actually, *DT* can be strengthened somewhat. We can strengthen the restricted Tarski-biconditionals in the following way:[1]

$\forall \vec{x} : T(\phi(\vec{x})) \leftrightarrow \phi(\vec{x})$ for all $\phi(\vec{x}) \in \mathcal{L}_{PA}$,

where $\forall \vec{x}$ is a list of quantifiers $\forall x_1, \forall x_2, \ldots$, and $\vec{x}$ is the corresponding list $x_1, x_2, \ldots$ of variables. After all, if the restricted Tarski-biconditionals in which

---

1. For this to make sense, we must be able to quantify into gödel quotes. This can be coherently done using the substitution function mentioned earlier (see section 3.6).

ϕ is required to be a sentence is acceptable, then the universal closure of the restricted Tarski-biconditionals in which ϕ is allowed to contain free variables is acceptable too. We could introduce a new name for this slightly stronger theory, but for our purposes there is no need to do so.

Note that *DT* is not a *definition* of truth; it is not even a definition of truth for $\mathcal{L}_{PA}$. A definition allows a defined term to be eliminated in every context in which it appears. But suppose that we have a sentence of the form

$$\exists x \in \mathcal{L}_{PA} : T(x) \wedge \phi(x),$$

with $\phi(x)$ an arithmetical formula. Then *DT* does not provide, in general, a way of finding a truth-free sentence that is provably equivalent with this sentence. So *DT* can only be understood as a *theory* of truth. Because we are looking for a theory of truth for our whole language, *DT* should be evaluated as a theory of truth not just for $\mathcal{L}_{PA}$ but for the entire language $\mathcal{L}_T$.

4.3 The Soundness of the Disquotational Theory

The reader will appreciate that, in the light of unpleasant past experiences, we are at this point worried about the soundness of *DT*. After all, we have merely blocked the argument that we used to prove *NT* inconsistent. Who knows, maybe another argument can be found to show that *DT* suffers the same fate as *NT*?

Fortunately, this is not the case. We know that by the completeness theorem, finding a model for *DT* is enough to prove it consistent. In fact, we do more than that: We find a *nice* model for *DT*.

A nice model is a model that is based on the natural numbers (i.e., a model $\mathfrak{M}$ which is of the form $\langle \mathbb{N}, \mathcal{E} \rangle$ for some collection $\mathcal{E}$ of formulae). Here $\mathbb{N}$ of course serves as the interpretation of the mathematical vocabulary, and $\mathcal{E}$ is the set of (codes of) sentences that serves as an interpretation of the truth predicate.

There must also be models that are not nice in this sense. The incompleteness theorem, in conjunction with the completeness theorem, entails that there must be models in which the negation of the gödel sentence is true. But we know from section 3.4.1 that the negation of the gödel sentence is false. Moreover, it is an arithmetical sentence. So such models are not nice.

Proposition 19 *DT has a nice model.*

Proof *Consider the model*

$$\mathfrak{M} =: \langle \mathbb{N}, \{\phi \mid \phi \in \mathcal{L}_{PA} \wedge \mathbb{N} \models \phi\} \rangle,$$

i.e., the model in which as the extension of the truth predicate we take all arithmetical truths. An induction on the length of proofs in DT verifies that

$\mathfrak{M} \models DT$.

We only consider the restricted Tarski-biconditionals. For any $\phi \in \mathcal{L}_{PA}$:

$\mathfrak{M} \models T(\phi) \Leftrightarrow \phi \in \mathcal{E} \Leftrightarrow \mathbb{N} \models \phi$.

But because ϕ is a purely arithmetical sentence, the extension of the truth predicate does not matter for its evaluation:

$\mathbb{N} \models \phi \Leftrightarrow \mathfrak{M} \models \phi$.

So, putting our findings together, we obtain:

$\mathfrak{M} \models T(\phi) \Leftrightarrow \mathfrak{M} \models \phi$. ∎

$\mathfrak{M}$ is the *minimal* nice model for *DT*: It contains the minimal extension of the truth predicate that is needed to make all the restricted Tarski-biconditionals true.

Corollary 20 *DT is consistent.*

Proof   This follows from proposition 19 via one direction of the completeness theorem. ∎

But why are models based on the standard natural numbers structure nice? They are nice because they prove more than just consistency of the theories that they model. A moment's reflection shows that proposition 19 shows that *DT* proves only true arithmetical sentences:

Corollary 21 *DT is arithmetically sound.*

Proof   Suppose $DT \vdash \phi$ for an arithmetical ϕ. Then by proposition 19,

$\langle \mathbb{N}, \{\phi | \phi \in \mathcal{L}_{PA} \wedge \mathbb{N} \models \phi\}\rangle \models \phi$.

But because ϕ does not contain the truth predicate, this entails that $\mathbb{N} \models \phi$. ∎

Note that this second corollary is strictly stronger than the first one. For it is a lesson of the first incompleteness theorem that consistency does not entail soundness. The first incompleteness theorem entails that if we add the negation of the gödel sentence for *PA* as an extra axiom to *PA*, the resulting theory is consistent. But because the negation of the gödel sentence for *PA* is false, this theory is unsound.

Perhaps we can go further and declare that *DT* is a *sound* theory of truth. Not only does *DT* prove only true arithmetical sentences; also all the sentences containing the truth predicate that it proves seem correct. After all, the restricted Tarski-biconditionals seem unproblematic: They make no claims about paradoxical sentences like the liar sentence. Of course, our assertion of the soundness of *DT* as a theory of truth cannot be proved as a theorem: It is a *philosophical* claim.

4.4 Climbing Tarski's Ladder

Thus, we have obtained our first successful axiomatic theory of truth. Let us now take first steps in investigating how close *DT* comes to truth-theoretic completeness. It emerges that the Tarskian treatment of the liar syndrome has the effect of a poison pill that leaves the patient cured but anemic and short of breath.

Suppose that you overhear the following fascinating conversation:

A: It is true that $0 = 0$.

B: What you have just said is true.

The assertions of A and B seem equally correct. A and B appear to assert trivial truths that are not in any way paradoxical. A's assertion can be expressed in $\mathcal{L}_T$ as $T(0 = 0)$, and B's assertion can be expressed as $T(T(0 = 0))$. So it seems that in English we can truthfully predicate truth of sentences that contain the concept of truth.

In this scenario, B might just as well have repeated what A said. So in a sense, B does not really have to iterate truth to get her message across. But avoiding truth iteration is not always possible. B might know that A has asserted the truth of some mathematical sentence without knowing what this mathematical sentence is. If B believes that A is reliable in matters mathematical, then B might still be prepared to assert that what A said is true. But now B is not in a position to avoid at least implicit truth iteration by repeating what A has said.

Unfortunately, *DT* does not prove $T(T(0 = 0))$. Indeed, the nice model that we have constructed for *DT* shows that *DT* does not prove *any* sentence of the form $T(\phi)$ where ϕ contains an occurrence of the truth predicate. It does not even prove $\exists x \in \mathcal{L}_{PA} : T(T(x))$.

So the question arises whether the Tarskian treatment has been too severe. Can the Tarskian approach validate the feeling that some truth iterations are genuinely unproblematic? Well, yes, to some extent.

Nothing prevents us from, instead of PA, taking DT as the theory against the background of which we formulate our truth theory. Let $\mathcal{L}_{T,T_1}$ be defined as $\mathcal{L}_T \cup \{T_1\}$. T_1 serves as our new, more broadminded truth predicate. Let PA^{T,T_1} be Peano arithmetic formulated in the extended language $\mathcal{L}_{T,T_1}$. Now we define DT_1 to consist of:

1. PA^{T,T_1};
2. $T(\phi) \leftrightarrow \phi$ for all $\phi \in \mathcal{L}_{PA}$;
3. $T_1(\phi) \leftrightarrow \phi$ for all $\phi \in \mathcal{L}_T$.

Just like DT, the theory DT_1 proves truth-ascribing sentences such as $T(0 = 0)$. But then the restricted Tarski-biconditionals for T_1 can be used to derive from $T(0 = 0)$ the sentence $T_1(T(0 = 0))$. This looks like just the sort of truth iteration that we wanted to assert.

As in the case of DT, we want to satisfy ourselves that DT_1 has nice models. Because DT is formulated in the language $\mathcal{L}_{T,T_1}$, nice models of it are of the form $\langle \mathbb{N}, \mathcal{E}, \mathcal{E}_1 \rangle$, where $\mathcal{E}$ as before serves as an extension of T and $\mathcal{E}_1$ serves as an extension of T_1.

Proposition 22 DT_1 *has a nice model.*

Proof   *Consider the model*

$$\mathfrak{M}_1 =: \langle \mathbb{N}, \{\phi \mid \phi \in \mathcal{L}_{PA} \wedge \mathbb{N} \models \phi\}, \{\phi \mid \phi \in \mathcal{L}_T \wedge \mathfrak{M} \models \phi\}\rangle,$$

An induction on the length of proofs in DT verifies that $\mathfrak{M}_1 \models DT_1$. This proof is similar to that of proposition 19.   ∎

Now suppose the conversation above were to be extended as follows:

A: It is true that $0 = 0$.

B: What you have just said is true.

C: Yes, B, that is very true.

It seems in effect that C asserts $T(T(T(0 = 0)))$. This appears just as acceptable as A and B's assertions.

If we want a truth theory that even proves a threefold truth iteration, then we must repeat the trick. We have to add a third truth predicate to our language and construct in the appropriate way a theory DT_2 that proves $T_2(T_1(T(0 = 0)))$.

So we can go on, up the *Tarskian hierarchy*. Let

$$\mathcal{L}_{T,T_1,T_2,\ldots} = \mathcal{L}_{PA} \cup \{T, T_1, T_2, T_3, \ldots, T_n, \ldots\}.$$

And let DT_ω be DT plus for every $n > 0$

$T_n(\phi) \leftrightarrow \phi$ for all $\phi \in \mathcal{L}_{T,T_1...T_{n-1}}$.

Proposition 23 DT_ω *has a nice model.*

Proof *The obvious generalization of the model that we have constructed for DT_1 will make DT_ω true.* ∎

Must we stop here? No, we can go on into the transfinite and formulate:

$DT_{\omega+1}, DT_{\omega+2}, \ldots,$

If we want to do this in $\mathcal{L}_T$, then we somehow have to code transfinite ordinal numbers such as $\omega + 2$ as natural numbers. Up to some transfinite ordinals, this can indeed be done; let us not go into the details here. Anyhow, this exercise somehow seems philosophically a bit pointless. Transfinitely many truth iterations occur infrequently in natural language.

4.5 The Uniformity of the Concept of Truth

Let us recapitulate. We have seen that $DT_1 \vdash T_1(T(0=0))$. But the fact that $\mathfrak{M}_1 \models DT_1$ entails that $DT_1 \nvdash T_1(T_1((0=0)))$. This follows via the completeness theorem from the construction of the model $\mathfrak{M}_1$, for $\mathfrak{M}_1 \nvDash T_1(T_1((0=0)))$. For similar reasons, $DT_1 \nvdash T(T((0=0)))$.

So in some sense, DT_1 gives rise to truthful iteration of truth predicates. But in a strict sense, the Tarskian diagnosis is upheld: No truth predicate can be truthfully predicated of a sentence containing that *same* truth predicate.

In other words, according to the Tarskian hierarchical conception, truth is not a *uniform* notion. There is in reality not one property of truth, but there are many properties of truth, ordered in levels in a linear way.

There are objections to the Tarskian hierarchy account. For one thing, *our* notion of truth seems at first sight to be a uniform notion. If there were more than one property of truth, then one would expect this to be reflected in natural language. One would expect there to be many truth predicates in English, but there is only one. As it stands, this objection is not compelling because English does contain homonyms.[2] But homonyms in natural languages have only a couple of different meanings. There are no established cases of homonyms that have an infinite number of meanings.

A second objection is due to Kripke. He has emphasized that the level of a token use of the truth predicate can depend on contingent factors: It can

---

2. Thanks to Henri Galinon for stressing this point.

depend on what things have been (or will be) said by the speaker or by others [Kripke 1975, section I]. Because of that, it is in certain situations practically impossible for a speaker to determine which level his truth predicate should take for his utterance to express the intended proposition.

To illustrate this, suppose that you are convinced that on the subject of the history of the Mayan civilization, Anna is extremely reliable. Suppose that even though you were not in Anna's company yesterday evening, you know that the conversation in which she was engaged was restricted to the subject of the history of the Mayan civilization. Then you may say today:

Everything Anna said yesterday evening is true.

Because you do not know which specific sentences Anna asserted yesterday evening, you do not know how far she got carried away after a few drinks in nesting occurrences of the truth predicate. Therefore, *you* have no means of determining how high you have to crank up the level of your use of the truth predicate in the sentence you assert about Anna.

Can the Tarskian hierarchy be resisted? One might be tempted to say that iterated occurrences of the truth predicates are simply redundant. Iteration of the truth predicate does not add content to a sentence. "It is true that it is true that the sun is a star" says no more than "It is true that the sun is a star." And "It is true that it is not true that frogs have descended from humans" says nothing more than "It is not true that frogs have descended from humans." Each sentence with iterated occurrences of the truth predicate has the same logical form as a sentence not containing truth iteration. One might even want to push this *redundancy view of truth* further. Perhaps every sentence containing one or more occurrences of the truth predicate has the same form as some truth-free sentence.

But the redundancy view of truth, even in its less radical form, is untenable. First, the view implies a marked divergence between the surface grammar and the logical form of sentences of English. Now one might reply to this that postulating such a divergence is not without antecedents: Look at Russell's theory of definite descriptions. But there is a second objection to the redundancy view that is more serious. There are sentences containing implicit truth iteration for which a truth iteration-free sentence with the same content is not easily found: Try your hand on the liar sentence!

4.6 Contextual Theories of Truth

Tyler Burge has developed a theory of truth which admits that truth is a uniform notion but still makes use of a Tarski-like hierarchy to hold the semantic

The Disquotational Theory

paradoxes at bay [Burge 1979].[3] On Burge's theory, the truth predicate indeed has a uniform meaning. But its extension varies over contexts. In this respect, the truth predicate semantically behaves like indexical expressions such as "I" and "here": These words have a uniform meaning, but their reference differs from context to context.

From the prior Kripkean considerations, it is clear that the speaker's intentions cannot in general determine the extension of the truth predicate in a given context. If anything fixes the level of the property of truth that my use of the truth predicate expresses, it must be the conversational context (in the widest sense of the word) plus the world as we find it.

Burge's theory of truth deals with the liar paradox in roughly the following manner. Consider the liar sentence once again:

(S) Sentence S is not true.

Let us evaluate sentence S. The truth predicate occurring in S must be "indexed" to a particular context, which we call context 0. So, semiformally, we can say that sentence S expresses that S is not $true_0$. For the familiar liar argument reasons, S cannot be $true_0$. If S were $true_0$, then what it says of itself, namely, that it is *not* $true_0$, would have to be the case, and this would yield a contradiction. But if sentence S is not $true_0$, then it should be in some sense *true* that it is not $true_0$. This is where, in the original argument of the liar paradox, we were led into trouble. Burge's indexical theory of truth has it that when we assert that it is true that S is not $true_0$, we are shifting to a new context. It is not that we intentionally make the shift: It happens automatically. The occurrence of "true" in "It is true that S is not $true_0$" must be given an index different from that of "$true_0$"; let its index be 1. Then we have both:

Sentence S is not $true_0$.

Sentence S is $true_1$.

Because of the indexical shift in extension of the truth predicate between contexts 0 and 1, this is not a contradiction.

Thus, we have a way of maintaining the uniformity of the notion of truth while helping ourselves to Tarski's hierarchy. Of course, strictly speaking, we do not have a hierarchy of *languages* anymore—our language contains only one truth predicate with only one meaning. We have, so to speak, pushed Tarski's hierarchy into semantics. Or you may say that we have pushed the hierarchy

---

3. Structurally similar theories of truth have been proposed by Barwise and Etchemendy [Barwise & Etchemendy 1987], Gaifman [Gaifman 1992], and Simmons [Simmons 2007].

into pragmatics: It depends on where the line between semantics and pragmatics is drawn.

Unfortunately, it appears that the liar paradox can strike back. Consider the sentence:

(S') Sentence S' is not true in any context.

This is called a *strengthened liar sentence*. It is not hard to figure out that there is no context in which S' can be coherently evaluated.

Burge was always acutely aware of this temptation to try to produce a "super-liar" sentence. In his view, it is simply impossible to successfully quantify into the index of the truth predicate. He says that an attempt to quantify out the indexical character of "true" "has some of the incongruity of 'here at some place' " [Burge 1979, p. 108]. But it is not clear how convincing this reply really is. For the indexical "here," the phrase "at some place" does the job: A sentence such as "It rains at some place" is, in contrast to "It rains (here)," not sensitive to spatial context shifts. But apparently, for the indexical notion of truth, no qualifier can successfully carry out the corresponding task. The only reason that this is so appears to be that if there were one, the liar paradox would rear its head. A more principled reason would surely be more satisfying.

5 Deflationism

Deflationism is the most popular philosophical view of truth these days. Many philosophers believe that the view is essentially correct. But there is surprisingly little agreement on what the view is committed to. This is to some extent due to the fact that just as mechanism is not really a physical theory, deflationism is not a theory of the laws of truth. It is rather a view on the nature and role of the concept of truth.

In this chapter, we look at what philosophers mean when they say that truth should be approached in a deflationary way. We outline the differences of opinion as to how the view should be stated. Along the way, and especially toward the end of the chapter, I take a stance on the question of what deflationism should and should not commit itself to.

5.1 The Unbearable Lightness of Truth

Deflationism is a vague doctrine, and it comes in many flavors. It is important to distinguish among these senses and to carve out a tenable version of the theory. It is argued that progress has been made on this front. Formulations of deflationism have been evolving in the past decades: We are slowly arriving at more robust formulations of deflationism.

Truth is sometimes described as one of the three principal domains of philosophy: Truth, Good, and Beauty. In a "superficial" way, it used to be said, the special sciences are also occupied with truth, namely, with truth in special domains. But in philosophy, we are concerned with the nature of Truth in general, with Truth in the deep and profound sense, as one of the absolutely fundamental categories of Being.

Deflationists dismiss this as babble from the sick bed. If anything, the situation is quite the reverse. The sciences are concerned with truth in a substantial sense, namely, with the specific propositions (concerning a given domain) that are true. Philosophy is the most general intellectual discipline. It is concerned with truth in a less substantial and more formal sense: It is concerned with the *concept* of truth.

Even the different branches of philosophy count in this respect as special sciences. According to deflationism, a satisfactory theory of truth does not substantially contribute to resolving disputes in epistemology or metaphysics. Deflationists are wont to quote Tarski himself on this issue [Tarski 1944, p. 362]:

> [W]e may accept [Tarski's] conception of truth without giving up any epistemological attitude we may have had; we may remain naive realists, critical realists or idealists, empiricists or metaphysicians—whatever we were before. [Tarski's] conception is completely neutral toward all these issues.

This is reflected in the fact that, among the proponents of deflationism about truth, one indeed finds empiricists, realists, nominalists, and platonists.

So the idea is that, unlike most other philosophical disciplines, the theory of truth does not have a substantial domain of its own. The domain of the theory of truth consists of the bearers of truth. These are linguistic entities (sentences), and therefore the theory of truth should be considered as a subdiscipline of the philosophy of language. Other philosophical fields do have nonlinguistic domains of their own (knowledge, reality as a whole, value, etc.), which are interconnected. The truths of the theory of truth merely supervene on facts that lie within the domain of investigation of other disciplines.

But then, what kind of notion *is* truth, and what is it good for? At a first approximation, deflationism claims that the notion of truth is akin to logical notions like "and," and "not." Logical notions are usually not regarded as *deep* philosophical notions. In a similar fashion, truth should be regarded as a superficial notion. This is what is meant when it is said that the notion of truth should be *deflated*. Traditional discussions of truth are like hot air balloons: They contain little substance.

5.2 Commitments of Deflationist Theories

A deflationist theory of truth consists of two parts [Gupta 1993, pp. 283–284]. First, it contains an account of the *meaning* of the concept of truth. Second, it contains a description of the *role* that truth should play in our intellectual practices, in particular in philosophy. The second part is based on the first part. A deflationist theory of truth should also tell us what *kind* of concept the notion of truth really is.

5.2.1 The Meaning of the Concept of Truth

We have seen that contemporary deflationists do not aim at defining truth. Nevertheless, deflationism does aim at explicating the meaning of the concept of truth.

Some versions of deflationism hold that the meaning of the concept of truth is given by the restricted Tarski-biconditionals. If someone knows the Tarski-biconditionals, then she knows all there is to know about the meaning of the concept of truth. In this sense, some deflationists take the theory DT to be truth-theoretically complete. Indeed, Michael Williams states that when we have endorsed the truth axioms of DT, we have said "just about everything there is to be said about truth" [Williams 1988, p. 424].

This should not be taken to imply that, in order for a language user to possess the concept of truth, she should know every restricted Tarski-biconditional because this would violate the finiteness of the human condition. In Gupta's terminology: Knowledge of all the Tarski-biconditionals would involve "massive conceptual resources." Rather, the language user must know the scheme, which can be seen as the application condition of the concept of truth. In other words, the competent language user knows the restricted Tarski-biconditionals in a dispositional sense: For any sentence that she recognizes, she is willing to assert the corresponding Tarski-biconditional. This entails that when our language is extended, the language user is prepared to accept more Tarski-biconditionals.

So in a sense, knowing the meaning of truth is, on this picture, like knowing a *rule*. This of course raises a philosophical question: What does knowledge of a rule consist of? This question is not really new. It has been with us since Wittgenstein, and it has since then been firmly put back on the philosophical agenda by the work of Kripke on Wittgenstein on following a rule [Kripke 1982]. We postpone this discussion until later,[1] but merely note here that it raises a concern. Namely, it may be that in our knowledge of what it means to follow a rule, knowledge of the concept of truth is involved. If that turns out to be so, then we have not advanced: We will have failed to fully explicate what knowledge of the concept of truth consists of.

But it is not clear why the meaning of truth has to be so intimately tied to the Tarski-biconditionals. We have argued that a case can be made for the thesis that DT is a philosophically sound theory of truth. But it is just *one* theory of truth. In the following chapters, we encounter other axiomatic theories of truth. Some of them are stronger than DT, and for some of these a case can also be

---

1. Compare infra, section 10.2.

made that they are philosophically sound. If they are indeed sound, then it is hard to see in which sense the Tarski-biconditionals can completely give the meaning of the concept of truth.

One reason that many philosophers think it is reasonable to ask of a theory of truth that it fully captures the meaning of the concept of truth is that truth is by many assumed to be a particularly *simple* notion. Horwich puts it thus [Horwich 1998, p. 51]:

> ...[the Tarski-biconditionals] could be explained only by principles that are simpler and more unified than they are—principles concerning propositional elements and the conditions in which truth emerges from combining them. But the single respect in which the body of minimal axioms is not already perfectly simple is that there is that there are so many of them—infinitely many; and no alleged explanation could improve on this feature. For there are infinitely many constituents to take into account; so any characterisation of them will also need infinitely many axioms.

To the logician, this passage raises a proof-theoretic question:

Is DT finitely axiomatisable over PA?

The answer to this question is indeed no. This proof-theoretic fact lends support to Horwich's claim about the irreducible simplicity of the Tarski-biconditionals.

So let us concede that if *DT* turns out to be truth-theoretically complete, then truth is indeed simple. Indeed, our demand that a theory of truth should somehow be natural is motivated by the conviction that truth is not a gerrymandered concept. If truth were a complicated notion, one would not expect ordinary human beings to be so adept at using it in a reliable manner in their everyday reasoning. So truth cannot be too complicated. Nevertheless, to say that truth is so simple that *DT* fully captures its meaning is a strong statement. It remains to be seen whether it is true. In fact, in subsequent chapters, we cast doubt on this assertion.

It may be too much to ask of any theory of truth to completely capture the meaning of the concept of truth. After all, axiomatic theories of truth would appear to be on a par with axiomatic theories of other concepts. One does not usually expect of an axiomatic theory of sets, for instance, that it completely conveys the meaning of the concept of set. Rather, one is inclined to say that ZFC, for instance, gives a *partial* explication of the meaning of the concept of set.[2] So too with theories of truth. The closer a truth theory comes to capturing the meaning of truth, the better. But perhaps it is unreasonable to expect of a theory of truth that it captures the meaning of truth completely.

---

2. ZFC stands for *Zermelo-Fraenkel* set theory with the axiom of *Choice*. See [Enderton 1977, chapter 2].

5.2.2 The Function of the Concept of Truth

Let us now try to get a perspective on the functions or roles that the concept of truth can *validly* perform. How can we legitimately make use of the concept of truth? Let us count the ways.

The truth predicate allows us to systematically relate terms to sentences and *vice versa*. By placing quotation marks around it, we transform a sentence into a term. By removing the quotation marks, the original sentence is retrieved. The theory *DT* allows us to treat a sentence as if it were an object. If one is willing to assert a sentence ϕ, one might as well put it in quotation marks and assert $T(\phi)$ instead.[3] In other words, instead of *asserting* a sentence, we can turn the sentence into an object and assert that this object has the property of truth. This is what Quine means when he says that truth is a *disquotational device* [Quine 1970, pp. 10–13], and this is why we call *DT* the *disquotational theory of truth*.

Positive Adding and removing quotation marks is no doubt a fascinating pastime for people of a certain bent. But because the relation between the assertion of a sentence and the attribution of truth to that same sentence in quotation marks is well nigh a logical equivalence, one may wonder what is gained in the process. Can we not always eliminate the concept of truth by erasing it and removing the quotation marks? Isn't truth a *redundant* notion?

Deflationists are quick to point out that even aside from the liar sentence and its ilk, the concept of truth is anything but redundant. The concept of truth allows us to express things that we would be hard pressed to express without it.

There first are the so-called *blind ascriptions*. Ramsey was perhaps the first to notice that occurrences of the truth predicate in blind ascriptions are not so easily eliminated.[4] Suppose you are engaged in a spirited discussion. You want to deny what Judy said yesterday evening, but in the heat of the debate you have forgotten what she said. Then the truth predicate comes in handy. You just say:

What Judy said yesterday evening is false.

But you may find yourself in an even stickier spot. Perhaps the discussion turns deeply philosophical. You find second-order logic[5] deeply objectionable (say), and yet you feel compelled to assert the principle of mathematical induction. Again you turn to the truth predicate, and say:

---

3. Recall that because of our deliberate sloppiness, we have invisible quotation marks.
4. See [Ramsey 1927, pp. 142–143].
5. Compare infra, section 7.2.2.

$$\forall \phi \in \mathcal{L}_{PA} : T\{[\phi(0) \wedge \forall y(\phi(y) \rightarrow \phi(s(y)))] \rightarrow \forall x \phi(x)\}.$$

In plain English, what this sentence says is the following: for every arithmetical property, it is true that if the property holds of the number 0 and "jumps" from numbers to their immediate successors, then the property holds of every natural number.

The first-order principle of mathematical induction is a *scheme* (i.e., an *infinite* collection of sentences). As finite beings, we cannot make an infinite number of assertions. But the truth predicate (in tandem with the first-order universal quantifier) allows us to assert in one sentence the *infinite conjunction* of all instances of the scheme. In a similar way, the truth predicate allows us to express infinitely long disjunctions. This, then, is a second way in which the truth predicate extends the *expressive strength* of our language.

So the truth predicate does expressive work for us. But we do not only want to express propositions using the concept of truth. We also want to assert some such propositions. In some cases, sentences containing the concept of truth can be derived from *DT* in the context of some background assumptions. For instance, if you are already prepared to assert that snow is white, *DT* allows you to derive from this that it is true that snow is white. Now in this latter sentence, the truth predicate is redundant. So one wonders whether *DT* helps us in proving general statements containing the concept of truth that are not redundant. This question is addressed in detail in [Halbach 1999b]. We postpone the discussion of it until the next chapter.

Negative It was traditionally thought that a theory of truth can and must do work in metaphysics and epistemology. For instance, received wisdom had it that the doctrine of realism in philosophy of science is intimately tied to a correspondence theory of truth, and it was thought that Kant's metaphysics is wedded to some sort of coherence theory of truth.

Deflationism denies this. If truth is not a deep philosophical notion, one would not expect it to do serious philosophical work. If truth is somehow "like conjunction," then it is not expected to substantially contribute to the resolution of philosophical problems. Just as theories of conjunction are not expected to solve any deep philosophical problem, neither should we expect this from a theory of truth.

Therefore, deflationism will claim that truth just is not a significant parameter in the solution space of substantial philosophical problems. Metaphysical theories, epistemological theories, and theories of meaning may partially depend on each other, but they are largely independent of theories of truth.[6]

---

6. An interesting exchange of views on these matters can be found in [Greenough & Lynch 2006].

5.2.3 Truth as a Logico-Linguistic Notion

Perhaps a theory of truth does not have to give the full meaning of the concept of truth. But as we have seen in section 2.2, a theory of truth should frame the concept of truth correctly. It should explicate what *kind* of notion the concept of truth is. Again, an analogy with set theory is instructive. One of the strengths of *ZFC* is that it shows how the concept of set is a mathematical concept. This was not at all evident when *ZFC* was first formulated in the beginning of the twentieth century: Many then took the concept of set to be a logical concept. But *ZFC* makes mind-boggling existence claims for sets. Such existence claims should surely not follow if set were a logical concept.

It was mentioned earlier that, according to deflationism, truth is *not* a philosophically substantial notion. But this tells us only what kind of notion truth is not. We also want to know what sort of concept the notion of truth is. Our previous remarks already hinted at a deflationist reply to this question.

Deflationists sometimes say that truth is a *logical notion*, or that truth expresses a *logical property* ([Field 1992, p. 322], [Field 1999, p. 534]). At least in part, truth indeed is a *logical* notion. We have seen that, like the first-order quantifiers, the truth predicate is a tool for expressing generality. But the notion of truth also allows us to formulate logical principles. For instance, using the concept of truth, we can express in one sentence a law of logic for $\mathcal{L}_{PA}$:

$$\forall \phi, \psi \in \mathcal{L}_{PA} : T((\phi \wedge \psi) \rightarrow \psi).$$

Without the concept of truth, we could not finitely express this principle in the object language.

But this statement of the kind of notion that truth is should be amended. In our framework, the concept of truth is portrayed as a logico-*linguistic* notion because, in part, truth clearly is a *linguistic* notion [Halbach & Horsten 2002a]. After all, the bearers of the property of truth are linguistic entities. More in particular, the bearers of truth are meaningful sentences (i.e., interpreted syntactic objects).

We have observed that the structural principles governing syntax are much like the structural principles for the natural numbers. Both can be seen as aspects of finite combinatorics. So if we are picturing the concept of truth as a logico-linguistic notion, then we are also picturing it as a *logico-mathematical* notion.

It is this aspect that Frege missed when he situated the theory of truth squarely in the province of logic. Of course we cannot really blame him for this. The importance of coding for the theory of truth only became clear through the work of Gödel and Tarski. Moreover, Frege (mistakenly) believed that mathematics in the final analysis reduces to logic.

The concept of elementhood is a *very* powerful mathematical notion: It is the central notion of the strongest mathematical theories that we have. The mathematical aspect of truth is connected to finitary combinatorics. So at first blush it seems that, insofar as truth is a mathematical notion, it is a comparatively light mathematical notion. It may carry mathematical commitments. But at least at first sight, one does not expect these mathematical commitments to be heavy.

But picturing truth as a logico-linguistic notion is picturing it as more than a logico-mathematical notion. The truth of a sentence is not only determined by its syntactical structure, but also by the meaning and reference (extension) of its component parts. Whereas linguistics comprises the theory of meaning and reference, mathematics does not.

But why stop there? It is surely a matter for the special sciences to decide what the extension of specific predicates is. For instance, it is the business of biologists to delineate the extension of the predicate "is a reptile." Therefore, one may have to consult a biologist to determine whether the sentence "Eddy is a reptile" is true. Does this not make truth partly a biological notion? I should think not. To determine whether a given metal rod will break if it is bent slightly more may require calculation. But this does not make facts about the breaking of metals in part mathematical. In the same way, the fact that specific referential facts belong to the provinces of the special sciences is compatible with the logico-linguistic nature of the notion of truth.

The fallacy here is the same as the fallacy that led philosophers to believe that truth is one of the most central notions of the most general science of all: *metaphysics*. It is correct to say that the truth of "It rains," for instance, depends on a metereological fact, and that this should not make the theory of truth a logico-linguistic-metereological enterprise. But in theories of truth, we are not interested in truths *per se*. We want to uncover the *laws* of truth (and thereby shed light on the concept of truth).

5.3 Foreign Tongues

Throughout we have maintained that truth is a property of sentences. But a sentence of one language is no less a candidate for being true than a sentence of another.

DT is intended to be a truth theory for a simplified and regimented version of *our* language: English. If *DT* is our theory of truth, then it is a theory of truth for the English language. *DT* does not say anything about truth of sentences of other languages, or even of truth of sentences of future extensions of English that do not already belong to the English language as we find it.

In contrast to sentences, propositions are language independent. This is one reason that it is attractive to take, as Horwich does, the bearers of truth to be propositions. But to the extent that propositions are different from sentences, they are also mysterious. The move from sentences to propositions does not really advance our understanding until a theory of propositions is given that is as explicit and precise as our theory of sentences (i.e., the theory of syntax). A circularity threat may be lurking here: It may be that a satisfactory theory of propositions presupposes the notion of truth.

Davidson has long emphasized that extending our theory of truth of sentences so as to give an account of sentences of other languages imports substantial commitments [Davidson 1973]. To connect our notion of truth to sentences of foreign languages, a *translation function* is needed that transforms sentences from foreign languages to sentences of our language. Such a translation function must evidently meet certain standards. In particular, it must be meaning-preserving, or at the very least it must preserve truth conditions. Then the question arises how we can know of a given translation manual that it preserves meaning or truth-conditions, and whether there is even always a matter of fact whether a given translation manual preserves meaning.

These questions have been pursued in a famous debate between Davidson and Quine, and in an extensive body of philosophical literature that springs from this debate. For us, the burning question is whether an account of meaning and truth-conditions can be given, which answers these questions adequately and which at the same time can justly be labeled deflationist. But we take no stance on this issue. We concentrate on the question of whether a deflationist account of truth can be given for *our* language. If this were the case, then this would already count as a major success for the deflationist. We leave it open whether such an account can be extended to other languages.[7]

---

7. For more about this problem, see [Field 1994, section 8].

6 The Compositional Theory

In this chapter, we investigate a second axiomatic theory that is directly inspired by Tarski's work on truth. Tarski's definition of truth in a model inspires an axiomatic theory of truth that explicates the compositional nature of truth. We see that the compositional theory has several advantages when compared with the disquotational theory.

6.1 Clouds on the Horizon

The following two propositions are typical illustrations of the proof-theoretic strength of the disquotational theory.

Proposition 24 *For all $\phi \in \mathcal{L}_{PA}$: $DT \vdash T(\phi) \vee T(\neg\phi)$*

Proof *Already propositional logic alone proves $\phi \vee \neg\phi$. Two restricted Tarski-biconditionals are $T(\phi) \leftrightarrow \phi$ and $T(\neg\phi) \leftrightarrow \neg\phi$. Combining these facts yields the desired result.* ∎

Proposition 25 (Tarski) $DT \nvdash \forall \phi \in \mathcal{L}_{PA} : T(\phi) \vee T(\neg\phi)$

Proof *Take any proof $\mathcal{P}$ in DT. And suppose, for a reductio, that*

$$\forall \phi \in \mathcal{L}_{PA} : T(\phi) \vee T(\neg\phi)$$

belongs to $\mathcal{P}$. $\mathcal{P}$, being a finite object, can contain only finitely many restricted Tarski-biconditionals. Let us list these Tarski-biconditionals:

1. $T(\varphi_1) \leftrightarrow \varphi_1$
2. $T(\varphi_2) \leftrightarrow \varphi_2$
3. ...
⋮
n. $T(\varphi_n) \leftrightarrow \varphi_n$

Now we will construct a model $\mathfrak{M} =: \langle \mathbb{N}, \mathcal{E} \rangle$ which makes all sentences of $\mathcal{P}$ true. Let $\mathcal{E}$ consist precisely of those true arithmetical sentences ψ such that either ψ or $\neg\psi$ is among $\{\varphi_1, \varphi_2, \ldots, \varphi_n\}$. The model $\mathfrak{M}$ makes all the arithmetical axioms true because it is based on $\mathbb{N}$. And it makes all the restricted Tarski-biconditionals of $\mathcal{P}$ true by the construction of $\mathcal{E}$. But for every true arithmetical sentence ϑ, such that neither ϑ nor $\neg\vartheta$ is in $\{\varphi_1, \varphi_2, \ldots, \varphi_n\}$, the restricted Tarski-biconditional $T(\vartheta) \leftrightarrow \vartheta$ is false in $\mathfrak{M}$. Thus,

$$\mathfrak{M} \not\models \forall \phi \in \mathcal{L}_{PA} : T(\phi) \vee T(\neg\phi).$$

By one direction of the completeness theorem for first-order logic, this yields a contradiction with our supposition that $\forall \phi \in \mathcal{L}_{PA} : T(\phi) \vee T(\neg\phi)$ belongs to $\mathcal{P}$. ∎

So somehow *DT* proves all the instances of an intuitively plausible logical principle concerning the notion of truth, but it is unable to collect all these instances together into a general theorem.

In a similar way, it can be shown that *DT* cannot prove:

$$\forall \phi, \psi \in \mathcal{L}_{PA} : (T(\phi) \wedge T(\psi)) \leftrightarrow T(\phi \wedge \psi).$$

Something similar can be said for seemingly basic laws of truth concerning negation and the quantifiers. In summary, *DT* fails to fully validate our intuitions concerning the *compositional nature* of the notion of truth (i.e., the fact that the property of truth "distributes" over the logical connectives). In fact, our intuition that truth is compositional is (perhaps independent from but) just as basic as our intuition that truth is a disquotational device. Our truth theory has an obligation to either do justice to it or explain what is wrong with it.

Earlier we insisted against inflationists about truth (such as Patterson) that proving many Tarski-biconditionals is a necessary condition for being a good truth theory.[1] But now we see that deriving many Tarski-biconditionals is not a sufficient condition for being a good theory of truth. A good theory of truth must in addition do justice to the compositional nature of truth.

The inability of *DT* to fully explicate the compositional nature of truth is a motivation for taking the principles that do explicate it as *axioms* of a theory of truth. We already know beforehand that if this is done, then there is a sense in which the resulting theory is stronger than *DT*. These principles of composition are of course contained in Tarski's clauses for recursively explicating the notion of truth of a formula in a model.

---

1. Compare supra, section 2.2.

6.2 The Compositional Theory of Truth

The axioms of our new axiomatic theory of truth can be directly read off from Tarski's definition of truth in a model. Indeed, Tarski's concept of a first-order model serves as the direct motivation for our new truth theory.

Tarski's axiomatic compositional theory of truth is denoted as TC.[2] The axiomatic theory of truth TC is formulated in $\mathcal{L}_T$ and consists of the following axioms:

TC1 PA^T;

TC2 $\forall$ atomic $\phi \in \mathcal{L}_{PA} : T(\phi) \leftrightarrow val^+(\phi)$;

TC3 $\forall \phi \in \mathcal{L}_{PA} : T(\neg \phi) \leftrightarrow \neg T(\phi)$;

TC4 $\forall \phi, \psi \in \mathcal{L}_{PA} : T(\phi \wedge \psi) \leftrightarrow (T(\phi) \wedge T(\psi))$;

TC5 $\forall \phi(x) \in \mathcal{L}_{PA} : T(\forall x \phi(x)) \leftrightarrow \forall x T(\phi(x))$.

So the idea behind this axiom system is straightforward. An explicit definition of the class of true atomic arithmetical sentences can be given by means of the arithmetical formula val^+.[3] Truth for complex arithmetical sentences can be reduced to truth of atomic arithmetical formulae through the compositional truth axioms.

Davidson championed the compositional theory. But it is typical, not just of him but of analytical philosophy during his lifetime, that he never bothered to write down the axioms of his theory of truth in detail. Field at one time was also a defender of the compositional theory of truth.[4]

It is important that each compositional truth axiom is expressed as a universally quantified sentence rather than as an axiom scheme. From the axiom scheme, the corresponding universally quantified sentence cannot be derived. But we have seen that each instance can be derived from DT, whereby the schematic version of TC is a consequence of DT. The whole motivation of TC lies in our desire for the universally quantified truth axioms to be provable in our truth theory.

---

2. It would be more felicitous to abbreviate it as CT were it not for the fact that the latter is the canonical abbreviation of *Church's Thesis*. In the literature, the theory TC is often referred to as $T(PA)$.

3. Compare supra, section 3.6.

4. See [Field 1999]. In more recent times, Field has developed a formal theory of truth of which it is not prima facie clear whether it can be accepted by a deflationist. Field's recent truth theory is discussed later in section 10.2.2.

As in the case of the disquotational theory, we can make a case for the soundness of *TC*. First of all, *TC* has models that are as nice as those of *DT*:

Proposition 26 *TC has nice models.*

Proof *It can be shown that the model $\mathfrak{M}$ that was constructed in the proof of proposition 19 is also a model of TC. As in the case for DT, the only nontrivial question is whether $\mathfrak{M}$ makes the truth axioms true. We do the case of the truth axiom for conjunction as an example:*

$\mathfrak{M} \models T(\phi \wedge \psi) \Leftrightarrow$

$\phi \wedge \psi \in \mathcal{E} \Leftrightarrow$

$\mathbb{N} \models \phi \wedge \psi \Leftrightarrow$

$\mathbb{N} \models \phi$ *and* $\mathbb{N} \models \psi \Leftrightarrow$

$\phi \in \mathcal{E}$ *and* $\psi \in \mathcal{E} \Leftrightarrow$

$\mathfrak{M} \models T(\phi)$ *and* $\mathfrak{M} \models T(\psi) \Leftrightarrow$

$\mathfrak{M} \models T(\phi) \wedge T(\psi).$ ∎

Tarski's diagnosis of the paradoxes is upheld in *TC*. As before, no sentences of the form $T(\ldots T \ldots)$ are provable in *TC*. Also as before, we can construct a whole hierarchy *TC*, $TC_1, \ldots, TC_n, \ldots$ of axiomatic compositional theories of truth—but there is no need to dwell on this now.

As in the case of *DT*, it seems somewhat plausible that *TC* is *truth-theoretically* sound. It appears to accurately explicate the commonsense view that the truth value of a complex sentence is determined by the truth values of its component parts. We might call this the compositionality intuition. In summary, *TC* is an attractive theory of truth.

One caveat must be made at this point. Natural language contains vague expressions. Most semanticists hold that sentences containing vague expressions sometimes lack a truth value.[5] The sentence "Italy is a large country" may, on this view, not have a truth value: The complex predicate "large country" is vague, and Italy seems to be a borderline case of being a large country. One of the most popular ways of extending partial logic to complex sentences is based on supervaluation [Fine 1975].[6] On this approach, truth is not compositional. If "Italy is a large country" does lack a truth value, then so, too, presumably, does "Italy is not a large country." But "Italy is or is not a large country" is true,

---

5. Timothy Williamson is a notable exception: see [Williamson 1994].
6. Supervaluation models are discussed in more detail in section 9.1.2.

on the supervaluationist account, because it is a truth of classical propositional logic. However, some disjunctions of truth-valueless sentences are just as truth-valueless. If the sentence "Great Britain is a large country" also lacks a truth value, then "Italy is a large country or Great Britain is a large country" is yet another sentence without a truth value. This shows that on the supervaluationist account, the truth value of a disjunction is not determined by the truth values of its disjuncts.

According to some, this shows that the compositional theory of truth is not sound as a theory of truth of English. In this book, we simply set aside the problems induced by vague predicates. Also, truth value gaps (if any) caused by other factors such as presupposition failure[7] are not taken into account. So one may take the theories of truth that are considered here as theories of truth for the fragments of ordinary English that do not contain vague expressions, presupposition failures, and so on. The task before us is already difficult enough without these added complications. Now it may be the case that the notion of truth causes certain sentences to lack a truth value. If such turns out to be the case, then we have phenomena that we cannot set aside because the notion of truth is our core business.

6.3 Truth and Satisfaction

In the formulation of the compositional theory of truth, a simplifying assumption has been made that is not completely innocuous. The assumption is related to the compositional axiom *TC*5, which says that truth commutes with the universal quantifier. But to see this, we have to look "through" our non-well-formed notation.

When axiom *TC*5 is made grammatical, we see that the substitution function appears. It then *really* says that a universally quantified sentence is true if and only if all the instantiations by standard numerals are true. Now this works fine for arithmetic: Every number is named by a standard numeral. But of course the compositional theory of truth is intended to be quite general. It should also work for an interpreted ground language such that not every element of its domain of discourse has a name, let alone a standard name. Indeed, the number of English expressions is denumerably infinite. But Cantor's theorem can be used to show that there are nondenumerably many real numbers.[8] So not every real number has a (simple or complex) name in English. Perhaps there are even

---

7. According to certain philosophers of language, the sentence "The queen of France is intelligent" *presupposes* rather than asserts that there is a queen of France (see e.g., [Strawson 1950]). Because this presupposition is not met, they say the sentence is not truth-evaluable.

8. See [Enderton 1977, pp. 132–133].

real numbers that are somehow inherently unnameable even in extensions of English that humans can master.

This problem is well known, and there is a standard solution. The solution is due, not surprisingly, to Tarski. It says that the truth predicate should be defined in terms of the more primitive *satisfaction relation*: the relation of being *true of*. The fundamental notion is that of a formula (containing free variables) being true of a sequence of objects (that serve as values of these variables).

A *rough* sketch of the solution goes as follows. Let $Sat(x, y)$ be the satisfaction predicate, where now x stands for a number rather than for a sequence of numbers. Then a satisfaction axiom for (one-place) atomic formulae looks roughly like this:

$$\forall \text{ atomic } \phi(x), \forall y : Sat(y, \phi(x)) \leftrightarrow \phi(y)$$

The compositional axioms for the propositional logical connectives are the analogues of $TC3$ and $TC4$. The compositional axiom governing the interaction between satisfaction and universal quantification is (roughly):

$$\forall x, \forall \phi(y) : Sat(x, \forall y \phi(y)) \leftrightarrow \forall y Sat(y, \phi(y)))$$

Truth is then defined as satisfaction by all sequences of objects of the domain.

In summary, the situation is not *very* different from the case where all objects have standard names. Nevertheless, one should be mindful. In the general case, satisfaction is a more primitive notion than truth. It is also even more susceptible to semantical paradox than the truth predicate: Even stronger no-go theorems can be proved for axiomatic theories of satisfaction than can be proved for axiomatic theories of truth.[9] This means that one has to be even more cautious in the formulation of a theory of satisfaction than in the formulation of a formal theory of truth.

We leave this complication behind us from now on. Therefore, we effectively work under the assumption that every element of the domain has a standard name. But as a matter of fact, the truth theories that we consider in this book can be fairly straightforwardly reformulated as theories of satisfaction.

6.4 The Power of Truth

The concept of *conservativeness* has played an important role in recent philosophical discussions of axiomatic theories of truth.

Intuitively, we say that a theory of truth is conservative over a background theory S if and only if no sentences in the language of S can be proved using

---

9. See [Horsten 2004].

The Compositional Theory

the axioms of the truth theory and the axioms of the background theory that cannot already be proved in S alone. We have taken a theory of syntax as our background theory. We have for convenience identified this theory of syntax with the arithmetical theory *PA*. So we focus on the notion of arithmetical conservativeness of a truth theory:

Definition 27 *A theory of truth S is* arithmetically conservative *over PA if for every sentence $\phi \in \mathcal{L}_{PA}$, if $S \vdash \phi$, then already $PA \vdash \phi$.*

The question then arises whether truth theories are arithmetically conservative over *PA*.

It can be shown that:

Proposition 28 *DT is arithmetically conservative over PA.*

Proof We demonstrate how every proof in *DT* of an arithmetical statement can be transformed into a proof in *PA* of that very same statement.
Suppose we are given a proof $\mathcal{P}$ of an arithmetical sentence ϕ. Because the number of sentences occurring in this proof is finite, there must be an upper bound to the complexity of sentences occurring in $\mathcal{P}$. Suppose the most complex sentence in $\mathcal{P}$ is Σ_n. We know that there exists an arithmetical partial truth predicate for Σ_n-sentences, and that *PA* can prove for all Σ_n-sentences the Tarski-biconditionals for this partial truth predicate. So we replace all occurrences of the primitive truth predicate T in $\mathcal{P}$ by occurrences of the partial truth predicate for for Σ_n-sentences. This results in a modified (but elliptical) proof $\mathcal{P}'$, which is a proof in *PA*. Moreover, the conclusion of $\mathcal{P}'$ remains ϕ, because ϕ does not contain any occurrences of T. ∎

This is not really a surprising result. *DT* differs from *PA* only in having, in addition, logical axioms concerning the notion of truth. One feels an inclination to believe that truth is a *philosophical* notion (even if it is, as the deflationists would have it, a shallow one) and not a mathematical notion. Logical axioms concerning philosophical notions will not help with the solution of *mathematical* problems that *PA* cannot solve.

We have seen that *TC* proves intuitively valid principles concerning the notion of truth that *DT* fails to prove. In fact, it is not hard to see that *DT* is a subtheory of *TC*:

Proposition 29 $TC \vdash T(\phi) \leftrightarrow \phi$ *for all $\phi \in \mathcal{L}_{PA}$.*

Proof *This fact is proved by an induction on the complexity of ϕ. The basis case follows by the first truth axiom of TC. We only do one inductive case. Suppose that by the inductive hypothesis, $T(\psi) \leftrightarrow \psi$ is provable in TC; we want to establish that $T(\neg\psi) \leftrightarrow \neg\psi$ is then also provable in TC. By the second truth* axiom of TC, we have $T(\neg\psi) \leftrightarrow \neg T(\psi)$. But by the inductive hypothesis, TC proves $\neg T(\psi) \leftrightarrow \neg\psi$. Combining these facts, we see that TC then indeed proves $T(\neg\psi) \leftrightarrow \neg\psi$. The other inductive cases can be proved in a similar way using the remaining truth axioms of TC. ∎

This is as it should be. Proving the restricted Tarski-biconditionals is an adequacy condition for truth theories.

We now show that the theory TC is even *arithmetically* stronger than DT: The collection of arithmetical theorems of DT is a proper subset of the collection of arithmetical theorems of TC. This implies, of course, that TC is *not* arithmetically conservative over PA.

First, it is shown how TC proves the *global reflection principle* for PA:[10]

Theorem 30 $TC \vdash \forall\phi \in \mathcal{L}_{PA} : Bew_{PA}(\phi) \rightarrow T(\phi)$.

Proof (Sketch) The theorem is proved by carrying out, inside TC, an induction on the length of proofs in PA.

For the basis case, it has to be shown that the logical axiom schemes are true and that the arithmetical axioms of PA (including the axiom scheme of mathematical induction) are true. We do not dwell on the logical axioms here. We sketch how it is shown that the axiom of PA that says that there is a least number is true, and how it is shown that all instances of mathematical induction are true. Suppose $\phi =: \neg\exists y\,(0 = s(y))$. By the previous proposition, TC proves

$$\neg\exists y\,(0 = s(y)) \leftrightarrow T(\neg\exists y\,(0 = s(y))).$$

Combining this with the PA-axiom $\neg\exists y\,(0 = s(y))$, TC indeed infers that

$$T(\neg\exists y\,(0 = s(y))).$$

Let us now turn to the proof that all instances of mathematical induction are true. The following is an instance of the induction axiom of TC:

$$\forall\phi(x) \in \mathcal{L}_{PA} : [T\phi(0) \wedge \forall y(T\phi(y) \rightarrow T\phi(y+1))] \rightarrow \forall x T\phi(x).$$

The compositional axioms of TC entail that the truth predicate can be moved to the front:

$$T\{\forall\phi(x) \in \mathcal{L}_{PA} : [\phi(0) \wedge \forall y(\phi(y) \rightarrow \phi(y+1))] \rightarrow \forall x \phi(x)\}.$$

And this is precisely what we were asked to prove.

For the induction step, we consider the case where ϕ is obtained by modus ponens from ψ and $\psi \rightarrow \phi$. In other words, we need to show in TC that $T(\phi)$ if

---

10. A detailed exposition of this proof can be found in [Halbach 2010, chapter 2].

$Bew_{PA}(\psi) \wedge Bew_{PA}(\psi \to \phi)$.

By the inductive hypothesis, we have $T(\psi)$ and $T(\psi \to \phi)$. By the compositional truth axioms of TC, we infer from $T(\psi \to \phi)$ that $\neg T(\psi) \vee T(\phi)$. Combining this with $T(\psi)$, we obtain $T(\phi)$. ∎

Corollary 31 $TC \vdash Con(PA)$.

Proof *We reason inside TC. We instantiate the TC-theorem that we have just proved by letting $\phi =: 0 = 1$, obtaining*

$Bew_{PA}(0=1) \to T(0=1)$.

By proposition 29, we also have $T(0=1) \leftrightarrow 0 = 1$. Combining these findings, we obtain, in TC, that

$Bew_{PA}(0=1) \to 0 = 1$.

But because TC of course also proves $\neg(0=1)$, we obtain in TC the conclusion that $\neg Bew_{PA}(0=1)$, i.e., $Con(PA)$. ∎

When first learning about this theorem, it appears to a philosopher like a tale

[...] whose lightest word
Would harrow up thy soul, freeze thy young blood,
Make thy two eyes, like stars, start from their spheres,
Thy knotted and combined locks to part
And each particular hair to stand on end,
Like quills upon the fretful porpentine
[Shakespeare 1600, Hamlet, Act I, Scene 5]

Indeed, this result concerning the power of *TC* is really surprising. *PA* fails to prove certain arithmetical sentences, such as $\neg Bew_{PA}(0=1)$. It is surprising that by just adding to *PA* principles concerning the notion of *truth*, we increase the *mathematical* strength of *PA*. This means that, contrary to our expectations, the "philosophical" notion of truth has real mathematical content. It reveals the power of truth!

We have seen how Gödel's second incompleteness phenomenon shows that *PA* cannot prove its own consistency. So *TC* is mathematically stronger than *PA*, because it can prove the consistency of *PA*. All this does not imply that *TC* escapes the incompleteness phenomenon. The moral of the second incompleteness theorem is that a (sufficiently strong) consistent theory cannot prove its own consistency. Because we know *TC* to be consistent, this moral holds also for *TC*: It cannot prove *its own* consistency.

The phenomenon that we have just described is robust. If we move one step up the Tarskian hierarchy and consider TC_1, for instance, we see that we have again gained arithmetical strength. TC_1 proves the consistency of TC for pretty much the same reasons as TC proves the consistency of *PA*.

We conclude this section by highlighting two aspects of TC that are essential for the nonconservativeness proof to go through.

First, it is essential that the compositional axioms are formulated as single (quantified) sentences and not as axiom schemes. We have seen before that this is necessary for proving sentences such as

$$\forall \phi, \psi \in \mathcal{L}_{PA} : T[\phi \to (\phi \vee \psi)]$$

Such theorems are appealed to in the basis case of the proof of the uniform reflection principle.

Second, allowing T to occur in the induction scheme is *essential* for the proof of the uniform reflection theorem to work. The truth predicate not only occurs in the property that is proved in the TC-induction on the length of proofs to hold universally, but the truth predicate also occurs in the instance of mathematical induction that is used to show that all instances of the induction axiom of *PA* are true.

Let us reserve a special name for the truth theory, which is just like TC except that the induction scheme is restricted to formulae of $\mathcal{L}_{PA}$: call this theory TC^-. It can be proved that TC^- is arithmetically conservative over *PA*. However, this proof is complicated, so we do not discuss it here.[11]

Now we are ready to make a preliminary comparative evaluation of the disquotational and compositional theories.

The compositional theory of truth contains the disquotational theory as a proper subtheory. It is mathematically sound. It appears to be (modulo vagueness, presupposition failure, etc.) philosophically sound. It is truth-theoretically more complete than the disquotational theory. It suffers from the same philosophical defect as the disquotational theory in that iterated truth ascriptions are not provable. The best that both the disquotational and compositional theories can do in this respect is to distinguish levels of truth. In this way, acceptance of truth iteration can to some extent be simulated: Truth of a higher level can correctly be ascribed to sentences containing only lower level truth predicates.

But unlike *DT*, the compositional theory is arithmetically not conservative over Peano arithmetic. This comes as a surprise; it is not immediately clear what to think of it. Until this issue has been cleared up, we cannot be quite confident that TC is, from a philosophical point of view, as unobjectionable as *DT*.

---

11. See [Halbach 1999a] for an elegant proof. The first proof of this theorem was given in [Kotlarski et al. 1981].

7 Conservativeness and Deflationism

In this chapter, we explore the relation between deflationism and the arithmetical nonconservativeness of the compositional theory of truth. In this context, we also describe the role that the concept of truth plays in specific philosophical disciplines such as epistemology, philosophy of language, and metaphysics.

7.1 Defining Conservativeness

Deflationist theories hold that truth is somehow an "insubstantial" notion, that it does not carry much ontological weight. This claim is sometimes combined with the view that the purpose of the notion of truth is to *express* certain things (infinite conjunctions) that we could not otherwise express, but not to *prove* things about matters not concerning truth that we cannot otherwise prove. In other words, some deflationists hold that the notion of truth is *argumentatively weak*.

Some believe that deflationism is wedded to conservativeness claims: A reasonable truth theory should be *conservative over* an underlying reasonable philosophical (metaphysical, epistemological, semantic, etc.) theory.[1] Shapiro expresses this conviction in the following manner [Shapiro 1998, pp. 497–498]:

I submit that in one form or other, conservativeness is essential to deflationism. Suppose, for instance, that Karl correctly holds a theory [A] in a language that cannot express truth. He adds a truth predicate to the language and extends [A] to a theory [A'] using only axioms essential to truth. Assume that [A'] is not conservative over [A]. Then there is a sentence Φ in the original language so that Φ is a consequence of [A'] but not a consequence of [A]. That is, it is logically possible for the axioms of [A] to be true yet Φ false, but it is not logically possible for the axioms of [A'] to be true and Φ false. This undermines the central deflationist theme that truth is insubstantial. Before

---

1. See [Horsten 1995] and [Field 1999]. The author of the former article now regrets the (cautious) remarks that he made in this direction.

Karl moved to [A'], $\neg \Phi$ was possible. The move from [A] to [A'] *added* semantic content sufficient to rule out the falsity of Φ. But by hypothesis, all that was added in [A'] were principles essential to truth. Thus, those principles have substantial semantic content.

In fact, most attention in the literature has been devoted to the question of conservativeness of a reasonable theory of truth not over reasonable philosophical but over reasonable *mathematical* theories ([Ketland 1999], [Halbach 2001]).

We can generalize the concept of conservativeness that we have discussed so far. Consider a theory Th formulated in a language $\mathcal{L}_{Th}$. Th may be a scientific (physical, mathematical, etc.) or a philosophical theory. Consider a theory of truth Tr that is intended to apply to the language of the theory Th. The theory Tr may be thought of as being formulated in the language $\mathcal{L}_{Tr}$, which is defined as $\mathcal{L}_{Th} \cup \{T\}$, where T is a truth predicate.

Now we say that the theory Tr of truth is conservative over Th if and only if for every sentence ϕ of the language of $\mathcal{L}_{Th}$ in which the truth predicate does not occur the following holds:

If $Th \cup Tr \vdash \phi$, then $Th \vdash \phi$.

Some philosophers insist that the language $\mathcal{L}_{Th}$, in which the theory Th is formulated, must not already contain the truth predicate [Field 1999]. If this restriction is accepted, then it can usually be shown for reasonable choices of Th and Tr that the conservativeness property indeed holds. If this restriction is rejected, then for many reasonable choices of Th and Tr the conservativeness property will not hold.

Already in the case where Th is a mathematical theory, it seems somewhat artificial to impose such a restriction on the language of Th. Suppose, for concreteness, that Th is Peano arithmetic. Then the restriction that the language of Th should not contain the truth predicate entails that in instances of the induction scheme, the truth predicate is not allowed to occur. This seems awkward because the induction scheme is intended to apply to *all* property-expressing predicates. So let us from now on allow that the language $\mathcal{L}_{Th}$ in which the theory Th is formulated may already contain the truth predicate.

Instead of the proof-theoretic characterization of conservativeness, one can opt for a semantic conception of conservativeness. We say that the theory Tr of truth is *semantically conservative* over Th if and only if for every sentence ϕ of the language of $\mathcal{L}_{Th}$ in which the truth predicate does not occur the following holds:

If $Th \cup Tr \models \phi$, then $Th \models \phi$.

Conservativeness and Deflationism

But given the completeness theorem for first-order logic, the proof-theoretic and the semantic conception of conservativeness coincide, so there is little point in distinguishing them.[2]

7.2 Conservative Over What?

We need to distinguish specific conservativeness requirements. If the question is raised whether truth is conservative, one should reply with a counter-question: conservative over what?

7.2.1 Conservativeness Over Logic

The strongest conservativeness requirement for a theory of truth says that the theory must be conservative over first-order logic. A truth theory Tr is conservative over logic if and only if all sentences that are provable from Tr but that do not contain the truth predicate are provable from the laws of logic alone.

It was pointed out by Halbach that not even weak truth theories can meet this requirement [Halbach 2001, pp. 178–180]. Already the weakest version of DT is nonconservative in this sense. Consider the following restricted Tarski-biconditionals:

$T(\forall x : x = x) \leftrightarrow \forall x : x = x$

$T(\forall x : x \neq x) \leftrightarrow \forall x : x \neq x$

Again these formulae are not well formed. The arguments of the truth predicate in these formulae are really names of numerical codes of sentences expressed by means of mathematical vocabulary. Because we only have the laws of *logic* at our disposal here, nothing of interest can be proved about these terms: We cannot even prove that they code sentences! Nevertheless, first-order logic implies that the right-hand side of the first sentence is true, whereas the right-hand side of the second sentence is false. So by Leibniz' principle that identical objects have the same properties, the sentence "$\forall x : x = x$" must be a different thing than the sentence "$\forall x : x \neq x$". So even in the absence of *PA*, the theory DT entails that there are at least two objects, which we may call "the True" and "the False." This is more than pure logic can do for us because logic alone does not entail $\exists x \exists y (x \neq y)$.

Now in the end, this is not surprising. It is not hard to see that DT is not *very* nonconservative over logic: It proves the existence of no more than two

---

2. Besides these two notions, there are notions of conservativeness that do not coincide with either of them. These other notions are not discussed in this book.

objects. This is not impressive given the fact that classical predicate logic alone already is nonconservative over *das Nichts*.

One wonders whether, from a philosophical point of view, a logical conservativeness requirement makes much sense. For in the absence of an arithmetical theory functioning as a theory of syntax, it is not even clear what a truth theory such as *DT means*. One would expect that in the axiomatic frame of mind, not only the meaning of the truth predicate but also the meaning of the syntax theory is given by axioms describing syntactical operations. In the setting we work in, this role is played by Peano arithmetic.

7.2.2 Conservativeness Over Arithmetic

If we take arithmetic on board, then we arrive at the requirement that a truth theory must be conservative over the background arithmetical theory, Peano arithmetic.

The disquotational theory is conservative over *PA*. It may be thought that the concept of arithmetical conservativeness gives us a handle on a problem that we were stuck with earlier. In section 4.2, it was noted that trying to collect as many Tarski-biconditionals as consistently possible is not a promising strategy: None of these collections is computably axiomatizable. One might hope that the extra constraint of conservativeness helps. We might look for a maximally strong, consistent, and axiomatizable extension of *DT*, which is conservative over *PA*. Unfortunately, this does not work either. Cieśliński has shown that the set of consistent axiomatizable extensions of *DT*, which are conservative over *PA*, does not have a maximal element under the inclusion ordering [Cieśliński 2007]. So we are again confronted with an embarrassment of choice.

We have seen that the compositional theory of truth is not conservative over *PA*. But this nonconservativeness is somehow of a different nature than the nonconservativeness of *DT* over logic. Although the disquotational theory turns out to be ontologically productive over logic, the compositional theory is *ideologically* nonconservative over arithmetic, to use Quine's phraseology.

Shapiro and Ketland were tempted to infer from the arithmetical nonconservativeness of *TC* that deflationism about truth cannot rationally be upheld ([Shapiro 1998], [Ketland 1999]). But Field has resisted this conclusion [Field 1999].

Field at one point cautiously accepted that deflationism is wedded to arithmetical conservativeness of truth. Specifically, he says [Field 1999, p. 536]:

> Since truth can be added in ways that produce a conservative extension (even in first-order logic), there is no need to disagree with Shapiro when he says that "conservativeness is essential to deflationism."

But Field takes issue with the contention that truth is arithmetically nonconservative.

Field's argument goes roughly as follows. The pure truth axioms are $TC1-TC5$. The induction axioms of TC do not count as "genuine" truth principles. So the fact that TC is not conservative over Peano arithmetic does not entail that truth is not arithmetically conservative. If we want to find out whether truth is conservative, we must add the *pure* truth axioms $TC1-TC5$ to PA. This of course yields the theory TC^-, which is, as we have seen, arithmetically conservative over PA.

This is a specious argument. It is difficult to see why the new induction instances count less as truth principles than the compositional axioms do. After all, is not $TC4$, for instance, as much about the logical connective of conjunction and about the natural numbers (which serve as names of sentences) as about truth? But even leaving this worry aside, if the truth-containing instances of the induction scheme are less than 18-carat truth principles, then what kind of principles are they?

One option is to regard the truth-containing instances of the induction scheme as *mathematical* principles. This is the position that McGee advocates [McGee 2003, pp. 19-20]:

Mathematics is the common background to all the sciences; this includes the principle of induction. If the chemist wants to establish some property of plastics by induction on the length of polymer chains, she allows the introduction of chemical vocabulary into induction axioms, without any worry that perhaps induction is only legitimate within pure mathematics, so that it's no longer applicable when chemical concepts are involved. The rule of mathematical induction is part of the scientist's standard mathematical toolkit, and in applying it as she does, the chemist is not reaching beyond the bounds of classical mathematics; she is extending the bounds of known chemistry.

Field also seems to express sympathy with this view [Field 1999, p. 538]:

[that the truth of the induction axioms containing the truth predicate depends only on the nature of truth] just seems false: the corresponding axioms would hold for any other predicate, and what they depend on is a fact about the natural numbers, namely, that they are linearly ordered with each element having only finitely many predecessors.

But if the induction axioms containing the truth predicate are *mathematical* principles, then we might as well take PA^T as our mathematical base theory. (Recall that PA^T is the version of Peano arithmetic where the truth predicate is allowed to occur in instances of the induction scheme.) If we then add the pure truth principles $TC1-TC5$, we of course obtain the nonconservative theory TC once more.

Another option consists of taking the new induction axioms to be interaction principles: bridge principles between truth and mathematics. On this view, what Field's argument brings out is the importance of these bridge principles. His argument highlights the difficulty of cleanly separating mathematical principles from truth principles.

If one favors second-order logic, then one can avoid taking the truth-containing induction axioms as basic.

The language of second-order logic also contains, besides first-order variables that range over objects and first-order quantifiers, variables $(X, Y, \ldots)$ that range over properties, and quantifiers $(\forall X, \forall Y, \ldots)$ that quantify over properties. These second-order quantifiers are governed by the natural analogues of the introduction and elimination rules for the first-order quantifiers.[3] Therefore, in second-order Peano arithmetic,[4] the first-order induction scheme can be synthesized into its second-order closure:

$$\forall X : [X(0) \wedge \forall y(X(y) \rightarrow X(s(y)))] \rightarrow \forall y X(y).$$

This second-order induction axiom, then, does not contain the notion of truth. So presumably it counts as a mathematical principle. Now we can add the compositional truth axioms and re-run the nonconservativeness argument.[5]

The nub seems to be that, after all is said and done, the arithmetical nonconservativeness of *TC* leaves the deflationist with two options. Either she distances herself from the claim that truth is argumentatively insignificant or she must argue that *TC* is somehow philosophically unsound.

The second option seems unappealing. It is clear that *TC* is mathematically sound. It just seems hard to come up with a theorem of *TC* that contains the truth predicate but that does not sit well with our commonsense conception of truth. So perhaps we are well advised to treat the mathematical power of truth as a *phenomenon* that we have uncovered. This phenomenon is to be explored rather than disputed. Perhaps one day we can somehow chart the boundaries of the nonconservativeness phenomenon.

If the latter line is taken, then we should take a hard look at the deflationist motives behind the conservativeness claims. The deflationist might want to say that truth is a *logical* notion, and logic should not carry any substantial

---

3. For a good and concise introduction to second-order logic, see [Boolos & Jeffrey 1989, chapter 18].
4. Second-order Peano arithmetic and some of its important subsystems are discussed in some detail in section 7.7.
5. We need to work with a satisfaction predicate instead of a truth predicate; but, as intimated earlier, we leave this complication aside.

Conservativeness and Deflationism

ontological or ideological commitments. But this is not convincing. As was pointed out in section 5.2.3, the notion of truth is wrapped up with syntax, which is wrapped up with finite combinatorics, which finally reduces to arithmetic. Instead of being a purely logical notion, truth should at least be called a *logico-linguistic* or *logico-mathematical* notion.

Shapiro has suggested a radical way out for the deflationist [Shapiro 2002]. The deflationist could question the terms in which the conservativeness debate is conducted. Specifically, she could object to the *definition* of conservativeness that is employed. She could insist that a version of the *semantical* notion of conservativeness is used in which the notion of consequence is not that of first-order logical consequence but of *second-order* logical consequence. In a second-order setting, the natural arithmetical base theory is second-order Peano arithmetic.[6] This theory is *categorical*: All its models are isomorphic to the standard model. So there is absolutely no hope of consistently extending it by means of truth axioms in such a way that new arithmetical facts become logical consequences. So in *that* sense, every reasonable truth theory will be arithmetically conservative.

It is doubtful whether Shapiro's proposal will be met with much enthusiasm by the deflationist community. The notion of first-order consequence is effective. This means that if one takes the logical consequences of a theory to be its first-order consequences, then there is a strong (albeit still idealized) sense in which one knows the content of one's theory. Second-order consequence is a highly noneffective notion. If the content of a theory is given by its second-order consequences, then it is not so clear in which sense one can be taken to grasp the content of a theory. In summary, if arithmetical conservativeness of truth can only be had by inflating the notion of logical consequence, then perhaps it is better not to have it.[7]

7.2.3 Conservativeness Over Empirical Science and Metaphysics

There seems on the face of it to be some plausibility to the claim that truth is conservative over empirical science, at least when we have the *natural* sciences in mind. It would be suspicious if someone were to claim that in order to find out whether atoms really exist, we need to reflect on the notion of truth.[8]

Perhaps this is because semantic concepts do not appear to be involved in the natural sciences. Nevertheless, a clean empirical conservativeness claim is not easy to state because, as Galilei taught us, theories belonging to the natural

---

6. See section 7.7.
7. For a defense of second-order logic, see [Shapiro 1991].
8. For a more in-depth discussion of these matters, see [Leeds 1978].

sciences are always formulated in a mathematical framework. Especially arithmetic is used everywhere in empirical science. We have seen that the notion of truth affects precisely this part of mathematics.

The question of whether truth is conservative over metaphysics has not received much attention in the philosophical literature. Metaphysics is sometimes described as the most general science. If that is a fair description, then perhaps our tentative conclusions concerning truth and empirical science also hold for truth and metaphysics. If we set the metaphysics of linguistic notions (such as concepts) aside, then semantic concepts do not seem to figure largely in metaphysics. At least this holds if we side with the currently dominant philosophical trend. If, in contrast, one is sympathetic to the older view that metaphysics reduces to the analysis of concepts, then the question of the conservativeness of truth over metaphysics may well reduce to the question of the conservativeness of truth over the theory of meaning.

Nevertheless, all of this is extremely speculative. There simply is no hard evidence at the moment. The question of whether truth is conservative over science and metaphysics must be regarded as wide open.

7.3 Truth and Epistemology

Deflationism about truth claims that the notion of truth does not play a central role in the resolution of metaphysical, epistemological, and semantic problems. Horwich expresses this sentiment as follows [Horwich 1998, p. 52]:

A deflationist attitude toward truth is inconsistent with the usual view of it as a deep and vital element of philosophical theory. Consequently the many philosophers who are inclined to give the notion of truth a central role in their reflections in metaphysical, epistemological, and semantic problems must reject the minimalist account of its function. Conversely, those who sympathise with deflationary ideas about truth will not wish to place much theoretical weight on it. They will maintain that philosophy may employ the notion only in its minimalist capacity [...] and that theoretical problems must be resolved without it.

Let us take a closer look at the question of whether truth is conservative over one particular philosophical discipline: epistemology. We adopt the attitude of Zermelo when he sought to defend the Axiom of Choice. He scrutinized the standard textbooks of mathematical analysis with an eye on essential uses of the Axiom of Choice. Likewise, we look at "textbook epistemology" with an eye on essential uses of strong principles of truth.

Consider, for instance, the "traditional analysis of knowledge." Its central commitment is that knowledge is true justified belief, which is most naturally expressed along the following lines:

$\forall x \in \mathcal{L} : K(x) \leftrightarrow (T(x) \wedge J(x) \wedge B(x))$,

where $\mathcal{L}$ is some language that we need not specify in detail, K is a knowledge predicate, J is a justification predicate, and B is a belief predicate.

Clearly, if we want to use this principle to derive that some particular proposition is known, we need truth axioms. So, in this sense, truth is not conservative over epistemology.

Of course, in a way this is cheating because it is clear that, for many applications, we do not need to express the central commitment of the traditional analysis of knowledge in one single sentence using a truth predicate. For the ordinary applications of the traditional analysis of knowledge, the *schematic* version of the central commitment will do just as well. This schematic version can be expressed without the truth predicate:

$K(\phi) \leftrightarrow (\phi \wedge J(\phi) \wedge B(\phi))$,

where ϕ ranges over all sentences of $\mathcal{L}$. To give a trite example, suppose our epistemological theory entails $0 = 0$, $J(0 = 0)$, and $B(0 = 0)$. Then the schematic version of our central commitment entails $K(0 = 0)$.

But the use of the truth predicate is not *always* so easily eliminated in epistemology. We demonstrate this on the basis of a variation on an epistemological argument that has been widely discussed recently. Fitch has constructed an argument to show that a certain version of verificationism is untenable [Fitch 1963]. Williamson convincingly argued that Fitch's argument is sound—even if it should be left open whether the conclusion of Fitch's argument is a faithful rendering of a main tenet of verificationism [Williamson 2000, chapter 12].

Fitch's argument is usually not formulated in modal-epistemic first-order logic, but in modal-epistemic propositional logic, where quantification over propositions is allowed. We work in an intensional language $\mathcal{L}_P$ that contains a possibility operator $\Diamond$ and a knowledge operator K ("it is known that").

In this language $\mathcal{L}_P$, we formulate two verificationist principles:

WV $\forall p : p \to \Diamond Kp$;

SV $\forall p : p \to Kp$.

The principle *WV* ("weak verificationism") has been taken by many philosophers to have some plausibility. The principle *SV* ("strong verificationism"), by contrast, has been taken by most philosophers to be false: It seems that we know that there are unknown truths. Fitch now shows how, using plausible principles, *SV* can be derived from *WV*. This argument can then be taken as a refutation of weak verificationism.

Aside from the principles of the minimal modal logic **K**, which contains the axiom

$$[\Box\phi \wedge \Box(\phi \to \psi)] \to \Box\psi$$

and the rule of Necessitation, the principles that are used in Fitch's argument are:

FACT $Kp \to p$;

DIST $K(p \wedge q) \to (Kp \wedge Kq)$.

Fitch's derivation of *SV* from *WV* goes as follows:

Proposition 32 $WV \vdash SV$

Proof

1. $\forall p : p \to \Diamond Kp$ *WV*
2. $\forall p : (p \wedge \neg Kp) \to \Diamond K(p \wedge \neg Kp)$ *Logic, 1*
3. $\forall p : (p \wedge \neg Kp) \to \Diamond(Kp \wedge K\neg Kp)$ *DIST, 2*
4. $\forall p : (p \wedge \neg Kp) \to \Diamond(Kp \wedge \neg Kp)$ *FACT, 3*
5. $\forall p : \neg(p \wedge \neg Kp)$ *Logic, 4*
6. $\forall p : p \to Kp$ *Logic, 5*   ∎

Our common understanding of quantification is in terms of objectual quantification. A formula of the form

$$\exists p : p$$

simply appears to be ill formed because an object is not a candidate for having a truth value. The received view is that, from the conventional *objectual* quantification point of view, perfect sense can be made of propositional quantification using a truth predicate [Kripke 1976]. A sentence of the form $\exists p : p$ is then taken to be short for a sentence of the form

$$\exists x : x \in \mathcal{L} \wedge T(x).$$

If this line is adopted, then Fitch's argument is really an argument that involves a truth predicate. It is worth spelling out this argument in detail because it will teach us something about the role of the concept of truth in epistemology.

We work in an intensional *first-order* language $\mathcal{L}$ that contains a possibility operator $\Diamond$, a knowledge operator K ("it is known that"), and a Tarskian truth predicate T for $\mathcal{L}^- = \mathcal{L}\setminus\{T\}$. It is assumed that the language $\mathcal{L}^-$ contains the

Conservativeness and Deflationism

required coding machinery. We shall, as has by now become our customary practice, be ignoring the details of coding in what follows.

Let *FI* ('Fitch') be the theory that consists of:

1. The axioms of first-order logic and of the minimal normal logic **K**;
2. $\forall x \in \mathcal{L}^- : \Box(T(Kx) \to T(x))$;
3. $\forall x, y \in \mathcal{L}^- : \Box(T(K(x \wedge y)) \to (T(Kx) \wedge T(Ky)))$;
4. $\forall x \in \mathcal{L}^- : \neg T(x) \leftrightarrow T(\neg x)$;
5. $\forall x, y \in \mathcal{L}^- : T(x \wedge y) \leftrightarrow (T(x) \wedge T(y))$.

As in the truth theories that we have considered before, *FI* has the axioms of Peano arithmetic as its theory of syntax. *FI* is the theory in which Fitch's argument can be formalized.

The first three of the principles of *FI* (modal logic, *FACT*, *DIST*) are used in the derivation of the orthodox version of Fitch's argument. The next two principles are versions of the Tarskian compositional truth clauses for propositional logical connectives. Because T is intended to be a truth predicate for the language $\mathcal{L}^-$, they are unproblematic.

Weak and strong verificationism can be expressed as follows:

WV^* $\forall x \in \mathcal{L}^- : T(x) \to \Diamond T(Kx)$;

SV^* $\forall x \in \mathcal{L}^- : T(x) \to T(Kx)$.

Now we can reformulate Fitch's argument without quantification over propositions:

Proposition 33 $WV^* \vdash_{FI} SV^*$

Proof

1. $\forall x \in \mathcal{L}^- : \Box[T(K(x \wedge \neg Kx)) \to (T(Kx) \wedge T(K \neg Kx))]$
   DIST
2. $\forall x \in \mathcal{L}^- : \Box[T(K(x \wedge \neg Kx)) \to (T(Kx) \wedge T(\neg Kx))]$
   FACT, 1
3. $\forall x \in \mathcal{L}^- : \Box[T(K(x \wedge \neg Kx)) \to (T(Kx) \wedge \neg T(Kx))]$
   Comp Ax for $\neg$, 2
4. $\forall x \in \mathcal{L}^- : \Box \neg T(K(x \wedge \neg Kx))$
   K, 3
5. $\forall x \in \mathcal{L}^- : \neg \Diamond T(K(x \wedge \neg Kx)) \to \neg T(x \wedge \neg Kx)$
   WV^*

6. $\forall x \in \mathcal{L}^- : \neg \Diamond T(K(x \wedge \neg Kx)) \to \neg(T(x) \wedge T(\neg Kx))$
   Comp Ax for $\wedge$, 5
7. $\forall x \in \mathcal{L}^- : \neg \Diamond T(K(x \wedge \neg Kx)) \to \neg(T(x) \wedge \neg T(Kx))$
   Comp Ax for $\neg$, 6
8. $\forall x \in \mathcal{L}^- : \neg \Diamond T(K(x \wedge \neg Kx)) \to (T(x) \to T(Kx))$
   Logic, 7
9. $\forall x \in \mathcal{L}^- : T(x) \to T(Kx)$
   Logic, 4,8   ∎

The principles concerning K and $\Diamond$ that play a role in this argument are those that are used in Fitch's original argument. The principles concerning truth state (roughly) that truth commutes with the propositional logical connectives.

There is absolutely no threat of paradox here: In the truth axioms, object-language and metalanguage are scrupulously kept apart. Indeed, a simple consistency proof goes as follows. Consider first the *translation function* τ that erases all occurrences of $\Box$ in a given proof of *FI*. τ translates proofs of *FI* into proofs of a system *FI**, which has as its axioms all the sentences $\tau(\phi)$ such that ϕ is an axiom of *FI*. Thus, for a consistency proof for *FI*, it suffices to show that *FI** has a model. We construct a model $\mathfrak{M}$ for *FI** as follows. The domain of $\mathfrak{M}$ consists of the natural numbers, and the arithmetical vocabulary is given its standard interpretation by $\mathfrak{M}$. A sentence ϕ is in the extension of the truth predicate according to $\mathfrak{M}$ if and only if the result of erasing all occurrences of $\Box$ and of K from ϕ results in an arithmetical truth. Then it is routine to verify that $\mathfrak{M}$ makes all axioms of *FI** true.

In sum, the version of Fitch's argument where propositional quantification is dispensed with by using a Tarskian truth predicate seems unobjectionable. This shows that Fitch's argument cannot be faulted on account of its use of supposedly ungrammatical quantification over propositions.

As mentioned earlier, Fitch's argument is generally seen as a refutation of Weak Verificationism. But to obtain $\neg WV^*$, proposition 33 has to be combined with $\neg SV^*$, which can be taken to be eminently plausible on empirical grounds. This means that in our reconstruction of Fitch's argument, we *have* to use more than restricted Tarski-biconditionals. If one believes (as Horwich does) that *DT* is truth-theoretically complete, and if one also believes that propositional quantification has to be interpreted using a truth predicate (as received opinion has it), then one simply cannot accept Fitch's refutation of Weak Verificationism as valid.

However, it also deserves remark that, for the reconstruction of Fitch's argument, the full compositional truth theory *TC* is not needed. The principle stating that truth commutes with the quantifiers plays no role in the argument. Also, it is immaterial for the argument whether the truth predicate is allowed in the induction scheme.

Fitch's argument crucially involves the notion of knowledge, and it relies on basic epistemological principles. So it seems fair to characterize it as an epistemological argument. Weak and Strong Verificationism involve the notion of truth as well. So our argument for $\neg WV$ does not show that truth is in the technical sense of the word nonconservative over epistemology. But it does appear to show that the theory of truth plays a substantial role in epistemology.

An objection to this line of reasoning runs as follows.[9] Weak Verificationism is, so the objection goes, a verificationist and hence substantial theory of *truth*. The fact that the compositional theory of truth that is part of the theory *FI* can be used to refute a substantial theory of truth shows that the former is substantial and thus nondeflationist. Indeed, Horwich might see the fact that Fitch's argument does not go through if only the truth principles of *DT* are used as an argument in favor of *DT*. If deflationism is correct, then our theory of truth should be neutral in substantial philosophical disputes. The compositional truth theory that is part of *FI* is not neutral in the dispute about Weak Verificationism, so it cannot possibly be an acceptable truth theory. *DT* does remain neutral in this dispute, so it is a more likely candidate for being a satisfactory theory of truth.

But this line of reasoning is unacceptable. We have no compelling independent reasons for thinking that the compositional theory of truth is unsound. The fact that it can be used to refute Weak Verificationism may be surprising. But it is not a sufficient reason for taking *TC* to be unsound.

The discussion of whether Weak Verificationism is a chapter in epistemology or in the theory of truth strikes me as unprofitable. The thesis *WV* involves both the concept of knowledge and the concept of truth. Fitch's argument against *WV* uses both laws of epistemology (such as *FACT*) and compositional truth laws (laws of *TC*). In any case, Weak Verificationism is a substantial philosophical thesis. If one wants to appeal to Fitch's argument to argue that Weak Verificationism is false, then one had better accept more laws of truth than just the restricted Tarski-biconditionals.

7.4 Truth and Meaning

The question of whether truth plays a substantial role in the theory of meaning has received a great deal of attention in the closing decades of the twentieth century. In this book, we do not delve deeply into these matters.

---

9. Thanks to Igor Douven for formulating it.

Some philosophers of language advocate using theories or inferential theories of meaning. Brandom and Horwich are famous cases in point ([Horwich 1999], [Brandom 2000]). If they are right, then there is a chance that truth is conservative over the theory of meaning for fragments of English. Davidson's semantical program, in contrast, aims at articulating the meaning of sentences in terms of their truth-conditions [Davidson 1967]. If Davidson's semantic program is on the right track, then the theory of meaning cannot even be expressed without making heavy use of the truth predicate. In that case, it is silly to require the theory of truth to be conservative over the theory of meaning.

But even if Davidson's semantic program is fundamentally sound, there is a legitimate question about what kind of theory of truth is required to make this program work. Davidson thought that deflationism is untenable *because* truth plays an explanatory role in the theory of meaning [Davidson 1990]. But it can be objected that he adopted an excessively narrow conception of deflationism. In other words, perhaps we should divorce deflationism from the claim that the concept of truth has no explanatory function in specific philosophical disciplines. Davidson thought that something like the theory TC would be sufficient for his theory of meaning. If that is the case, and if TC counts as a deflationary theory of truth, then it can still be maintained that Davidson's semantic program is compatible with deflationism.[10]

7.5 Deflating Arithmetical Nonconservativeness

From the foregoing, we may conclude that the question of the conservativeness of truth over philosophy and empirical science is open. But with respect to the question of the conservativeness of truth over mathematics, the situation is different. This question can no longer be treated as open: The nonconservativeness of truth over mathematics is a *phenomenon*.

So Halbach is right when he states that if deflationism about truth is to be given a chance at all, it must be dissociated from mathematical conservativeness claims [Halbach 2001]. Conservativeness over mathematics should not be regarded as an essential component of deflationism about truth. This leaves us with this question: What *is* essential to deflationism?

On the conception of deflationism that is developed in this book, the prime positive role of the truth predicate is twofold. Truth serves, first, as a device for expressing generalities, and, second, as an inferential tool. The role of truth as a

---

10. The question of whether Davidson's semantic program is compatible with deflationism about truth is investigated at length in [Fischer 2008].

device for expressing generalities is well documented. The role of the concept of truth as an inferential tool deserves more comment.

Halbach has emphasized that a theory of truth must allow us to prove generalities about the notion of truth. But we have seen that the notion of truth also allows us to infer "new" mathematical propositions: consistency statements, for example.

A comparison between the notion of truth and the concept of negation may be instructive here. It is known from the discussion between constructive and classical mathematics that some purely positive arithmetical existence statements can (as far as we know) only be proved by relying on the law of excluded middle. In other words, some mathematical statements not containing the concept of negation can only be proved by making use of the concept of negation. The deflationist emphasizes that the notion of truth is in this respect similar to that of negation. Truth, like education, is not so much a putting in as a drawing out. It helps to draw out implicit commitments of theories that we have postulated.

It is for this reason that the comparison with Hilbert's program and the notion of elementhood is misleading. It is true that the nonconservativeness of set theory over first-order arithmetic has done much to establish set theory as a substantial theory indeed. But a closer look at the theory of elementhood (set theory) reveals that the situation here is different. Set theory postulates a whole new ontology over and above the theory of the natural numbers. In this sense, set theory is much more than an inferential tool for arithmetic. Set-theoretically provable facts about some of these new entities (sets of natural numbers, in particular) allow us to prove many new first-order arithmetical statements. Truth theories, according to deflationism, should not postulate "new" entities with natures of their own. But they should be inferentially useful.

Nevertheless, one may start to feel worried about deflationism at this stage. In this chapter, it was suggested that deflationism should be stripped of a number of commitments that are often attributed to it. It was argued that it is compatible with deflationism that truth is not conservative over its background theory. It was also argued that deflationism should not commit itself to the claim that truth plays no explanatory role in specific philosophical disciplines. At about this point, the question arises: What is the positive content that remains after such a deflation of deflationism? Merely claiming that truth is a logico-linguistic or logico-mathematical notion is not enough to alleviate this concern. We return to this important issue in section 10.2. There I inject new content in the deflationist view about truth.

7.6 Substantiality and Irreducibility

Nothing stated previously excludes that there are senses in which truth is a substantial notion. Some have suggested that truth is a substantial notion in the sense that it is not reducible to other notions.

7.6.1 Reducibility and Interpretability

The prospects of this proposal of course depend on what is meant by conceptual reducibility. If in this context reducibility is identified with definability, then truth is indeed substantial because we have seen in chapter 3 how Tarski proved that truth is undefinable. But it is well known from the literature in philosophy of science that theoretical reducibility should not be identified with definability. A better suggestion, perhaps, is that reducibility should be spelled out in terms of *relative interpretability* [Niebergall 2000]. Roughly, a relative interpretation from a formal theory T_1, formulated in $\mathcal{L}_{T_1}$, to another theory T_2, formulated in $\mathcal{L}_{T_1}$, is a translation that preserves provability and that preserves the logical structure of sentences.[11] More precisely:

Definition 34 *A relative interpretation from a theory T_1 into a theory T_2 is a computable function σ from $\mathcal{L}_{T_1}$ to $\mathcal{L}_{T_2}$ such that:*

1. $\sigma(\phi \wedge \psi) = \sigma(\phi) \wedge \sigma(\psi)$;
2. $\sigma(\neg\phi) = \neg\sigma(\phi)$;
3. $\sigma(\forall x \phi(x)) = \forall x (\delta(x) \rightarrow \sigma(\phi(x)))$ *for some formula* $\delta(x) \in \mathcal{L}_{T_2}$ *such that* $T_2 \vdash \exists x \delta(x)$;
4. *For all* $\phi \in \mathcal{L}_{T_1}$: *if* $T_1 \vdash \phi$, *then* $T_2 \vdash \sigma(\phi)$.

Definability and interpretability do not amount to the same thing. In particular, although arithmetical truth is not definable in *PA*, we have:[12]

Theorem 35 *DT is relatively interpretable in PA.*

So in some sense *DT* does not endow the concept of truth with genuinely new conceptual power.

The notion of relative interpretability provides a way to articulate the double demand that truth should be conservative yet nonreducible. Maybe we should look for a truth theory that is conservative but not interpretable into

---

11. [Lindström 1997, chapter 6] is a good introduction to the theory of relative interpretability.
12. For a proof of this statement, see [Fischer 2010].

Conservativeness and Deflationism

its arithmetical background theory.[13] This would give rise to a new version of deflationism about truth. This form of deflationism would hold that conservativeness is an adequacy condition for theories of truth. But it would claim at the same time that truth is not reducible to the background theory. Truth is a notion that we did not implicitly have before it was introduced; however, this has been done. Its inferential behavior cannot be simulated by our background theory.

Variants of the notion of relative interpretability are currently under investigation. One such notion is that of *truth-definability*.[14] A truth theory T_2 is said to be truth-definable in a theory T_1 if there is a predicate $\phi(x)$, definable in the language of T_1, such that T_1 can prove that the truth laws of T_2 hold for $\phi(x)$. The notion of truth-definability is stricter than that of relative interpretability because it requires that the interpretation by T_1 of the truth-free predicates of T_2 is left unchanged, and it does not allow that the domain of the quantifiers of T_2 is restricted. It is currently a matter of debate which variant on the idea of relative interpretability best captures the informal idea of conceptual reduction.

7.6.2 A Conservative but Noninterpretable Truth Theory

Although I argued earlier in this chapter against taking conservativeness as an adequacy condition for truth theories, it must be admitted that the present suggestion is an interesting dialectical move in the debate. Conservativeness and interpretability in general do not amount to the same thing. There exist, for instance, theories that are conservative over *PA* and yet are not relatively interpretable in *PA*.

TC^- is conservative over *PA*, as we saw in section 6.4. But, somewhat surprisingly, it turns out that TC^- is relatively interpretable in *PA*.[15] Nonetheless, it turns out that there is an interesting formal truth theory that is conservative but not relatively interpretable in *PA*. The theory in question is called PT^-, and it is discussed in [Fischer 2010]. As usual, the theory PT^- is formulated in $\mathcal{L}_T$. To state the theory, it is helpful to define an auxiliary notion:

Definition 36 *$tot(\phi(x))$ ($\phi(x)$ is total, or truth-determinate) is defined as:*

$\forall x : T(\phi(x)) \vee T(\neg\phi(x))$.

Then the theory PT^- consists of the following principles:

---

13. This standpoint is defended in [Fischer 2010].
14. See [Fujimoto 2010].
15. See [Fischer 2010].

PT-1 PA^T without the induction axiom;

PT-2 $\forall \phi(x) \in \mathcal{L}_T : [tot(\phi(x)) \wedge T(\phi(0)) \wedge \forall y(T(\phi(y)) \to T(\phi(y+1)))] \to \forall x T(\phi(x))$;

PT-3 $\forall$ atomic $\phi \in \mathcal{L}_{PA} : T(\phi) \leftrightarrow val^+(\phi)$;

PT-4 $\forall$ atomic $\phi \in \mathcal{L}_{PA} : T(\neg\phi) \leftrightarrow \neg val^+(\phi)$;

PT-5 $\forall \phi, \psi \in \mathcal{L}_{PA} : T(\phi \wedge \psi) \leftrightarrow (T(\phi) \wedge T(\psi))$;

PT-6 $\forall \phi, \psi \in \mathcal{L}_{PA} : T(\neg(\phi \wedge \psi)) \leftrightarrow (T(\neg\phi) \vee T(\neg\psi))$;

PT-7 $\forall \phi(x) \in \mathcal{L}_{PA} : T(\forall x \phi(x)) \leftrightarrow \forall x T(\phi(x))$;

PT-8 $\forall \phi(x) \in \mathcal{L}_{PA} : T(\neg \forall x \phi(x)) \leftrightarrow \exists x T(\neg \phi(x))$;

PT-9 $\forall \phi \in \mathcal{L}_{PA} : T(\neg\neg\phi) \leftrightarrow T(\phi)$.

In certain respects, PT^- resembles truth theories that we discussed earlier. First, in the spirit of TC and DT, the theory PT^- adheres to Tarski's strict separation between objectlanguage and metalanguage: PT^- does not prove truth-iterations. Second, like TC, the system PT^- is a compositional theory of truth: It explains how the truth value of more complex sentences is determined by the truth values of its components.

Nevertheless, PT^- also differs from TC in certain respects. First, PT^- does not contain an axiom stating that negation commutes with the truth predicate. Axioms PT6 and PT8 do explain how the truth of negated complex formulae reduces to the truth values of simpler formulae. However, their truth is not determined by simpler formulae lacking the property of truth, but by certain simpler formulae *having* the property of truth. Second, the principle of induction is restricted in two ways. First, the principle of induction is formulated as an axiom and not as an axiom scheme.[16] Second, the principle of mathematical induction is not postulated to hold for all sentences of $\mathcal{L}_T$, but only for those that are truth-determinate.

These initially puzzling features of PT^- can to some extent be motivated. PT^-'s way of handling negation could be supported by an appeal to *truthmaker theory*.[17] Suppose one holds that to every true atomic or negated atomic sentence there corresponds a fact that makes it true or false, and that the basic laws of a truth theory should explain how the truth of sentences reduces to the truth of other sentences that ultimately are made true by atomic facts and their negations. Then one will not be satisfied with TC because this theory does not explain

---

16. For more on the distinction between mathematical induction interpreted as a scheme and interpreted as an axiom, compare supra, section 5.2.2.

17. Compare supra, section 2.1.

how the truth of complex negated sentences reduces to the truth of positive and negative atomic facts. PT^-, in contrast, does provide such an explanation. In favor of restricting mathematical induction to truth-determinate formulae, the following can be said. From the literature on the problem of vagueness, we know that it is dangerous to perform an induction along a sorites sequence. We would accept that one grain of sand does not make a heap. It may seem plausible that if n grains fail to make a heap of sand, then so do $n + 1$ grains of sand. Yet we would definitely not want to conclude that any number of grains fail to make up a heap. The problem is that there are collections of grains for which it is indeterminate whether they make up a heap. Similarly, there are predicates of $\mathcal{L}_T$ that are truth-indeterminate for some arguments. Therefore, we should be hesitant to perform mathematical induction on such predicates.

PT^- satisfies minimal formal adequacy requirements. For one thing, it is certainly formally coherent:

Proposition 37 PT^- *has nice models.*

Proof   *It can be easily verified that PT^- is a subtheory of TC, and we have seen in proposition 26 that TC has nice models.* ∎

Furthermore, an induction on the buildup of arithmetical formulae shows that PT^- proves the restricted Tarski-biconditionals:

Proposition 38 *For all $\phi \in \mathcal{L}_{PA}$:*

$PT^- \vdash T(\phi) \leftrightarrow \phi.$

But what makes PT^- of special significance are the following facts:

Theorem 39 (Cantini) PT^- *is arithmetically conservative over PA.*

Theorem 40 (Fischer) PT^- *is not relatively interpretable in PA.*[18]

These properties make PT^- an interesting theory for those deflationists who hold, on the one hand, that truth is a conservative notion, and hold, on the other hand, that the concept of truth adds genuine power to our conceptual apparatus.

7.6.3 Disquotationalism Revisited

Notions such as definability and relative interpretability can be used to argue that seemingly weak theories turn out on closer inspection to be quite powerful after all. Halbach considers a disquotational truth theory that he calls *PUTB*

---

18. For a proof, see [Fischer 2010].

[Halbach 2009]. As always, this theory has Peano arithmetic (with truth allowed in the induction scheme) as its background theory. Aside from this, it contains those uniform Tarski-biconditionals in which the truth predicate only occurs *positively* (i.e., within the scope of an even number of negation symbols). Halbach shows that this truth theory is consistent,[18] arithmetically sound, and arithmetically highly nonconservative over *PA*.

Halbach observes that *PUTB* can *define* a predicate that provably (in *PUTB*) satisfies strong compositional truth principles, for example, those of *TC*.[19] (*DT* do no such thing.) In other words, the truth predicates of strong truth theories are truth-definable in *PUTB*. So in a way, *PUTB* can make sense of the compositionality intuition: It can simulate it. This shows that the difference between disquotationalist and compositional truth theories is in the final analysis not as absolute as it would appear.

Nevertheless, *PUTB* does not prove the compositional truth axioms for essentially the same reasons that *DT* does not prove them. Thus, *PUTB* cannot be seen as a vindication of disquotationalism.

But a proposition due to Vann McGee shows that disquotational axioms *can* generate the compositional truth axioms as theorems. In fact, more is true. For any truth theory T, there exists a disquotational theory that is equivalent to it [McGee 1992]:

Theorem 41 *For any theory T, formulated in $\mathcal{L}_T$, there exists a (computably enumerable) collection of Tarski-biconditionals $Dis(T)$ such that for every sentence $\phi \in \mathcal{L}_T$:*

$T \vdash \phi \Leftrightarrow Dis(T) \vdash \phi$.

Proof *Consider an arbitrary sentence ϕ that is provable in T. Using the extended strengthened diagonal lemma, find a sentence λ corresponding to ϕ such that*

$PA^T \vdash \lambda \leftrightarrow (T(\lambda) \leftrightarrow \phi)$.

Then it is immediate from the asssociativity of $\leftrightarrow$ that the Tarski-biconditional $T(\lambda) \leftrightarrow \lambda$ is provably equivalent to ϕ. So if we let $Dis(T)$ consist of all the Tarski-biconditionals corresponding to diagonal sentences for theorems of ϕ in this way, then $Dis(T)$ will be provably equivalent to T. ∎

---

19. Observe, in this connection, that the liar sentence contains the truth predicate in the scope of an odd number of negation signs!
20. A predicate can even be defined of which *PUTB* proves that it satisfies the principles of the truth predicate of the strong truth theory *KF*, which is investigated in section 9.2.

Unfortunately, even McGee's theorem does not show that disquotationalism is right after all. After all, in general, there is no reason to expect $Dis(T)$ to be a *natural* theory of truth. In particular, it seems unlikely that the compositionality of truth follows from Tarski-biconditionals via the diagonal lemma. The connection between compositionality and disquotation must be more immediate.

7.7 A Serious Game

TC can prove more arithmetical statements than PA: It can prove the consistency of PA. It turns out that TC can even prove the consistency of $PA + Con(PA)$, and so on. Then the question arises whether it is possible to characterize the exact first-order arithmetical power of TC. Proof theorists have solved this problem.

Consider the language $\mathcal{L}_{PA^2}$ of *second-order* arithmetic. This language is just like the language of first-order arithmetic, except that it also contains second-order variables $X, Y, \ldots$ that range not over natural numbers but over *sets* of natural numbers.

The laws of second-order logic are just like the laws of first-order logic except that they also contain the obvious analogues for second-order quantification of the first-order quantifier laws. Second-order Peano arithmetic, PA^2, is just like PA, except that:

1. it is formulated in second-order logic;

2. it contains the *full comprehension scheme*

$\exists Y \forall x [Y(x) \leftrightarrow \phi(x)]$,

where $\phi(x)$ contains no free occurrences of Y;[20]

3. it contains the induction scheme for all formulae of the language of *second-order* arithmetic.

In fact, we have seen that if we wanted to, we could express the induction principle now as an *axiom* instead of a scheme:

$\forall X : [X(0) \wedge \forall y (X(y) \rightarrow X(s(y)))] \rightarrow \forall y X(y).$

It is easy to see that this would yield the same class of theorems as PA^2.

---

21. If free occurrences of Y in $\phi(x)$ would be allowed, then $\exists Y \forall x [Y(x) \leftrightarrow \neg Y(x)]$ would be a comprehension axiom, thus rendering the system inconsistent.

PA^2 is a strong theory indeed. It not only proves second-order arithmetical statements that PA cannot prove. Even the collection of first-order arithmetical consequences of PA^2 is *much* larger than the collection of theorems of PA.

The first-order arithmetical strength of TC lies in between that of PA and that of PA^2. In fact, its first-order arithmetical strength is (loosely speaking) much closer to PA than to PA^2. The mathematical strength of TC is related to the mathematical strength of a particular subsystem of PA^2, which is called ACA in the literature. The system ACA is exactly like PA^2, except for one difference. ACA only contains a severely truncated version of the full comprehension scheme, which is known as *arithmetical comprehension*:

$$\exists Y \forall x [Y(x) \leftrightarrow \phi(x)],$$

where $\phi(x)$ contains *no bound occurrences of second-order variables* and does not contain the second-order variable Y free.

The restriction on the comprehension axiom causes ACA to be proof-theoretically much weaker than PA^2. The idea behind the system ACA is that not all second-order formulae with a free first-order variable determine sets of natural numbers. Only those among them that do not contain bound second-order quantifiers do. The motivation for this restriction is the following. A school in the foundation of mathematics known as *predicativism* has it that a mathematical object (such as a set of numbers) cannot be defined by quantifying over a collection that includes that same mathematical object. To do so would be a violation of the vicious circle principle.

The arithmetical strength of TC has been exactly calibrated. It can be expressed in terms of the predicative system ACA:[21]

Theorem 42 *The arithmetical consequences of TC are exactly the arithmetical consequences of the second-order system ACA.*

We found that TC is an attractive truth theory: We appear to have reasons to believe that it is truth-theoretically sound. The question arises whether there exist natural, philosophically sound theories of truth, which are arithmetically stronger than TC.

Thus, a project takes shape. The aim is to calibrate the power of the notion of truth. A natural measure (although by no means the only natural measure) of the strength of truth is to look at its first-order arithmetical consequences. This can be seen as a game: Let us call it the *power game*. Like all games, especially among people of a mathematical bent, the power game quickly turns

---

22. For a proof of this theorem, see [Halbach 1994].

competitive. The challenge is to find the arithmetically strongest axiomatical truth theory that is both natural and truth-theoretically sound.

At some point, a limit of the power of truth will be reached in this way. We will have reached a point where increase in arithmetical strength can only be reached by either making our truth theory artificial or by proposing a truth theory about which doubts can be raised with respect to its philosophical soundness. It is unclear at the moment how close we are to reaching this point.

8 Maximizing Classical Compositionality

We now investigate to what extent Tarski's compositional theory of truth can be consistently extended. In particular, we look at a theory of truth that was formulated by Harvey Friedman and Michael Sheard, and we discuss its relation with the revision theory of truth.

8.1 Typed and Untyped Theories

We have seen that Tarski's compositional and disquotational theories fail to validate certain seemingly unproblematic sentences containing iterations of the truth predicate. Remember, for example, that both DT and TC fail to prove $T(T(0=0))$. We know that the naive attempt to solve this by lifting the restriction in DT of the Tarski-biconditionals to sentences of $\mathcal{L}_{PA}$ results in inconsistency.

We have seen that Tarski proposed languages that contain a hierarchy of truth predicates. In an axiomatic vein, Tarski's proposal inspires axiomatic theories that do not prove sentences such as $T(T(0=0))$, but that do prove sentences such as $T_1(T(0=0))$. Here T_1 is a "higher level" truth predicate for the language $\mathcal{L}_T$. Truth theories that are formulated in languages that contain truth predicates of different levels and that prove iterated truth ascriptions only if the hierarchy constraints are satisfied are called *typed theories of truth*.

There also exist consistent axiomatic truth systems that contain a single truth predicate but that do prove sentences of the form $T(T(\phi))$. These systems are called *untyped theories of truth*. Sometimes they are also called *reflexive* or *semantically closed* theories of truth.

Untyped theories of truth abandon Tarski's strictures on truth iteration. We have seen that the self-referential paradoxes are related to *particular* iterations of the truth predicate. So the idea is to distinguish carefully between sentences that contain problematic iterations of the truth predicate, such as $T(L) \leftrightarrow L$, where L is the liar sentence, and sentences that contain innocuous truth iterations, such as $T(T(0=0))$. The latter may be proved by an untyped truth theory but not the former.

We have already seen one example of a type-free theory of truth: the system *PUTB* of section 7.6.3. The theory *PUTB* proves many sentences that contain nested occurrences of the truth predicate. As a simple example, the reader might try to work out why $T(T(0=0))$ is a theorem of *PUTB*.

In this chapter, we look at classical untyped theories of truth that extend the compositional theory *TC*. In the next chapter, we discuss untyped theories of truth that are formulated in partial logic.

8.2 The Friedman–Sheard Theory

Friedman and Sheard have proposed an axiomatic theory of self-referential truth that is called *FS* [Friedman & Sheard 1987]. Friedman and Sheard give a slightly different list of axioms (and they did not call their system *FS*), but the following list is equivalent to their system:[1]

FS1 PA^T;

FS2 $\forall$ atomic $\phi \in \mathcal{L}_{PA} : T(\phi) \leftrightarrow val^+(\phi)$;

FS3 $\forall \phi \in \mathcal{L}_T : T(\neg\phi) \leftrightarrow \neg T(\phi)$;

FS4 $\forall \phi, \psi \in \mathcal{L}_T : T(\phi \wedge \psi) \leftrightarrow T(\phi) \wedge T(\psi)$;

FS5 $\forall \phi(x) \in \mathcal{L}_T : T(\forall x \phi(x)) \leftrightarrow \forall x T(\phi(x))$.

Moreover, *FS* contains two extra rules of inference, which are called *Necessitation* (NEC) and *Co-Necessitation* (CONEC), respectively:

NEC From a proof of ϕ, infer $T(\phi)$;

CONEC From a proof of $T(\phi)$, infer ϕ.

Let us consider the axioms and rules of *FS*. The compositional axioms of *FS* show that it seeks to reflect, like *TC*, the intuition of the *compositionality* of truth. In this sense, *FS* can be seen as a natural extension of *TC*. In fact, the *axioms* are exactly like the axioms of *TC*, except that the compositional axioms quantify over the entire language of truth instead of only over $\mathcal{L}_{PA}$. But if we disregard the rules of inference NEC and CONEC, this does not help us in any

---

1. This formulation of *FS* is due to Halbach: see [Halbach 1994].

way in proving *iterated* truth statements. The reason is that the truth axiom for atomic sentences only quantifies over atomic *arithmetical* sentences.

FS is the result of maximizing the intuition of the compositionality of truth. Nevertheless, the truth of truth attribution statements is in *FS* only in a weaker sense compositionally determined than the truth of other statements. *FS* only claims that if a truth attribution has been *proved*, then this truth attribution can be regarded as true (and conversely), whereas for a conjunctive statement, for instance, *FS* makes the stronger hypothetical claim that *if* it is true, then both its conjuncts are true also (and conversely). But it is necessarily that way. If we replace NEC and the CONEC by the corresponding *axiom schemes*, an inconsistent theory results.

8.3 The Revision Theory of Truth

We want to investigate the theory *FS* from both philosophical and technical vantage points. A first question is whether *FS* is coherent at all (i.e., whether it is consistent). We see that it can indeed be shown that *FS* has models but, surprisingly, no nice ones. A second question is: which conception of truth can we take *FS* to express? A brief exploration of a semantical theory of truth is instructive here. It turns out that there is a deep connection between *FS*, on the one hand, and a popular semantic theory of truth, on the other hand.

The semantic truth theory in question is the revision theory of truth of Gupta, Belnap, and Herzberger [Gupta & Belnap 1993]. It is an untyped truth theory that aims to classify many sentences that express truth-iterations as true. Let us take a look at a simplified version of the theory.

The general idea is the following. We start with a classical model for $\mathcal{L}_T$. This model is transformed into a new model again and again, thus yielding a long sequence of classical models for $\mathcal{L}_T$, which are indexed by ordinal numbers. The official notion of truth for a formula of $\mathcal{L}_T$ is then distilled from this long sequence of models.

As before, we only consider models that are based on the standard natural number structure. For simplicity, let us start with the model

$$\mathfrak{M}_0 = \langle \mathbb{N}, \emptyset \rangle :$$

the model that regards no sentence whatsoever as true. Suppose we have a model $\mathfrak{M}_\alpha$. Then the next model in the sequence is defined as follows:

$$\mathfrak{M}_{\alpha+1} = \langle \mathbb{N}, \{\phi \in \mathcal{L}_T \mid \mathfrak{M}_\alpha \models \phi\} \rangle.$$

In other words, the next model is always obtained by putting those sentences in the extension of the truth predicate that are made true by the last model that has already been obtained.

Now suppose that λ is a limit ordinal and that all models $\mathfrak{M}_\beta$ for $\beta < \lambda$ have already been defined. Then

$$\mathfrak{M}_\lambda = \langle \mathbb{N}, \{\phi \in \mathcal{L}_T \mid \exists \beta \forall \gamma : (\gamma \geq \beta \wedge \gamma < \lambda) \Rightarrow \mathfrak{M}_\gamma \models \phi\}\rangle.$$

In words: We put a sentence ϕ in the extension of the truth predicate of $\mathfrak{M}_\lambda$ if there is a "stage" β before λ such that, from $\mathfrak{M}_\beta$ onward, ϕ is *always* in the extension of the truth predicate. The sentences in the extension of the truth predicate of $\mathfrak{M}_\lambda$ are those that have "stabilized" to the value *True* at some stage before λ.

This yields a chain of models that is as long as the chain of the ordinal numbers. Elementary cardinality considerations (Cantor's theorem) tell us that there must be ordinals α and β such that $\mathfrak{M}_\alpha$ and $\mathfrak{M}_\beta$ are identical. In other words, the chain of models must be periodic.

On the basis of this long sequence of models, we can now define the notion of *stable truth* for the language $\mathcal{L}_T$. A sentence $\phi \in \mathcal{L}_T$ is said to be stably true if at some ordinal stage α, ϕ enters in the extension of the truth predicate of $\mathfrak{M}_\alpha$ and stays in the extension of the truth predicate in all later models. A sentence $\phi \in \mathcal{L}_T$ is said to be stably false if at some ordinal stage α, ϕ is outside the extension of the truth predicate of $\mathfrak{M}_\alpha$ and stays out forever thereafter. A sentence that is neither stably true nor stably false is said to be *paradoxical*.

The reader can easily verify that the sentence $T(T(0 = 0))$, for instance, enters the extension of the truth predicate in $\mathfrak{M}_3$ and stays in forever after. So this sentence is stably true. The reader can also verify that the liar sentence L, governed by the principle $L \leftrightarrow \neg T(L)$, is coy, vascillating, and flippant. She enters the truth predicate in $\mathfrak{M}_1$, but jumps out again in $\mathfrak{M}_2$, then comes back, jumps out again, and so on. In brief, she never settles down.

Revision theorists have tentatively proposed to identify truth simpliciter with stable truth and falsehood simpliciter with stable falsehood. Sentences that never stabilize, such as the liar, are classified as paradoxical. But they hesitate to fully endorse this identification. Another strong contender for identification with truth simpliciter (falsehood simpliciter) is the slightly more complicated notion of *nearly stable truth* (nearly stable falsehood). A sentence $\phi \in \mathcal{L}_T$ is said to be nearly stably true if, for every stage α after some stage β, there is a natural number n such that for all natural numbers $m \geq n$, ϕ is in the extension of the truth predicate of $\mathfrak{M}_{\alpha+m}$. A sentence $\phi \in \mathcal{L}_T$ is said to be nearly stably false if, for every stage α after some stage β, there is a natural number n such that for all natural numbers $m \geq n$, ϕ is outside the extension of the truth predicate of $\mathfrak{M}_{\alpha+m}$. In other words, for this notion of truth, we do not care what happens before any fixed finite number of steps after any limit ordinal.

The notions of stable truth and nearly stable truth do not coincide. It shall be shown that there exists a connection between the notion of nearly stable truth, on the one hand, and provability in the theory *FS*, on the other hand.

The revision theory of truth was developed as an attempt at explicating our naive patterns of reasoning with self-referential sentences containing the truth predicate. Indeed, when we naively go about trying to decide whether a sentence ϕ is *true*, we consider the situation we think we find ourselves in and evaluate whether ϕ holds in this situation. Such a situation is like a model. So what we in fact do is to use the naive Tarski-biconditional $T(\phi) \leftrightarrow \phi$. When we find out that ϕ indeed holds in the "model" we are considering, we add ϕ to the extension of T, thus generating a revised model. In other words, we use the naive Tarski-biconditionals to keep on adjusting our view of the situation in which we find ourselves. This results in *diachronic inconsistency*: We keep changing our minds about the truth status of the liar sentence, for example. It must be conceded that it is not so easy to explain how the limit rule for constructing models is connected to our naive reasoning practice. But at the same time, the limit rule appears to be the only natural one that springs to mind.

8.4 Probing the Friedman–Sheard Theory

Let us now return to the axiomatic theory *FS*. Like *TC*, the system *FS* is a thoroughly *classical* theory of truth. Not only is it formulated in classical logic, but it also *proves* that the notion of truth is consistent and complete: No sentence and its negation are both true, and for every sentence either it or its negation is true. Unlike *TC*, the theory *FS* proves not only that these properties hold for sentences of $\mathcal{L}_{PA}$, but also that they hold for all sentences of $\mathcal{L}_T$:

Proposition 43

1. $FS \vdash \forall \phi \in \mathcal{L}_T : \neg(T(\phi) \wedge T(\neg\phi))$;
2. $FS \vdash \forall \phi \in \mathcal{L}_T : T(\phi) \vee T(\neg\phi)$.

Proof   *The proof is completely straightforward. We only do 1 as an example. It is a law of logic that* $\forall \phi \in \mathcal{L}_T : \neg(T(\phi) \wedge \neg T(\phi))$. *Then we use FS2 to conclude* $\forall \phi \in \mathcal{L}_T : \neg(T(\phi) \wedge T(\neg\phi))$. ∎

It is comforting to know that *FS* meets a minimal coherence constraint:[2]

Theorem 44 (Friedman and Sheard) *FS is consistent.*

Proof *(Sketch)* *Consider the initial segment of the ordinal-length chain of revision models up to but not including $\mathfrak{M}_\omega$. In all successor models of this initial segment, the axioms of FS are true. Even though none of the models in this initial segment is closed under Necessitation and Co-Necessitation, it can be shown that for any natural number k, the model $\mathfrak{M}_{2 \times k}$ is closed under k applications of Necessitation and Co-Necessitation. Because every proof of FS only contains a finite number of applications of Necessitation and Co-Necessitation, FS must then be consistent.* ∎

Observe that this consistency theorem shows that the *inference rules* NEC and CONEC together are in the context of the other axioms of *FS* weaker than their corresponding *axioms* $\phi \to T(\phi)$ and $T(\phi) \to \phi$. Indeed, as mentioned earlier, including the latter axioms amounts to including the unrestricted Tarski-biconditionals, which results in inconsistency.

Because none of the models in the initial segment of the revision sequence of models is a model of all of *FS*, theorem 44 does not show that *FS* has a *nice* model. Indeed, $\mathfrak{M}_\omega$ is not a model for *FS* at all:

Proposition 45 $\mathfrak{M}_\omega \not\models F3$.

Proof *The liar sentence L oscillates forever below stage ω. So $\mathfrak{M}_\omega \not\models T(L)$, whereby $\mathfrak{M}_\omega \models \neg T(L)$. The sentence $\neg L$ oscillates every bit as much as L. So $\mathfrak{M}_\omega \not\models T(\neg L)$. Therefore*

$$\mathfrak{M}_\omega \not\models \neg T(L) \leftrightarrow T(\neg L).$$

∎

Not all of *FS* is stably true. Indeed, not only $\mathfrak{M}_\omega$ but every limit model fails to make axiom FS3 true, for instance. Nearly stable truth, in contrast, is a more suitable notion in this respect:

Proposition 46 *FS is nearly stably true.*

Proof *This is shown by a straightforward induction on the length of proofs in FS.* ∎

So *FS* is closely connected to the "near stable truth" variant of the revision theory of truth.

FS is a *self-referential* theory of truth, because it proves genuine truth iterations. This is accomplished mainly by the Necessitation rule:

---

2. The proof-sketch given here follows the proof in [Halbach 1994].

Proposition 47 *For all $n \in \mathbb{N}$: $FS \vdash T^n(0 = 0)$, where $T^n(0 = 0)$ stands for n iterations of T followed by $0 = 0$.*

Proof *PA already proves $0 = 0$. The proposition results from n applications of NEC to this sentence.* ∎

Proposition 48 *FS does not prove* transfinite *truth iterations.*

Proof *This follows from the proof of theorem 44 because in no model $\mathfrak{M}_\alpha$ for $\alpha < \omega$ are transfinite truth iterations true.* ∎

So although FS proves $T^n(0 = 0)$ for every $n \in \mathbb{N}$, it cannot synthesize these proof into a master proof of $\forall n T^n(0 = 0)$.

Because FS is consistent, it must by the completeness theorem have a model. Nevertheless, it follows from an important theorem of McGee[3] that no models based on the natural numbers *can* be constructed in such a way as to make FS true. McGee has proved that FS is *ω-inconsistent*, meaning:

Definition 49 *An arithmetical theory S is ω-inconsistent if for some formula $\phi(x)$, the theory S proves $\exists x \phi(x)$ while for every $n \in \mathbb{N}$, S proves $\neg \phi(\overline{n})$*

The proof that FS is ω-inconsistent goes as follows:[4]

Theorem 50 (McGee) *For some formula $\phi(x) \in \mathcal{L}_T : FS \vdash \exists x \phi(x)$ and $FS \vdash \neg \phi(\overline{n})$ for all $n \in \mathbb{N}$.*

Proof *There exists a computable function $f(x, y)$ that is such that if n is a natural number and $y = \phi$, then*

$$f(n, \phi) = \underbrace{T \ldots T}_{n} \phi.$$

This function f can be expressed in $\mathcal{L}_{PA}$. By the self-referential lemma, we find a sentence λ such that

$$PA^T \vdash \lambda \leftrightarrow \exists x \neg T(f(x, \lambda))$$

Now we reason in PA^T:

$$\neg \lambda \Rightarrow$$

$$\forall x T(f(x, \lambda)) \Rightarrow$$

---
3. See [McGee 1985].
4. I present the proof that is given in [Halbach 1996, pp. 158–159].

$$T(f(0,\lambda)) \Rightarrow$$

$$T(\lambda).$$

On the other hand, if we necessitate $\lambda \to \exists x T f(x,\lambda)$ and distribute the truth predicate over $\to$ using the compositional truth laws of FS, we obtain

$$T(\lambda) \to T(\exists x \neg T(f(x,\lambda))).$$

With this, we can continue the argument:

$$T(\lambda) \Rightarrow$$
$$T(\exists x \neg T(f(x,\lambda))) \Rightarrow$$
$$\exists x T(\neg f(x+1,\lambda)) \Rightarrow$$
$$\exists x T(\neg f(x,\lambda)) \Rightarrow$$
$$\lambda.$$

So we conclude that $FS \vdash \lambda$, i.e., $FS \vdash \exists x \neg T(f(x,\lambda))$. On the other hand, for any $n \in \mathbb{N}$ we can derive by n applications of NEC that $FS \vdash T^n(\lambda)$, i.e.,

$$FS \vdash T(f(0,\lambda))$$
$$FS \vdash T(f(1,\lambda))$$
$$FS \vdash T(f(2,\lambda))$$
$$\vdots$$

Thus, we reach the conclusion that FS is ω-inconsistent. ∎

Note that McGee's theorem actually proves a slightly stronger statement. In the theorem, CONEC was not used, so even $FS - CONEC$ is ω-inconsistent.

McGee's theorem is a strong no go-result. It can be seen as a strengthening of the impossibility result that we have seen earlier, namely, the Paradox of the Knower.[5] Even if we weaken the Tarski-biconditionals *considerably*, we land in the soup.

Nevertheless, FS is *arithmetically* sound: It proves only arithmetical truths. This follows from an analysis of theorem 44 (Exercise). In fact, FS is arithmetically quite a bit stronger than TC. FS is arithmetically equivalent to the ω-th level of the Tarskian hierarchy based on TC:[6]

---

5. See section 3.5.3.
6. For a proof of this theorem, see [Halbach 1994].

Theorem 51 (Halbach) *FS is arithmetically equivalent to* TC_ω.

The nonconservativeness of *FS* is of a peculiar kind. In section 7.2.2, we distinguished between *ontological* and *ideological* nonconservativeness. *DT* was shown to be ontologically productive over logic, in the sense that it proves the existence of more objects than classical logic alone is able to do. *TC* was shown to be ideologically productive over arithmetic, in the sense that it proves more statements about the natural numbers than *PA* does. We have seen that *FS* is even more ideologically nonconservative over Peano arithmetic than *TC*. But in addition to that, it also turns out to be ontologically productive over arithmetic: It forces the domain of its models to contain more than just the standard natural numbers.

8.5 Is the Friedman–Sheard Theory Sound?

The untyped system *FS* is more complete than its typed cousin *TC*. It proves truth iterations while *TC* doesn't. Also, it is arithmetically stronger than *TC*. *FS* is a natural compositional and reflexive extension of the natural system *TC*. So *if* a strong case can be made that *FS* is sound, then it scores higher in the power game than *TC*.

At first sight, the prospects of *FS* in this respect look dim. In words, McGee's theorem says that *FS* proves that there is a number x with a certain truth-theoretic property ϕ, but at the same time, for any number n, *FS* proves that n does not have the property ϕ. Most truth theorists for this reason find *FS* problematic as an axiomatic theory of self-referential truth. Even though *FS* is not outright inconsistent, its ω-inconsistency seems clear evidence of its unsoundness.

But things are not as bad as they seem at first sight. The *arithmetical* soundness of *FS* can be used to try to remove the appearance of unsoundness of *FS* that is created by McGee's theorem.[7]

In the formula $\neg T(f(x, \lambda))$, the formula λ occurs in the scope of the truth predicate T. The arithmetical soundness of *FS* entails that *any* formula witnessing the ω-inconsistency of *FS* must be a formula that essentially involves T. In fact, the formula in the proof of McGee's theorem is clearly *paradoxical*. It is reminiscent of the liar sentence: It is a sentence that says of itself that it can be turned into a falsehood by prefixing some finite but unspecified number of Ts to itself. Thus, the witness of the ω-inconsistency of *FS* that we have constructed is a statement about which we have no firm intuitions as to what its truth value should be. Perhaps it should not come as such a surprise that *FS* proves strange things about some paradoxical sentences.

---

7. In [Halbach & Horsten 2005], a more sustained defence of *FS* is presented than is given here.

At any rate, *FS* treats the liar sentence *L* in the way that it should be treated:

Proposition 52

1. FS ⊬ L;

2. FS ⊬ ¬L.

Proof *We prove 1 and leave 2 to the reader. As an application of the diagonal lemma, we have FS ⊢ L ↔ ¬T(L). Suppose FS ⊢ L. Then by the diagonal lemma, we have FS ⊢ ¬T(L). But by NEC, we have FS ⊢ T(L). So we reach a contradiction. But we know that FS is consistent.* ∎

This notwithstanding, there is still cause for concern. Earlier I have asserted that dialetheist theories of truth are unsatisfying.[8] *FS* is ω-inconsistent. To many, an ω-inconsistency is no more than a "sophisticated" inconsistency. So *FS* may seem just a bit too close to dialetheism for comfort. In view of this, it seems that *FS* would have been better off if it would have treated $\exists x \neg T(f(x, \lambda))$ like it treats the liar sentence: It should have left it undecided. After all, it is exceedingly difficult to imagine what it means for an existential statement to be true while all its instances are false.

In defense of *FS*, one might argue that the notion of nearly stable truth is an accurate explication of *our* notion of truth and point out that all of *FS* is nearly stably true. But against this it can be said that, in the notion of stable truth, the notion of nearly stable truth has a serious rival for the claim of coinciding with truth simpliciter. What independent reasons do we have to think that the more "technical" notion of nearly stable truth has a better claim of coinciding with truth than the simpler notion of stable truth? It is hard to believe that our notion of truth is *that* complicated. Moreover, one person's modus ponens is another's reductio. The fact that nearly stable truth is synchronically ω-inconsistent might be taken as a reason that it cannot be our notion of truth. This is not to say, of course, that the notion of stable truth, which is ω-consistent, must be the right one instead. We have seen that, in contrast to nearly stable truth, stable truth is not compositional, and this could be held against it.[9] Moreover, the notion of stable truth is already so complicated that doubts could be raised as to whether this could be *our* notion of truth.

In the light of these considerations, it seems safe to conclude that the philosophical soundness of *FS* is doubtful. So the question arises whether there is a way of fixing *FS*. The obvious move at this point would be to minimally weaken

---

8. See section 1.2.

9. The trade-off, from the revision theorist's perspective, between compositionality and ω-inconsistency is discussed in [Gupta & Belnap 1993, chapter 6, section D].

FS so as to restore ω-consistency or even obtain a system that is stably true. Attempts to do this would take us too far afield, so we let the matter rest here.

8.6 A Somewhat Frivolous Game

It turns out that *FS* is arithmetically stronger than the typed truth theory *TC*. It may be thought that arithmetical strength is a good measure for truth-theoretic completeness. But, as we will see, this is not always the case.

8.6.1 Subsystems of Second-Order Arithmetic

We have mentioned that *FS* is stronger than *TC*. In the light of theorem 42, this means that the arithmetical consequences of *FS* exceed those of *ACA*. The arithmetical power of *FS* again coincides with the first-order consequences of a natural system of second-order arithmetic. Let us have a brief look at it.

The system *ACA* can be strengthened in the following way to a system ACA_1. We can add a new collection of second-order variables $X^1, Y^1, \ldots$ to the language of *ACA*. These new second-order variables figure in exactly the same way in the logical and arithmetical axioms as the "old" second-order variables $X, Y, \ldots$. But the new second-order variables are governed in ACA_1 by a new collection of comprehension axioms, namely, all those sentences of the form

$$\exists Y^1 \forall x [Y^1(x) \leftrightarrow \phi(x)],$$

where $\phi(x)$ does not contain the second-order variable Y^1 free, contains no bound occurrences of the *new* second-order variables, *but is allowed to contain bound occurrences of the old second-order quantifiers* ($\exists X, \forall Y, \ldots$). The idea behind ACA_1 is that arithmetical formulae determine sets of natural numbers, but also those formulae that quantify over sets of formulae that are (first-order) arithmetically defined. The system ACA_1 has more first-order arithmetical consequences than *ACA* but fewer than PA^2 has.

Clearly, this is the beginning of a hierarchy of systems of second-order arithmetic. We can again add new second-order variables $X^2, Y^2, \ldots$, and add comprehension axioms which say that they range over sets that can be defined by quantifying over arithmetically defined sets and sets that can be defined by quantifying over *them*. We thereby obtain a system ACA_2, which has more first-order consequences than ACA_1. Thus, for each number n, a system ACA_n can be defined. ACA_ω is defined as the union of all the ACA_ns. The system ACA_ω again has more first-order consequences than any of the ACA_ns but fewer than PA^2 has. ACA_ω is often called *ramified analysis* up to level ω.[10] As with the

---

10. This system goes back to the work of Hermann Weyl on predicative number theory.

Tarskian hierarchy, there is no need to stop here. We can continue to construct theories $ACA_{\omega+1}$, $ACA_{\omega+2}$, etc.

8.6.2 The Strength of FS

The ACA hierarchy can be used to calibrate the mathematical strength of FS [Halbach 1994]:

Theorem 53 (Halbach) *The arithmetical consequences of FS are exactly the first-order consequences of the system ACA_ω.*

So the mathematical power of FS is much greater than that of TC.

Michael Sheard has investigated an interesting subsystem of FS, which he calls S_1 [Sheard 2001]. It consists of the following principles:

S1 PA^T;

S2 $\forall \phi \in \mathcal{L}_T : T(\phi) \to (\phi$ is a sentence of $\mathcal{L}_T)$;

S3 $\forall \phi, \psi \in \mathcal{L}_T : (T(\phi) \wedge T(\phi \to \psi)) \to T(\psi)$;

S4 $\forall \phi \in \mathcal{L}_T : (\phi$ is a first-order logical truth$) \to T(\phi)$;

S5 $\forall$ atomic or negated atomic arithmetical $\phi : \phi \to T(\phi)$;

S6 $\forall \phi(x) \in \mathcal{L}_T : T(\forall x \phi(x)) \leftrightarrow \forall x T(\phi(x))$;

S7 From a proof of $T(\phi)$, infer ϕ.

S7 is the inference rule CONEC, and S6 is axiom FS5. In fact, S6 is the only axiom that expresses an aspect of the compositionality of truth; the other compositionality principles (FS3–FS4) have been left out. The axioms S1–S5 together form a weak theory of truth: These principles are easily seen to be provable in FS. So we have:

Proposition 54 S_1 *is a subtheory of FS.*

From a truth-theoretic point of view, S_1 is quite weak. For instance, S_1 does not prove the statement

$$\forall \phi(x) \in \mathcal{L}_T : \neg(T(\phi) \wedge T(\neg \phi)).$$

We have seen that FS, in contrast, easily proves the consistency of the extension of the truth predicate. So S_1 is not very interesting as a theory of truth.

Proof-theoretically, S_1 is better behaved than FS: Sheard proves that S_1 is ω-consistent. Strangely and surprisingly, S_1 is arithmetically quite strong:

Theorem 55 (Sheard) *S_1 is arithmetically just as strong as FS.*

This surprising result has a truth-theoretic moral. It shows that mathematical strength and truth-theoretic strength do not always go hand in glove. In other words, the mathematical strength of a truth theory can be a poor yardstick for measuring its truth-theoretic completeness. Of course Sheard's results about S_1 do not detract from the importance of the project of calibrating the mathematical content of the notion of truth. But from the vantage point of truth-theoretic completeness, what we have called the power game seems somewhat frivolous.

8.6.3 The Weakness of FS

The revision theory is *very* complicated. Philip Welch has shown that the stable truth is from a recursion-theoretic point of view more complicated than almost all other formal proposals for defining reflexive truth [Welch 2001]. Moreover, he has shown that the collection of nearly stable truths is just as complex as the collection of stable truths. Now we have seen that *FS* is, mathematically, indeed a fairly strong truth theory. But, as we see in the next chapter, *FS* is not nearly as strong as some other truth theories.

Normally, one would expect that axiomatizations of very complicated truth sets are proof-theoretically strong. This is not the case here. Thus, it appears that we have been able to capture the motivation behind the concept of nearly stable truth only to a limited extent.[11] It must be admitted that, until now, we do not have a good axiomatic grip on revision-theoretic conceptions of truth. Much (if not all) of the semantical action is in the limit rule for constructing revision models, and it is hard to see how this limit rule can be proof-theoretically described in $\mathcal{L}_T$.

---

11. In [Horsten et al. in prep.], an attempt is made to axiomatically capture more of the concept of nearly stable truth.

9 Kripke's Theory Axiomatized

Kripke formulated what is currently probably the most influential semantical theory of truth [Kripke 1975]. In this chapter, we see that, like Tarski's semantical notion of a (classical) model, Kripke's semantical theory has been a rich source of inspiration for proof-theoretic approaches to truth. Some of our strongest and best axiomatic theories of truth result from attempts to axiomatize some of his models for the language of truth.

9.1 Kripke's Semantical Theory of Truth

Kripke has constructed a semantical theory of self-referential truth. He is not occupied with formulating an axiomatic theory of truth. For Kripke, models come first. His aim is to construct particularly nice models of the language $\mathcal{L}_T$, which do justice to the self-applicative nature of the concept of truth.

9.1.1 Constructing Models for Self-Referential Truth

The argument of the liar paradox puts us in the awkward position of recognizing that both the supposition that the liar sentence L holds and the supposition that its negation holds lead to a contradiction. Kripke takes the moral of the argument to show that neither L nor its negation holds.

In ordinary Tarskian models for $\mathcal{L}_T$, a given sentence either holds or its negation holds. So if we are to respect Kripke's diagnosis of the liar paradox, then we must modify our notion of model so as to leave room for the possibility that for some sentences, neither they nor their negation hold. This leads us to the notion of a *partial model*, to which we now turn.

We want to build a model for the language $\mathcal{L}_T$. The arithmetical vocabulary is interpreted throughout as in the standard model $\mathbb{N}$. The predicate T will be the only partially interpreted symbol: It will receive, at each ordinal stage, an *extension* $\mathcal{E}$ and an *anti-extension* $\mathcal{A}$. The set $\mathcal{E} \cup \mathcal{A}$ does not exhaust the domain because otherwise T would be a total predicate. The extension $\mathcal{E}$ of T is the collection of (codes of) sentences that are (at the given stage) determinately true; the anti-extension $\mathcal{A}$ of T is the collection of (codes of) sentences that are (at the given stage) determinately false. Because we do not want to allow for the possibility that a sentence is both true and false, we insist that $\mathcal{E} \cap \mathcal{A} = \emptyset$.

A partial model $\mathfrak{M}$ for $\mathcal{L}_T$ can then be identified with an ordered pair $(\mathcal{E}, \mathcal{A})$.[1] In general, the union of the extension and the anti-extension will not exhaust the collection of all sentences. Some sentences will at each ordinal stage retain their indeterminate status. An example of an eternally indeterminate sentence is the liar sentence L. The intuition that the liar-argument tells us that the sentence L cannot have a determinate truth value is the basic motivation for constructing a theory of truth in which T is treated as a partial predicate.

At stage 0, the extension and the anti-extension of T are empty. This yields a partial model,

$$\mathfrak{M}_0 = (\emptyset, \emptyset).$$

Next, a popular evaluation scheme for partial logic is used: the so-called *strong Kleene scheme*. The strong Kleene evaluation scheme $\models_{sk}$ is defined roughly as follows:

- For any atomic formula $Fx_1 \ldots x_n$:

1. $\mathfrak{M} \models_{sk} F(n_1, \ldots, n_k)$ if and only if the k-tuple $\langle n_1, \ldots, n_k \rangle$ belongs to the extension of F;

2. $\mathfrak{M} \models_{sk} \neg F(n_1, \ldots, n_k)$ if the k-tuple $\langle n_1, \ldots, n_k \rangle$ belongs to the anti-extension of F.

- For any formulae ϕ, ψ :

1. $\mathfrak{M} \models_{sk} \phi \wedge \psi$ if and only if $\mathfrak{M} \models_{sk} \phi$ and $\mathfrak{M} \models_{sk} \psi$;

2. $\mathfrak{M} \models_{sk} \neg(\phi \wedge \psi)$ if and only if either $\mathfrak{M} \models_{sk} \neg\phi$ or $\mathfrak{M} \models_{sk} \neg\psi$ (or both);

3. $\mathfrak{M} \models_{sk} \forall x \phi$ if and only if for all n, $\mathfrak{M} \models_{sk} \phi(n/x)$;

4. $\mathfrak{M} \models_{sk} \neg\forall x \phi$ if and only if for at least one n, $\mathfrak{M} \models_{sk} \neg\phi(n/x)$;

5. $\mathfrak{M} \models_{sk} \neg\neg\phi$ if and only if $\mathfrak{M} \models_{sk} \phi$.

The strong Kleene scheme is used to determine the collection $\mathcal{E}_1$ of sentences of $\mathcal{L}_T$ that are made true by $\mathfrak{M}_0$ and the collection $\mathcal{A}_1$ of sentences of $\mathcal{L}_T$ the negation of which are made true by $\mathfrak{M}_0$. Thus, a new partial model $\mathfrak{M}_1 = (\mathcal{E}_1, \mathcal{A}_1)$ is obtained. Using $\mathfrak{M}_1$, a new extension $\mathcal{E}_2$ and a new anti-extension $\mathcal{A}_2$ are then determined, and so on. In general, for any ordinal α,

---

1. We denote partial models as $(\mathcal{E}, \mathcal{A})$ and not as $\langle \mathcal{E}, \mathcal{A} \rangle$ to clearly distinguish them from classical models of the form $\langle \mathbb{N}, \mathcal{E} \rangle$.

$\mathcal{E}_{\alpha+1} =: \{\phi \in \mathcal{L}_T \mid \mathfrak{M}_\alpha \models_{sk} \phi\}$ and

$\mathcal{A}_{\alpha+1} =: \{\phi \in \mathcal{L}_T \mid \mathfrak{M}_\alpha \models_{sk} \neg\phi\}$.

For limit stages λ, we set

$$\mathcal{E}_\lambda =: \bigcup_{\kappa < \lambda} \mathcal{E}_\kappa,$$

$$\mathcal{A}_\lambda =: \bigcup_{\kappa < \lambda} \mathcal{A}_\kappa.$$

This means that at limit stages we collect in the extension (anti-extension) of T all sentences that have landed the extension (anti-extension) of T at some earlier stage.

Now we are going to consider the resulting transfinite sequence of models:

$(\mathcal{E}_0, \mathcal{A}_0), (\mathcal{E}_1, \mathcal{A}_1), \ldots, (\mathcal{E}_\omega, \mathcal{A}_\omega), \ldots$

It is not hard to see that the strong Kleene valuation scheme has the following (important) *monotonicity* property:

Theorem 56 *For any two partial models $(\mathcal{E}_a, \mathcal{A}_a)$ and $(\mathcal{E}_b, \mathcal{A}_b)$: If $\mathcal{E}_a \subseteq \mathcal{E}_b$ and $\mathcal{A}_a \subseteq \mathcal{A}_b$, then*

$\{\phi \mid (\mathcal{E}_a, \mathcal{A}_a) \models_{sk} \phi\} \subseteq \{\phi \mid (\mathcal{E}_b, \mathcal{A}_b) \models_{sk} \phi\}$.

Proof *This follows by an induction on the complexity of formulae of $\mathcal{L}_T$.* ∎

A consequence of this is that:

Corollary 57 *For all α, β with $\alpha < \beta$, we have:*

$\{\phi \mid (\mathcal{E}_\alpha, \mathcal{A}_\alpha) \models_{sk} \phi\} \subseteq \{\phi \mid (\mathcal{E}_\beta, \mathcal{A}_\beta) \models_{sk} \phi\}$.

In other words, as we proceed in the sequence of models, more and more sentences of $\mathcal{L}_T$ end up in the extension or in the anti-extension of T, and once a sentence is in the extension (anti-extension) of T, it stays in forever after. But by elementary cardinality considerations, this process must eventually come to an end. Intuitively, what happens is that at some ordinal stage, the basket of sentences that can be put in the extension or in the anti-extension of T is exhausted.

Proposition 58 *For some ordinal ρ, $\mathcal{E}_\rho = \mathcal{E}_{\rho+1}$ and $\mathcal{A}_\rho = \mathcal{A}_{\rho+1}$.*

Proof *This is an elementary argument in transfinite set theory.*
  Remember that for every ordinal α, $\mathcal{E}_\alpha$ is just a set of codes of sentences and thus is countable. There are uncountably many ordinal numbers. Suppose that

for uncountably many ordinals α at least one new sentence ϕ_α enters in $\mathcal{E}_\alpha$. Then there would be a one-to-one onto correspondence between an uncountable set O of ordinals and the union of all the $\mathcal{E}_\alpha$ for $\alpha \in O$. But because the language $\mathcal{L}_T$ is countable, the union of all the $\mathcal{E}_\alpha$ is countable. So by Cantor's Theorem, no such one-to-one onto correspondence can exist.

The argument for the anti-extension of the truth predicate is symmetrical. ∎

The partial model $\mathfrak{M}_\rho = (\mathcal{E}_\rho, \mathcal{A}_\rho)$ is called the *least fixed point* model or the least fixed point, for short. It is the particularly nice model for the language $\mathcal{L}_T$ we have been looking for. The ordinal stage at which this fixed point is attained is exactly known. It is the ordinal number ω_1^{CK}. The ordinal ω_1^{CK} is the first nonrecursive ordinal (i.e., it is (roughly) the smallest ordinal number that cannot be represented by a computable function on the natural numbers). The ordinal ω_1^{CK} is a countable ordinal, but it is a large countable ordinal number.[2]

9.1.2 Properties and Variations

This model is nice because it is based on the natural numbers. But why is this model *particularly* nice?

First, long truth iterations hold in the least fixed point. For one thing, the sentence $\forall x\, T^x(0 = 0)$ for the first time enters the extension of T at stage ω. The sentence $T \forall x\, T^x(0 = 0)$ enters the extension only at the next stage $\omega + 1$, so this sentence can be taken to "express" a sequence of Ts of inverse order type $\omega + 1$, followed by $0 = 0$. In general, we have:

Proposition 59 (Kripke) *(Exactly) for all $\alpha < \omega_1^{CK}$, $\mathfrak{M}_\rho \models_{sk} T^\alpha(0 = 0)$.*

We do not prove this proposition here, but merely pause to observe that these are *much* longer truth iterations than can be proved to hold in the axiomatic self-referential theory *FS*.

Second, the least fixed point is "consistent" in the sense that:

Proposition 60 *There is no sentence ϕ of $\mathcal{L}_T$ such that $\mathfrak{M}_\rho \models_{sk} T(\phi)$ and $\mathfrak{M}_\rho \models_{sk} T(\neg\phi)$.*

Proof *Suppose there were such a sentence ϕ. Then there would be an ordinal $\alpha < \rho$ such that $\mathfrak{M}_\alpha \models_{sk} \phi$ and $\mathfrak{M}_\alpha \not\models_{sk} \neg\phi$ —or conversely, but that case is symmetric. But then by monotonicity and the clauses of truth in a partial model, there can be no $\beta > \alpha$ such that $\mathfrak{M}_\beta \models_{sk} \neg\phi$. Contradiction.* ∎

---

2. For an exact definition of ω_1^{CK} and more about computable notations for ordinals, see [Rogers 1967, section 11.7].

Kripke's Theory Axiomatized   121

Third, and most important, *in a certain (partial) sense*, the *unrestricted* Tarski-biconditionals hold in $\mathfrak{M}_\rho$:

Theorem 61 *For all sentences ϕ in $\mathcal{L}_T$:*

$$\mathfrak{M}_\rho \models_{sk} \phi \Leftrightarrow \mathfrak{M}_\rho \models_{sk} T(\phi).$$

Proof *First, suppose $\mathfrak{M}_\rho \models_{sk} \phi$. Then by the definition of the sequence of partial models, $\mathfrak{M}_{\rho+1} \models_{sk} T(\phi)$. But because $\mathfrak{M}_\rho$ is a fixed point, we have $\mathfrak{M}_{\rho+1} = \mathfrak{M}_\rho$. So $\mathfrak{M}_\rho \models_{sk} T(\phi)$.*

Second, suppose $\mathfrak{M}_\rho \models_{sk} T(\phi)$. Then there must be an ordinal $\alpha < \rho$ such that $\mathfrak{M}_\alpha \models_{sk} \phi$. Therefore, by monotonicity, $\mathfrak{M}_\rho \models_{sk} \phi$. ∎

This is the brilliant insight that Kripke had: Tarski's undefinability theorem does *not* hold in an unqualified way for partial logic. Recall that Tarski's undefinability theorem 14 says that no *classical*, Tarskian model $\mathfrak{M}$ is such that for all sentences ϕ of $\mathcal{L}_T$, $\mathfrak{M} \models \phi$ exactly if $\mathfrak{M} \models T(\phi)$, or, equivalently, is such that for all sentences ϕ of $\mathcal{L}_T$, $\mathfrak{M} \models \phi \leftrightarrow T(\phi)$. But the previous theorem tells us that we *have* constructed a *partial* model $\mathfrak{M}_\rho$, such that for all sentences ϕ in $\mathcal{L}_T$: $\mathfrak{M}_\rho \models_{sk} \phi$ exactly if $\mathfrak{M}_\rho \models_{sk} T(\phi)$. However, this is *not* equivalent to saying that for all sentences ϕ in $\mathcal{L}_T$:

$$\mathfrak{M}_\rho \models_{sk} \phi \leftrightarrow T(\phi).$$

In fact—and this is a *fourth* reason that the least fixed point is a particularly nice model—this cannot be the case, for because the liar sentence L is left indeterminate by the least fixed point. To prove this, we first describe a way of obtaining a classical model for $\mathcal{L}_T$ from a partial model by *closing off* the partial model:

Definition 62 *For any partial model $(\mathcal{E}, \mathcal{A})$ with $\mathcal{E} \cap \mathcal{A} = \emptyset$, the closed off model corresponding to $(\mathcal{E}, \mathcal{A})$ is the classical model $(\mathcal{E}, \mathbb{N} \setminus \mathcal{E})$.*

Intuitively, a partial model is closed off by absorbing the gap into the antiextension of the truth predicate.

Theorem 63 $\mathfrak{M}_\rho \not\models_{sk} T(L)$ *and* $\mathfrak{M}_\rho \not\models_{sk} \neg T(L)$.

Proof *We concentrate on the first part of the theorem—the second part is proved in a similar way.*

Because $\mathfrak{M}_\rho$ has the fixed point property (theorem 61), we have $\mathfrak{M}_\rho \models_{sk} L$ exactly if $\mathfrak{M}_\rho \models_{sk} T(L)$. Now by closing off the model $\mathfrak{M}_\rho$ we obtain a classical model $\mathfrak{M}_\rho^c$. Suppose that $\mathfrak{M}_\rho \models_{sk} T(L)$ and thereby $\mathfrak{M}_\rho \models_{sk} L$. Then by monotonicity, also $\mathfrak{M}_\rho^c \models_{sk} T(L)$ and $\mathfrak{M}_\rho^c \models_{sk} L$. (Note that because $\mathfrak{M}_\rho^c$

*is a classical model, $\mathfrak{M}_\rho^c \models_{sk} \ldots$ amounts to the same as with $\mathfrak{M}_\rho^c \models \ldots$.)
But because $\mathfrak{M}_\rho^c$ is just a classical model, the strengthened extended diagonal
lemma (theorem 13) holds in it. So we have*

$$\mathfrak{M}_\rho^c \models_{sk} L \leftrightarrow \neg T(L).$$

*But putting these three facts together gives us a contradiction. So we deny our
supposition and conclude that $\mathfrak{M}_\rho \not\models_{sk} T(L)$.* ■

Because L and $T(L)$ are left undecided by $\mathfrak{M}_\rho$, so is (by the clauses of the strong Kleene valuation scheme) the sentence $L \leftrightarrow T(L)$. So in *this* sense, the unrestricted Tarski-biconditionals are not satisfied by $\mathfrak{M}_\rho$. But we have come close to getting what we want.

From a computability-theoretic point of view, the least fixed point is a complicated collection of sentences.[3] But its complexity is not as high as that of the collection of stable truths (or of the nearly stable truths) that we have discussed in the previous chapter.

Now we have discussed the least fixed point, the smallest fixed point model that exists. But there is a plethora of partial models that have the fixed point property, and these fixed point models have been intensively studied. It is no easy matter to decide which of these models should be preferred as the "intended" model(s) of the language $\mathcal{L}_T$.

The liar sentence is not the only paradoxical sentence of $\mathcal{L}_T$. Not all paradoxical sentences behave in the same way in all fixed points. Consider the sentence J such that

$$PA^T \vdash J \leftrightarrow T(J).$$

The diagonal lemma guarantees that J exists. This sentence says of itself (modulo coding) that it is true. It is called the *truth-teller* sentence. It can be shown that, like the liar sentence, the truth-teller is gappy in the least fixed point model. But whereas the liar sentence is gappy in *all* fixed point models, there are fixed point models in which J is true and fixed point models in which J is false. If we would have put J in the extension (anti-extension) of the truth predicate at the outset, it would have remained there throughout the process.

Nevertheless, the least fixed point model is special. In the first stage, the extension and anti-extension of the truth predicate were taken to be empty. Then we looked at the world (the world of the natural numbers, in this case) to include sentences in the extension and in the anti-extension. Then we built on that. As a result, the sentences in the extension and anti-extension of the

---

3. Complexity calculations for this and other fixed points of Kripke's construction can be found in [Burgess 1986].

least fixed point are all *grounded* in the world.[4] Their truth value is ultimately determined by facts in the (mathematical) world. For other fixed points, this is not always the case.

It was mentioned earlier that besides the strong Kleene scheme, there are other valuation schemes for partial logic. One of these schemes deserves special attention. This is the *supervaluation scheme*, which is due to van Fraassen. In the supervaluation approach, a formula $\phi \in \mathcal{L}_T$ is regarded as true in a partial model $\mathfrak{M} = (\mathcal{E}, \mathcal{A})$ if and only if ϕ is true in all total (or classical) models $\mathfrak{M}_c = \langle \mathbb{N}, \mathcal{C} \rangle$ for which the interpretation $\mathcal{C}$ of the truth predicate is such that $\mathcal{E} \subseteq \mathcal{C}$ and $\mathcal{A} \subseteq \mathbb{N}\backslash\mathcal{C}$. Intuitively, this means that ϕ is regarded as supervaluation-true in a partial model if ϕ comes out true in every way of extending this partial model to a total, classical model. Similarly, we say that a formula $\phi \in \mathcal{L}_T$ is regarded as false in a partial model $\mathfrak{M} = (\mathcal{E}, \mathcal{A})$ if and only if ϕ is false in all total (or classical) models $\mathfrak{M}_c = \langle \mathbb{N}, \mathcal{C} \rangle$ for which the interpretation $\mathcal{C}$ of the truth predicate is such that $\mathcal{E} \subseteq \mathcal{C}$ and $\mathcal{A} \subseteq \mathbb{N}\backslash\mathcal{C}$.

Of course, the notion of supervaluation-truth leaves room for a formula to be neither supervaluation-true nor supervaluation-false. But it is clear that every classical logical truth will come out supervaluation-true in all partial models. So in this sense, supervaluation logic is closer to classical logic than strong Kleene logic.

The considerations that we have gone through in this section establish that a minimal supervaluation fixed point model can be built for $\mathcal{L}_T$ in the same way as for the strong Kleene scheme. This minimal supervaluation fixed point model also judges neither the liar sentence nor its negation to be true. But unlike the strong Kleene fixed point, it judges $L \vee \neg L$ to be determinately true because this is an instance of the law of excluded third. So the supervaluation-incarnation of Kripke's theory of truth is noncompositional.

Kripke suggested that the way in which the extension and anti-extension of the truth predicate grow in stages mirrors the way in which the concept of truth is learned. A child is first told of scores of sentences not containing the truth predicate ("Snow is white," "$1 + 1 = 2$," etc.) that they are true. At some point, the child grasps what it means for a sentence not containing the truth predicate to be true. Then the child is taught that, for example, the sentence "It is true that $1 + 1 = 2$" is also true and that "It is true that it is true that $1 + 1 = 2$" is also true. Eventually the child is told in an off-hand way: "and so on." What is meant by "and so on" is taught in the child's mathematics classes. In primary school, it becomes clear that a potentially infinite number of levels of truth is covered by "and so on." Hellman asks how real people ever learn *transfinite*

---

4. For more about the notion of groundedness, see [Yablo 1982] and [Leitgeb 2005].

truth iterations [Hellman 1985]. The answer is that most people don't. But at the university some of the brighter children are taught that one can continue to count after the natural numbers are exhausted. If the young adult has done a bit of transfinite set theory, she can prove for herself that there must be a stage when the process yields nothing new: There is a fixed point.

There is, however, one pressing and damning philosophical objection to Kripke's theory of truth, both in its strong Kleene incarnation and in its supervaluation guise. In the least fixed point model, the liar sentence L ends up in the gap: It is neither in the extension nor in the anti-extension of T. This may be expressed as: *L is neither made true nor made false in the least fixed point*. But if it is made neither true nor false, then it is not made true. But that is exactly what L says of itself. So L seems true after all! Thus, the liar paradox strikes again—or so it seems. In Kripke's own words [Kripke 1975, p. 80]:

The ghost of the Tarski hierarchy is still with us.

So we have arrived at another variant of the strengthened liar problem. If you throw your mind back, you will recall that contextualist theories of truth were plagued by it.[5] It is in fact one of the most recalcitrant problems for theories of truth. Even a cursory look at the essays in [Beall 2007] can convince the reader of the seriousness of this problem for many contemporary formal theories of truth. Almost every truth theorist alleges that *his* theory escapes the strengthened liar problem, but all the other truth theories succumb to it. It would be considered most unsportsmanlike if I were not to follow suit. So, later on in this book, I do exactly like the others.[6]

9.2 Kripke–Feferman

It was argued earlier that semantic theories of truth do not meet the mark. Thus, Kripke's theory of truth cannot be accepted as it stands. But Kripke's theory of truth has inspired strong and natural axiomatic theories of truth. To these we now turn.

There exists an axiomatic theory of self-referential truth that is due to Feferman and that has more supporters than *FS* does. This theory is called *KF* (for "Kripke–Feferman"). It can be viewed as an attempt to axiomatically describe the construction of Kripke's fixed point models. Aside from PA^T, the theory *KF* consists of the following axioms:

---

5. See section 4.6.
6. Compare infra, section 10.2.2.

KF1 $\forall$ atomic $\phi \in \mathcal{L}_{PA} : T(\phi) \leftrightarrow val^+(\phi)$;

KF2 $\forall$ atomic $\phi \in \mathcal{L}_{PA} : T(\neg \phi) \leftrightarrow val^-(\phi)$;

KF3 $\forall \phi \in \mathcal{L}_T : T(\neg \neg \phi) \leftrightarrow T(\phi)$;

KF4 $\forall \phi, \psi \in \mathcal{L}_T : T(\phi \wedge \psi) \leftrightarrow (T(\phi) \wedge T(\psi))$;

KF5 $\forall \phi, \psi \in \mathcal{L}_T : T(\neg(\phi \wedge \psi)) \leftrightarrow (T(\neg \phi) \vee T(\neg \psi))$;

KF6 $\forall \phi(x) \in \mathcal{L}_T : T(\forall x \phi(x)) \leftrightarrow \forall y T(\phi(y))$;

KF7 $\forall \phi(x) \in \mathcal{L}_T : T(\neg \forall x \phi(x)) \leftrightarrow \exists y T(\neg \phi(y))$;

KF8 $\forall \phi \in \mathcal{L}_T : T(T(\phi)) \leftrightarrow T(\phi)$;

KF9 $\forall \phi \in \mathcal{L}_T : T(\neg T(\phi)) \leftrightarrow T(\neg \phi)$;

KF10 $\forall \phi \in \mathcal{L}_T : \neg(T\phi \wedge T\neg \phi)$.

Thus, *KF* is a strongly compositional ("positive") type-free theory of truth (KF1–KF7) that includes truth iteration axioms (KF8–KF9). The system *KF* stands to Strong Kleene truth roughly like *TC* stands to truth in a classical model, except that *KF* also contains truth iteration axioms.

KF10 expresses the consistency of the extension of the truth predicate. This axiom is a bit of an odd duck. Unlike the other truth axioms, it does not reduce the truth of statements to the truth of other statements or to elementary facts. But it allows *KF* to prove that truth is closed under modus ponens:

Proposition 64 $KF \vdash \forall \phi, \psi \in \mathcal{L}_T : [T(\phi) \wedge T(\phi \rightarrow \psi)] \rightarrow T(\psi)$

Proof *We reason in KF. Take any two sentences $T(\phi)$ and $T(\phi \rightarrow \psi)$, i.e., $T(\neg(\phi \wedge \neg \psi))$. By axiom KF10, $T(\phi)$ implies $\neg T(\neg \phi)$. Now assume, for a reductio, that $\neg T(\neg \neg \psi)$. Then we have $\neg(T(\neg \phi) \vee T(\neg \neg \psi))$. So by KF5, we obtain $\neg T(\neg(\phi \wedge \neg \psi))$, which yields a contradiction. So $T(\neg \neg \psi)$, from which we obtain $T(\psi)$ by KF3.* ∎

This proposition cannot be proved without making use of axiom KF10.

How do *KF* and *FS* compare? On the one hand, *KF* contains the full truth iteration principles as axioms, whereas *FS* only has the (weaker) rules of inference NEC and CONEC. On the other hand, *FS* states that *T* commutes with $\neg$. The theory *KF* only makes the weaker claim that *inside the scope of T*, $\neg$ commutes with *T*. Actually, it is not hard to verify (by induction on the length of formulae) that if the axiom stating that *T* and $\neg$ commute would be added to *KF*, the unrestricted Tarski-biconditionals would become derivable, whereby the system would slide into inconsistency. But *in a partial setting*, it seems that one should not want $\neg$ and T to commute: The liar sentence is not true, but we do not want to conclude from this that the negation of the liar sentence is true.

This seems to harmonize well with the truth-maker interpretation discussed earlier, except that now not every atomic sentence or its negation has a truth-maker. The liar sentence nor its negation, for instance, have a truth-maker. (But of course the defender of *KF* is not *forced* to accept facts in her ontology.)

Let us have a look at the formal properties of *KF*.

Theorem 65   *KF has nice models.*

Proof   *We start with a partial model: Any fixed point model as constructed in Kripke's semantical theory of truth will do. Then we close this model off so as to obtain a classical model. It is then routine to verify by an induction on the length of proofs that this model verifies all the axioms of KF.* ∎

Corollary 66   *KF is (ω-)consistent.*

Proof   *The nice models for KF that we have constructed are based on $\mathbb{N}$.* ∎

Corollary 67   *KF is arithmetically sound.*

Proof   *This follows for the same reason as corollary 66.* ∎

This leaves open the question of the strength of *KF*. Solomon Feferman solved this problem [Feferman 1991]. It turns out that *KF* is much stronger than *FS*. Let us define the ordinal ϵ_0 as is the supremum of the collection $\{\omega, \omega^\omega, \omega^{\omega^\omega}, \ldots\}$. Like ω_1^{CK}, the ordinal ϵ_0 is a transfinite countable number. But ϵ_0 is much smaller than ω_1^{CK}. The arithmetical strength of *KF* can be expressed as follows:

Theorem 68 (Feferman)   *KF is arithmetically equivalent with TC_{ϵ_0}.*

Because TC_{ϵ_0} is arithmetically as strong as ACA_{ϵ_0}, this means that the arithmetical strength of *KF* is exactly that of ACA_{ϵ_0}.

Theorem 68 is a deep theorem. Its proof is complicated and is not discussed here.

9.3   The Inner Logic of *KF*

So far, it seems that *KF* is an attractive theory of truth. However, we now turn to properties of *KF* that disqualify it from ever becoming our favorite theory of truth.[7]

---

7. These problems were first identified and discussed in [Reinhardt 1986].

Lemma 69 *For all sentences $\phi \in \mathcal{L}_T$, $KF \vdash T(\phi) \to \phi$.*

Proof *By induction on the complexity of ϕ.* ∎

This important lemma has an unwelcome consequence:

Corollary 70 $KF \vdash L \wedge \neg T(L)$, *where L is the liar sentence.*

Proof *We reason in KF. We know by the extended diagonal lemma that L is such that $KF \vdash L \leftrightarrow \neg T(L)$. So assume $\neg L$. Then $T(L)$. So by lemma 69, we obtain L, which gives us a contradiction. So we reject our assumption and conclude L. Then we apply the diagonal lemma again to obtain $\neg T(L)$.* ∎

In other words, *KF* proves sentences that *by its own lights* are untrue. This does not look good. To prove sentences that by one's own lights are untrue seems a sure mark of philosophical unsoundness: It seems that *KF* falls prey to the strengthened liar problem.

Note, incidentally, how close corollary 70 is to a property that all classical axiomatic truth theories (including *DT* and *TC*) have, namely:

Proposition 71 $PA^T \vdash (L \wedge \neg T(L)) \vee (\neg L \wedge T(L))$.

Proof *This is an immediate consequence of the property*

$PA^T \vdash L \leftrightarrow \neg T(L)$

that the liar sentence is guaranteed to have by the extended diagonal lemma. ∎

Perhaps even this proposition is hard to swallow because both disjuncts are hard to digest. The first disjunct is the unwelcome consequence of *KF* that was discussed earlier. But the second disjunct looks, for symmetry reasons, just as objectionable. But then *all* classical theories, typed or untyped, must be mistaken because the proof of this proposition does not make use of *any* laws of truth.

However, if this disjunction is accepted as true, then why can't in particular its left-hand side be true (i.e., why can't we then embrace *KF*)? Indeed, Tim Maudlin believes that it should not be held against *KF* that it proves $L \wedge \neg T(L)$.[8] Maudlin's defense of *KF* consists mainly of pragmatic considerations. In his view, the pragmatic rules of assertion dictate that no sentences may be asserted of which the negations are true, and no negations may be asserted of sentences that are known to be true. But, he argues, it is too much to ask of a truth theory to assert only sentences that are true and to deny only sentences of which the

---

8. See [Maudlin 2004], [Maudlin 2007].

negations are known to be true. Truth theories are *permitted* to assert sentences that are not true and to deny sentences the negations of which are not true.

The trouble with this defense of *KF* is that Maudlin's assertion rules are not closely related to any rules of assertion that are proposed in the literature. They do not belong to the usual candidates, such as "assert only what is true," "assert only what you know," or "assert only what you rationally believe."[9] A proposal of extraordinary rules of assertion such as Maudlin's seems to be badly in need of independent support. Otherwise, this proposal has an air of ad hockery about it.

The weakest norm of assertion that has received some attention in the literature is: "assert only what you believe." If this were the correct rule of assertion, then we would be permitted to assert $L \wedge \neg T(L)$ only if we could believe at the same time "this sentence is not true" and that *that* sentence is not true. But it seems that believing something is almost tantamount to believing that something is true.

It is true that in another context, some philosophers have taken exception to the claim that believing and believing to be true are closely linked. In the debate about doxastic attitudes toward indicative conditional sentences, one finds philosophers who claim that conditionals can be believed even though they have no truth value (and thus are not true). But this is a minority position. It is precisely because of the oddness of such a position that many philosophers of language nowadays claim that rather than being believed or disbelieved in the same sense as truth-apt assertions are believed or disbelieved, indicative conditionals are accepted or rejected.

Lemma 69 has another consequence, which allows us to situate *KF* vis-à-vis *FS*:

Corollary 72   *KF* + *NEC* *is inconsistent.*

Proof   *This follows from corollary 70. It would suffice to apply NEC to L in order to obtain an outright contradiction.*   ∎

Because *NEC* is a rule of *FS*, this means that *KF* and *FS* are incompatible with each other.

Our misgivings with *KF* can be restated in terms of our last consequence. It is *desirable* for a truth theory to be closed under *NEC* and *CONEC*. Thus, if it proves a sentence, then it judges this sentence to be true, and conversely. This is precisely what *KF* cannot do.

In response to the trouble with *KF*, Reinhardt has suggested that we look at a theory that is derivative of *KF* [Reinhardt 1986].

---

9. For a discussion of rules of assertion, see [Williamson 2000, chapter 11].

Definition 73 $IKF = \{\phi \mid KF \vdash T(\phi)\}$

IKF is called the *inner logic of KF*. It is closed under *NEC* and *CONEC*. *IKF* has certain nice properties. For one thing, with a little effort, it can be seen that *IKF* is mathematically as strong as *KF*:

Lemma 74 *For all sentences $\phi \in \mathcal{L}_{PA}$: $KF \vdash T(\phi) \vee T(\neg\phi)$*

Proof *This can be verified by an induction on the complexity of ϕ.* ∎

Theorem 75 *For all sentences $\phi \in \mathcal{L}_{PA}$: $KF \vdash \phi \Rightarrow KF \vdash T(\phi)$*

Proof *This follows from the combination of lemma 74 and lemma 69.* ∎

From this theorem, the desired result immediately follows:

Corollary 76 *IKF is arithmetically equivalent with KF.*

By theorem 68, this means that the arithmetical strength of *IKF* is exactly that of ACA_{ϵ_0}.

It is easy to see that *IKF* does not contain the liar sentence *L*, nor does it contain $\neg L$. The theory *IKF* is a thoroughly *partial* theory of truth. It does not contain the instance $L \vee \neg L$ of the principle of excluded third, for instance, because *KF* does not prove $T(L \vee \neg L)$. This shows that *KF* is only superficially a classical theory, so to speak. It is formulated in a classical logic, but scratch its surface and you find a partial core.

To summarize, we have learned two things. First, *IKF* is a mathematically strong theory of truth. Second, a case can be made that *IKF* is truth-theoretically sound (whereas *KF* isn't) because it proves only sentences that are in the least fixed point of the strong Kleene construction. For this reason, Reinhardt suggests that we adopt *IKF* as our preferred theory of truth.

McGee describes the procedure that we have followed in these words [McGee 1991, p. 93]:

Our [...] proposal for using Kripke's construction to overcome the limitations imposed by the usual object language/metalanguage policy is the proposal that we repudiate classical logic and henceforth work entirely within the object language with its 3-valued logic. According to this proposal, the unabashed use Kripke makes of classical logic in developing his construction must be regarded as merely a heuristic measure. Out of habit, we continue to use classical logic while we are getting our bearings in a nonclassical world. But, once we get a firm handhold, we shall kick away the ladder, and thenceforward we shall use only the weaker 3-valued logic.

But there is a problem. As it stands, *IKF* is not really a *theory*. Because *IKF* is a computably enumerable set of sentences, it is, by an old theorem of

Craig, axiomatizable. But the axiomatic first-order theory that results when Craig's method is applied to *IKF* is unnatural.[10] The "artificial" axioms that are generated by Craig's method do not give us any insight into the nature of the concept of truth.[11] In a strict sense of the word, *IKF* is not a theory of truth as it stands. So Reinhardt put it as a challenge to come up with a *natural* axiomatization of *IKF*. Until now, no one has been able to meet this challenge (although some have tried).

9.4 A Conservative Type-Free Theory

In section 7.6.2, the deflationist theory PT^- was discussed. It was suggested that this theory might appeal to deflationist philosophers who believe that truth is a conservative notion that nevertheless genuinely increases our conceptual repertoire.

In this and in the previous chapter, we have seen reasons for preferring type-free theories over typed truth theories. So it would be worthwhile to formulate a type-free variant of PT^-. As always, we want to do this in a philosophically controlled way (i.e., we want the principles of this type-free theory to be truth-theoretically sound).

In the case of PT^-, the principle of mathematical induction was restricted to truth-determinate predicates. This was done because the induction axiom was formulated for all predicates of $\mathcal{L}_T$, and many of them are "gappy" for some arguments. Because the compositional axioms only range over grounded and therefore truth-determinate sentences, there was no need to restrict the compositional axioms to truth-determinate sentences. But once we lift the type restrictions, it is advisable to extend the totality restrictions to the compositional principles to remain in keeping with the treatment of mathematical induction. This results in the truth theory that we call *RKF* ("restricted *KF*"). It contains the following axioms:

RKF1 PA^T without the induction axiom;

RKF2 $\forall \phi(x) \in \mathcal{L}_T : [tot(\phi(x)) \wedge T\phi(0) \wedge \forall y(T\phi(y) \rightarrow T\phi(y+1))] \rightarrow \forall x T\phi(x);$[12]

---

10. *IKF can* be naturally (completely) axiomatized in infinitary logic: see [Martin 2009]. But of course this axiomatization is not computably enumerable.
11. This philosophical drawback of Craig's method is a well-known chapter in the philosophy of science: see [Hempel 1958].
12. Recall that $tot(\phi(x))$ expresses that $\phi(x)$ is truth-determinate: see section 7.6.2.

RKF3 $\forall$ atomic $\phi \in \mathcal{L}_{PA} : T(\phi) \leftrightarrow val^+(\phi)$;

RKF4 $\forall$ atomic $\phi \in \mathcal{L}_{PA} : T(\neg\phi) \leftrightarrow \neg val^+(\phi)$;

RKF5 $\forall \phi, \psi \in \mathcal{L}_T : (tot(\phi) \wedge tot(\psi)) \to [T(\phi \wedge \psi) \leftrightarrow T(\phi) \wedge T(\psi)]$;

RKF6 $\forall \phi, \psi \in \mathcal{L}_T : (tot(\phi) \wedge tot(\psi)) \to [T\neg(\phi \wedge \psi) \leftrightarrow T(\neg\phi) \vee T(\neg\psi)]$;

RKF7 $\forall \phi(x) \in \mathcal{L}_T : tot(\phi(x)) \to [T(\forall x \phi(x)) \leftrightarrow \forall x T(\phi(x))]$;

RKF8 $\forall \phi(x) \in \mathcal{L}_T : tot(\phi(x)) \to [T(\neg\forall x \phi(x)) \leftrightarrow \exists x T(\neg\phi(x))]$;

RKF9 $\forall \phi \in \mathcal{L}_T : tot(\phi) \to [T(\neg\neg\phi) \leftrightarrow T(\phi)]$;

RKF10 $\forall \phi \in \mathcal{L}_T : T(T(\phi)) \leftrightarrow T(\phi)$;

RKF11 $\forall \phi \in \mathcal{L}_T : T(\neg T(\phi)) \leftrightarrow T(\neg\phi)$;

RKF12 $\forall \phi \in \mathcal{L}_T : tot(\phi) \to \neg(T\phi \wedge T\neg\phi)$.

In RKF8 and RKF9, the totality restrictions are absent because they would be redundant. (Exercise for the reader.)

RKF is like *KF*, except that no nonlogical claims are made about ungrounded sentences. Because *RKF* is a subtheory of *KF*, it is consistent and indeed arithmetically sound. Moreover, it is readily verified that it meets the minimal adequacy criterion of proving the restricted Tarski-biconditionals. We do not go into details of the proofs here, but we note that even though in *RKF* truth-iterations can be derived, the theory is in important proof-theoretic respects like PT^-:

Theorem 77 (Cantini) *RKF is conservative over PA.*

Theorem 78 *RKF is not interpretable in PA.*

The argument that *KF* proves propositions that by its own lights are not true does not carry over to *RKF*. So it may be hoped that, unlike *KF*, *RKF* is a philosophically sound theory of truth. In other words, the following question is presently unresolved:

Problem 79 *Can RKF be consistently closed under the rules of necessitation and co-necessitation?*

RKF is a truth theory that might appeal to deflationists of a certain bent. *RKF* is a strongly compositional type-free truth theory that contains truth iteration principles. It meets minimal adequacy conditions. It is mathematically conservative, but at the same time it shows how the notion of truth expands our conceptual repertoire.

9.5 Partial Kripke–Feferman

KF and *RKF* are classical type-free theories. Despite its artificiality, *IKF* is a truly *partial* theory of truth. We have seen that *IKF* does not contain the sentence $L \vee \neg L$, for instance, even though this is an application of the classical principle of excluded third. This gives us a diagnosis of what went wrong with *KF*. The system *KF* is only to some extent a partial theory of truth. It does not prove $T(L \vee \neg L)$, for instance. But *KF* is formulated in *classical* logic. So it does prove $L \vee \neg L$, which it should not. In other words, the aim should be to axiomatize partial models instead of the classical models that result from closing them off.

Unlike Reinhardt, we do not use *KF* as an instrument in terms of which a partial theory of truth is defined. If we want to formalize Kripke's theory of truth properly, we should work *directly* in partial logic, where the principle of excluded third is not assumed. This is what we do in this section.

We sketch a natural partial theory of truth, which is called *PKF*. For a more detailed description, investigation, and discussion of this system, the reader is referred to [Halbach & Horsten 2006].

9.5.1 Restricted Conditionalization

The language of our theory is, as before, $\mathcal{L}_T$. The theory *PKF* is formulated in the strong Kleene-version of partial predicate logic. Even the most elementary axiom schemes of classical logic, such as $\phi \to \phi$, will no longer be valid. For if ϕ has no truth value, then the corresponding material implication will also lack a truth value. The most perspicuous way to describe the proof theory of partial logic is as a *natural deduction system*.

The rules of inference of this natural deduction system are just like those of the natural deduction system for classical logic,[13] except for the rules of the material implication. The elimination rule for material implication (Modus Ponens) is valid. But the introduction rule for material implication is a more delicate matter.

As intimated before, we do not want theorems such as

$L \to L$

because we want to take seriously Reinhardt's admonition not to assert truth-indeterminate sentences. But the sentence $L \to L$ is immediately obtained by the rule of *conditionalisation* (*COND*):

---

13. For a presentation of the natural deduction system for classical logic, see, for instance, [Sundholm 1983].

Kripke's Theory Axiomatized

$$\phi \ (Hyp)$$
$$\vdots$$
$$\underline{\psi \ (Hyp)}$$
$$\phi \to \psi$$

Therefore, the rule *COND* has to be restricted—if not abandoned altogether.

However, we do want to allow hypothetical reasoning in our system *PKF*. Conditional reasoning plays a crucial role in the proof-theoretic strength of the system. Therefore, we assume the following *restricted* rule of conditionalization (*RCOND*):

$$T(\phi) \vee T(\neg\phi) \quad \phi \ (Hyp)$$
$$\vdots$$
$$\underline{\psi \ (Hyp)}$$
$$\phi \to \psi$$

In our partial setting, this rule is valid for the following reason. If it is known at some point in a derivation that a sentence is truth-determinate, then conditionalization can be validly applied. If ϕ is false, then $\neg\phi \vee \psi$ is determinately true. If ϕ is true and ψ follows from ϕ by truth-preserving rules, then ψ will also be true, whereby again $\neg\phi \vee \psi$ is determinately true.

In other words, there is a crucial difference between:

1. Suppose ϕ [were true]. Then ... ψ [is true].
2. (if ϕ then ψ) [is true].

This is the difference between hypothetical reasoning and the assertion of a conditional, the difference between truth under a hypothesis and truth of the corresponding conditional. In a partial setting, 1 constitutes acceptable hypothetical reasoning. But this should not automatically give rise to 2 because ϕ may not be truth-determinate.

The restriction of *COND* to *RCOND* is the distinctive feature of *PKF*.

9.5.2 Partial Arithmetic and Determinate Truths

The truth predicate is the only partial predicate of $\mathcal{L}_T$. So sentences that do not contain T should receive a determinate truth value. Therefore, we adopt as axioms of *PKF* all formulae of the form

$$\phi \vee \neg\phi$$

with $\phi \in \mathcal{L}_{PA}$.

The only axiom of PA^T that contains the truth predicate is the mathematical induction scheme. Therefore, all the axioms aside from the induction scheme are taken as axioms of *PKF*. With respect to the induction scheme, we have to be careful. For any formula $\phi(x)$ of which all the instances lack a truth value, for instance, the induction axiom for $\phi(x)$ also lacks a truth value. Therefore, in *PKF*, we adopt the following inference rule as our principle of induction:

$$\frac{\phi(0) \quad \phi(x)\,(Hyp) \quad \vdots \quad \phi(s(x))\,(Hyp)}{\forall x \phi(x)}.$$

Here $\phi(x)$ ranges over all formulae of $\mathcal{L}_T$.

9.5.3 The Truth Rules

The truth principles of *PKF* will be the rule-counterparts of the truth axioms of *KF*. To be precise, *PKF* contains the rules:

PKF1 $\quad \dfrac{val^+(t_1 = t_2)}{T(t_1 = t_2)} \quad \dfrac{T(t_1 = t_2)}{val^+(t_1 = t_2)}$

PKF2 $\quad \dfrac{T(\phi) \wedge T(\psi)}{T(\phi \wedge \psi)} \quad \dfrac{T(\phi \wedge \psi)}{T(\phi) \wedge T(\psi)}$

PKF3 $\quad \dfrac{T(\phi) \vee T(\psi)}{T(\phi \vee \psi)} \quad \dfrac{T(\phi \vee \psi)}{T(\phi) \vee T(\psi)}$

PKF4 $\quad \dfrac{\forall x\, T(\phi(x))}{T(\forall x \phi(x))} \quad \dfrac{T(\forall x \phi(x))}{\forall x\, T(\phi(x))}$

PKF5 $\quad \dfrac{\exists x\, T(\phi(x))}{T(\exists x \phi(x))} \quad \dfrac{T(\exists x \phi(x))}{\exists x\, T(\phi(x))}$

PKF6 $\quad \dfrac{T(\phi)}{T(T(\phi))} \quad \dfrac{T(T(\phi))}{T(\phi)}$

PKF7 $\quad \dfrac{\neg T(\phi)}{T(\neg \phi)} \quad \dfrac{T(\neg \phi)}{\neg T(\phi)}$

Here it is important to note that in these rules, t_1, t_2, ϕ, and ψ function as *variables* ranging over terms and formulae, respectively. So as in the truth axioms in *TC* and unlike the truth axioms of *DT*, the inference rules universally quantify over terms and formulae. It is just that in *PKF* this is done implicitly, using free variables that are always treated as universally quantified over, whereas in *TC* this is done explicitly.

This completes the description of the theory *PKF*.

If we look at *PKF*, we see that it hardly contains axioms. Most of its basic components are formulated as rules of inference. For this reason, even though strictly speaking it is not incorrect, it sounds odd to call *PKF* an *axiomatic* theory of truth. But it clearly harmonizes well with the proof-theoretic approach to truth.

Like all the truth theories that we consider, *PKF* meets minimal adequacy conditions. For instance, *PKF* proves the restricted Tarski-biconditionals.

9.6 Analysis and Evaluation

Let us now turn to the question of whether *PKF* is an attractive truth theory. In the process of addressing this question, let us compare *PKF* with the truth theories that were discussed before.

9.6.1 Naturalness

It is safe to say that, unlike *IKF*, *PKF* is in some sense a *natural* truth theory. It is a natural semantically closed extension of the compositional theory *TC*. Actually, this assertion needs to be taken with a grain of salt because *PKF* is not *really* an extension for we have weakened the background logic. But *PKF* does appear to explicate the compositional nature of the concept of truth in a natural and elegant way. Its introduction and elimination rules display a pleasing symmetry that is reminiscent of the symmetry between the introduction and elimination rules for the logical connectives.

But there is also a way in which *PKF* is less than natural. Feferman has observed that in three-valued logic, "nothing like sustained ordinary reasoning can be carried on" [Feferman 1984, p. 100]. It is simply awkward and painful to reason in partial logic.[14] Perhaps this is to a large extent an effect of our classical upbringing. If we had been taught to reason in partial logic from a tender age, we might have found it intuitive. But this is pure speculation.

For large fragments of our language, however, we can safely reason classically. For one thing, as long as we are doing pure mathematics, physics, or biology and are not using the concept of truth, we can reason classically without giving it a second thought. Only when our reasoning involves sentences containing the truth predicate do we need to be careful. But even then, purely hypothetical

---

14. This objection is also mentioned and discussed in [McGee 1991, pp. 100–101].

reasoning can be done exactly as we are accustomed to. There is just one thing that we must be mindful of: When we conditionalize, we have to check whether the hypothesis is truth-determinate.

9.6.2 Methodology

McGee has formulated the following methodological objection to moving to three-valued logic [McGee 1991, pp. 102–103]:

> […] our methodological standards in semantics ought not be any lower than our methodological standards in the empirical sciences. We shall contravene this admonition if we attempt to cover up the deficiencies of our naive theory of truth by abandoning classical logic.
>
> Imagine that we have a genetic theory to which we are particularly attached, perhaps on political grounds, and that this theory tells us that, if a certain DNA molecule has an even number of nucleotides, then all fruit flies are brown; that, if that particular molecule does not have an even number of nucleotides, then all fruit flies are green; and that fruit flies are not all the same colour. It would surely be absurd to respond to this circumstance by saying that our cherished genetic theory is entirely correct and that classical logic does not apply when we are doing genetics. What we have to say instead is that the genetic theory has been refuted....
>
> As preposterous as it would be to respond to the embarrassment faced by the genetic theory by saying that classical logic no longer applies when we are doing genetics, it would be no less preposterous to respond to the liar paradox by saying that classical logic no longer applies when we are doing semantics. The liar paradox refutes the naive theory of truth. It is our duty to come up with a better theory of truth. It is a dereliction of duty to attempt to obscure the difficulty by dimming the natural light of reason.

But genetics and the theory of truth are just not analogous in relevant respects. Genetical theories are complicated constructions. They are not intimately connected to the given. As the example shows, the theoretical tenets of the hypothetical genetical theory are only indirectly supported by a body of observations (nucleotides are not observable with the naked eye). With respect to the concept of truth, the situation is completely different. The argument of the liar paradox is breathtakingly short and simple and is based on arguably our most basic intuition concerning truth: the disquotational intuition. So we have little room to maneuver. This puts more pressure on the logical component of the argument than in McGee's hypothetical situation in genetics. Think about Quine's web of belief. Empirical refutation merely pulls at the edges. The liar paradox, in contrast, strikes directly at the heart of the web.

Moreover, we should not forget that there are situations even in the natural sciences where many investigators are willing to compromise on classical logic. When asked whether it is true or false that a given electron (which is not currently being measured) is located at a given position, many a quantum physicist will tell you with a straight face that the proposition in question is neither true nor false.[15]

This is not to say that on each occasion when pressure is put on the heart of a theory, it is classical logic that will have to yield. Consider the history of set theory.[16] The naive comprehension scheme says that every property determines a set. Russell's paradox shows that this scheme is inconsistent. This problem was resolved not by weakening classical logic, but by restricting the comprehension scheme. In this case, a conceptual motivation was found for motivating this restriction. According to the iterative conception, sets are formed in stages by applying the power set operation. This motivated Zermelo to restrict the comprehension scheme in a specific way. The problem is that, in the case of truth, no winning new conception of truth has hitherto been found that motivates some specific restriction of the Tarski-biconditional scheme. Or, rather, one might say that the disquotation intuition is correct. It is just that this inferential intuition does not support the categorical Tarski-biconditionals, which means that a wedge must be driven between valid rules of inference and conditional theorems. Hence, a restriction of the rule of conditionalization is called for.

9.6.3 Soundness

PKF can be shown to be a subtheory of *KF*. (This is left to the reader as a simple exercise.) We have seen that *KF* has nice models based on the standard natural numbers structure. Therefore, *PKF* is clearly be *mathematically* sound.

But a strong case can be made that *PKF* is in addition also truth-theoretically sound. In this respect, *PKF* is unlike *KF* (and also *FS*). Any partial fixed point of Kripke's construction for the Strong Kleene valuation scheme is a model of *PKF*. Because all paradoxical sentences such as the liar sentence do not receive a truth value in the minimal fixed point model, they are also not provable in *PKF*.

Thus, it is hard to see how there could be *any* sentence that is proved by *PKF* but that is not clearly philosophically acceptable. Philosophically, there is as little reason to doubt its soundness as there is reason to doubt the soundness of *TC*. Perhaps *PKF* has even better prospects in this respect because it does not prove doubtful propositions such as

$$(L \wedge \neg T(L)) \vee (\neg L \wedge T(L)).^{17}$$

---

15. McGee's objection is discussed more at length in [Restall 1994, chapter 1].
16. This case was raised by Øystein Linnebo in conversation.
17. Compare supra, proposition 71.

9.6.4 Strength

PKF is mathematically powerful. We have seen earlier how the Tarski-hierarchy for *TC* functions as a scale for measuring the arithmetical strength of truth theories. Somewhat surprisingly, the arithmetical strength of *PKF* is intermediate between the strength of *FS* and the strength of *IKF*. We have seen that *FS* has the strength of ACA_ω. We have seen that systems stronger than ACA_ω can be constructed by continuing the process of defining new systems of ramified analysis into the transfinite. In this way, the systems $ACA_{\omega+1}, \ldots, ACA_{\omega+\omega}, \ldots$ are defined. In terms of one of the systems in this sequence, the mathematical strength of *PKF* can be expressed [Halbach & Horsten 2006, section 6]:

Theorem 80 *The arithmetical consequences of PKF are exactly the first-order consequences of the system* ACA_{ω^ω}.

Thus, *PKF* is mathematically much stronger than *FS*. The system *PKF* is truth-theoretically also in some sense more complete than *FS*. In *FS*, one is allowed to conclude to $T(\phi)$ only if one has *proved* ϕ, whereas in *PKF* one is allowed to infer $T(\phi)$ even from the *hypothesis* that ϕ [Halbach & Horsten 2006, p. 695]:

Proposition 81

$$\frac{\phi}{T(\phi)} \quad \text{and} \quad \frac{T(\phi)}{\phi}$$

are admissible rules of inference of PKF.

This can be viewed as an expression of the extent to which fixed points of the strong Kleene construction make the unrestricted Tarski-biconditionals true. In this context, it may be worth emphasizing again that *KF* is not, and cannot consistently be, closed under these inference rules.

Corollary 76 has shown us that the "theory" *IKF* is mathematically even stronger than *PKF*: *IKF* and *KF* have the same arithmetical content. *IKF* has the advantage of over *KF* that it is truth-theoretically sound. Unfortunately, as we have seen, *IKF* is not a theory in the true sense of the word.

To repeat, there is a sense in which *PKF* is weaker than its classical rivals *TC*, *FS*, and *KF*. But the fact that *PKF* does not contain the law of excluded third does not compromise its soundness. After all, *PKF* does not *deny* that the law of excluded middle holds for all sentences; it just refrains from asserting it. But of course *PKF cannot*, on pain of inconsistency, assert the principle of excluded third. Does not this unavoidable truth-theoretic reticence compromise the completeness of *PKF*?[18] After all, mathematical strength is one thing, whereas truth-theoretic strength is another.

Perhaps a comparison with *vague predicates* is again instructive here. As a solution for solving the sorites paradox, it has been argued that predicates such as "is bald" and "is a heap" are partial predicates. Analogues of Kripke's semantic theory of truth have been proposed to model vague predicates. Among these, the *supervaluation* approach appears to have found most support. One of the main reasons for the popularity of the supervaluation approach in discussions about vagueness is surely that it allows us to retain the theorems of classical logic. Now truth does not appear to be a vague predicate.[19] But in the light of our deep-seated desire to retain classical logic, it might nevertheless seem attractive to axiomatize the supervaluation fixed points of Kripke's construction instead of the strong Kleene fixed points.

An ingenious attempt has been made by Andrea Cantini to do exactly this [Cantini 1990]. He formulated the axiomatic truth theory *VF* (for "van Fraassen," the inventor of the supervaluation approach to partial logic). We do not discuss Cantini's *VF* in detail. In fact, we do not even list its axioms. Suffice it to say that Cantini's theory suffers from much the same problems as Feferman's *KF*. Because *VF* formalizes the classical closed-off versions of supervaluation fixed points, instead of the supervaluation fixed points themselves, it simultaneously proves L and $\neg T(L)$. At the moment, it is unclear how a natural formalization of supervaluation fixed points would look.

---

18. McGee formulated this as an objection not to *PKF* but to *IKF*: see [McGee 1991, pp. 101–102].
19. McGee does think that the notion of truth is similar to vague notions. See [McGee 1991].

10 Truth and Philosophy

In this final chapter, we reflect on the relationship between the concept of truth and philosophy. We have seen that there are sound theories of truth that are considerably stronger even than the typed compositional theory of truth. First, we want to know what becomes of deflationism in the light of the existence of proof-theoretically strong truth theories. Second, we speculate about the extent to which even some of the stronger theories of truth that we have discussed play an essential role in philosophical discussions.

10.1 Strong Theories of Truth

As philosophers, we seek a theory of truth for our entire language. In such a situation, an axiomatic approach has clear advantages over a definitional or model-theoretic approach. An adequate definition of truth can only be given for the fragment of our language that does not contain the truth predicate. A model can never encompass the whole of the domain of discourse of our language. The axiomatic approach does not suffer from these deficiencies. Approaching the problem in an axiomatic spirit, we sought to formulate natural, philosophically sound theories that are as truth-theoretically complete as possible.

If we abstract from the self-reflexiveness of the concept of truth, the disquotational theory DT falls short of our expectations, and Tarski's compositional theory TC is perhaps still the most satisfactory collection of principles. Those who hold that truth is a conservative notion will find TC too strong and might be tempted to execute a strategic retreat to a subtheory such as TC^- or PT^-. But, as was argued in section 7.5, conservativeness should not be taken as an adequacy condition for truth theories.

Our concept of truth is self-reflexive. So in the second part of this book, we sought to articulate truth theories that reflect the self-reflexive nature of truth. Thus, we embarked on an investigation of type-free truth theories.

We first explored how far the type-free approach can be taken if we adhere to full classical logic. In the spirit of *TC*, it seemed natural to aim at articulating a compositional theory of truth. Thus, we were quickly led to consider the theory *FS*. Unfortunately, this theory turned out to be ω-inconsistent, which seemed a sure sign of truth-theoretic unsoundness.

Whereas *FS* is closed under the rules of necessitation and co-necessitation, it is not, and cannot consistently be, closed under the inference rule that allows us to conclude $T(\phi)$ from ϕ if ϕ depends on one or more undischarged hypotheses. A fortiori *FS* does not contain any truth iteration principles. If we want to include such rules or principles in our truth theory, then we have to compromise on classical logic.

We went on to do this, albeit not cheerfully but accompanied with soul searching and hand wringing. Compromising on classical logic can be done to a lesser or higher degree. Cantini's formalization *VF* of the Kripkean supervaluation fixed points only makes minimal nonclassical concessions. It can be labeled as a *semi-classical* theory. *VF* admits that the liar sentence is neither true nor false. But it is formulated in classical logic, and it does insist that all classical tautologies are true. *KF* departs slightly more from the true spirit of classical logic. Even though it is also formulated in classical logic, it does not insist that all classical tautologies are true. In addition, both *VF* and *KF* are mathematically strong. Unfortunately, we were stopped in our tracks when we found both of them to be truth-theoretically unsound. Again we made use of our strategic railroads to transport us to friendlier surroundings. An attempt to minimally weaken *KF* so as to regain soundness led us to the system *RKF*. Unfortunately, at present it is not known whether *RKF* satisfies all minimal adequacy conditions for type-free theories.

The two truly partial theories of truth that we have probed are *IKF* and *PKF*. They are formulated in partial logic, and there are reasons to believe that both theories are truth-theoretically sound. Also, at least of *PKF*, one can be quite confident that it does justice to the compositionality of truth. Unfortunately, *IKF* is unacceptable as it stands not because it is philosophically unsound, but because it is not a theory in the true sense of the word. It is not given in terms of inference rules and axioms that are recognizable as basic reasoning mechanisms and principles governing the notion of truth. *PKF* does not suffer from this defect: It is formulated in terms of natural and simple inference rules. *PKF* is mathematically weaker than *KF* and *IKF*, but the theoretical virtues of truth-theoretic soundness and naturalness override the virtue of mathematical strength.

10.2 Inferential Deflationism

PKF is, from a proof-theoretical point of view, a strong theory. Nevertheless, I now argue that adopting *PKF* as a truth theory harmonizes well with a deflationist stance. But then deflationism has to be reconceived.

10.2.1 Truth and Logical Notions

Let us return to the misty core of deflationism, which says that truth is a light, insubstantial notion. I have argued that it is a mistake to try to cash this vague thought out in terms of conservativeness claims. Let me now suggest an alternative way of making the deflationist *credo* more precise. This gives rise to a version of deflationism that is immune to the objections discussed earlier.

One commitment of most forms of truth-theoretic deflationism that is reflected by *PKF* is the simplicity of truth. It is scarcely imaginable that the introduction and elimination rules for the truth predicate that are contained in *PKF* could be simplified further. If the concept of truth is correctly described by *PKF*, then truth is indeed not a complicated notion at all. But there is another sense in which *PKF* harmonizes with the vague deflationist thesis that truth is an "immaterial" notion. To uncover this sense, a deeper reflection on the concept of truth is required.

Carnap held that the meaning of the logical connectives is fixed by linguistic convention. So in a derivative way, logical truths are on his account true by convention [Carnap 1934]. Quine showed that Carnap's position suffers from a vicious regress problem. If the meaning of the logical connectives were not already determined, the convention could never be applied [Quine 1936]. Although he never developed his own positive view in detail, Quine held that the meaning of the logical connectives is determined by our inferential behavior, not by convention.

In a Quinian spirit, it is a rather popular view nowadays that the meaning of the classical logical connectives is determined by their role in valid reasoning. More in particular, it is held by many that the meaning of the classical logical connectives is determined by the introduction and elimination rules of the natural deduction calculus [Prawitz 1978]. It seems that the familiar introduction and elimination rules for first-order logic are semantically complete: They completely determine the meaning of the logical connectives.

We have seen that, according to *PKF*, there are no unrestricted general principles of truth. This can be explained by the fact that there is no nature or essence of truth to be described by general principles. Classical theories of truth, such as *TC* or *FS*, do entail that there are fully general principles of truth. Thus, they provide no reason to believe that truth has no essence.

According to *PKF*, there are natural and fully general rules of inference governing the truth predicate. Although blanket generalizations about the notion of truth scarcely exist, there are simple and fully general ways of proceeding from one truth about truth to another. This, combined with the fact that the notion of truth has an important expressive function, suggests that truth should first and foremost be seen as an inferential tool.

Truth resembles the logical notions. There are contents that we could not express without logical connectives. The same holds for truth. Logical laws are the cogs in our reasoning processes. Likewise, truth assists us in our reasoning: It helps us to draw correct inferences. Like the logical connectives, the concept of truth is a handmaiden of reasoning. In this sense, there is after all something deeply right about Field's claim that truth is a logical notion—even if, as we have seen, in the strict sense we have to disagree with it. In a way, the inferential view applies even better to the truth predicate than to the logical connectives. All that the arguments in [Quine 1936] show is that at least one rule of inference is needed if logic is ever going to be applied. Moreover, in classical logic, the deduction theorem guarantees that each rule of inference corresponds to an axiom scheme. But for the reasons given earlier, there can be no deduction theorem for *PKF*: *None* of the truth rules of *PKF* can be validly replaced by axioms. Truth is *essentially* an inferential notion. Of course, if truth is indeed a thoroughly partial notion, then even the logical connectives are essentially inferential because not all instances of the laws of classical logic are then acceptable.

10.2.2 Silence

In Kripke's *Naming and Necessity*, a Wittgensteinian concern is mooted. Kripke expresses the hope that he is not proposing a *theory* of reference because, if he does, then it must certainly be wrong [Kripke 1980, p. 93]. It now seems that in the case of truth, such a Wittgensteinian attitude is even more appropriate. Kripke's theory of truth should be articulated as a nontheory. That is what happens in *PKF*. Thus, it seems ironic that Kripke's seminal article on truth bears the title "Outline of a Theory of Truth." Indeed, the problem of the strengthened liar that has haunted Kripke's theory of truth ("the ghost of Tarski") is a consequence of Kripke's insistence to formulate his theory in a classical metalanguage. The system *PKF*, in contrast, is not vulnerable to a strengthened liar attack because it makes no claim concerning the truth value of the liar sentence. *PKF* simply does not assert the liar sentence, nor its negation, nor that it is true, nor that it is not true.[1]

---

1. In this respect, *PKF* is in agreement with [Reinhardt 1986] and with [Soames 1999, chapter 6].

According to *PKF*, the inference rules corresponding to the unrestricted Tarski-biconditionals are acceptable. Thereby justice is done to the disquotational intuition that was discussed in section 3.5.2: If you are prepared to categorically or hypothetically assert a sentence ϕ, then you had better also be prepared to assert in the same mood that ϕ is true; and if you are prepared to categorically or hypothetically assert that ϕ is true, then you had better also be prepared to assert in the same mood that ϕ. Because there is no deduction theorem for partial logic, this does not give us the unrestricted Tarski-biconditionals.

Although he does not express his truth theory in a proof-theoretic way, Field in his recent work on truth agrees with *PKF* insofar as it goes.[2] When the biconditional is read as a material equivalence, the unrestricted Tarski-biconditionals are not all acceptable. But he insists that there must be a sense in which the Tarski-biconditionals are categorically assertible. So there is a sense in which there nevertheless is at least one fundamental law of truth. He also insists that there is a sense in which the liar sentence is not "really" or *determinately* true. Thus, he regards systems such as *PKF* as expressively incomplete.

Field proceeds in the following way. He begins by adding a new primitive conditional operator $\rightharpoonup$ to $\mathcal{L}_T$, resulting in the language $\mathcal{L}_{T,\rightharpoonup}$. He then constructs partial models for this extended language, which satisfy for every $\phi \in \mathcal{L}_{T,\rightharpoonup}$ the *Field-biconditional*

$$\phi \rightleftharpoons T(\phi),$$

where the biconditional $\rightleftharpoons$ is defined in terms of $\rightharpoonup$ and $\wedge$ in the obvious way.

On by now obvious pain of contradiction, the new conditional cannot satisfy all the principles that are satisfied by the material implication. In particular, it turns out that Field's models do not satisfy the "formalized modus ponens" principle

$$[\phi \wedge (\phi \rightharpoonup \psi)] \rightharpoonup \psi.$$

This should give us pause. Formalized modus ponens is not only satisfied by the familiar material implication but also by all of the implication relations that have been proposed in the recent literature as candidates for capturing central aspects of the semantics of indicative conditionals in English. Thus, it is questionable whether the Field-biconditionals are biconditionals in *our* sense of the word. Tony Martin expresses this worry as follows [Martin 2009, p. 9]:

Field remarks that some have said that his account does not really yield the Tarski schema because his conditional is different from the classical conditional Tarski is using. Field

---

2. See [Field 2008].

points out that it agrees with the classical conditional where the law of excluded middle holds. He says that it is a *generalisation* of the classical conditional. This reply is fine, so far as it goes. What bothers me is that I don't see how it is *a* generalisation.

Field's conditional operator allows the expression of a notion of determinacy in terms of which it can rightfully be said that the liar sentence is not determinately true. If $D(\phi)$ ("ϕ is determinately true") is defined as

$$\phi \wedge (\top \rightarrow \phi),$$

then in Field's models $\neg D(L)$ holds.

This is an open invitation to construct a strengthened liar sentence L^*, which says of itself that it is not determinately true. How do we express *its* indeterminateness? Field deals with this problem by defining a hierarchy of notions of determinacy. $D\phi$ is the first step in this hierarchy; the next level of determinacy for a given formula ϕ is $D(D(\phi))$. According to Field's models, the strengthened liar sentence L^* is not determinately true in this stronger but not in the weaker sense.

We can of course continue this game by constructing a super-strengthened liar sentence L^{**}, a new sense in which it is not determinately true, and so on. In the end, Field has to deny that there is a maximal sense of determinacy in which all the sentences in the sequence $L, L^*, L^{**}, \ldots$ are not determinately true [Field 2007].

But this is unsatisfactory. The whole point of moving to type-free theories of truth was that it seemed implausible that what seems to be one notion (truth) on closer inspection turns out to be an irrevocably fragmented concept. But then we should be equally skeptical of the view that a closely related notion (determinate truth) that appears to be every bit as much unified on closer inspection proves to be irrevocably fragmented. Conversely, arriving at the conviction that there exists no unified notion of determinate truth should be expected to dampen our enthusiasm for adopting a type-free theory of truth in the first place.

The gist of it all, in my view, is the following. It is simply an illusion to think that there are deep facts about truth that are either difficult to express or cannot be expressed at all. After the inferential moves that govern the truth predicate have been displayed, there are no more facts to be uncovered. There is nothing more to be said.

10.2.3 A Concept Without an Essence

So this is what deflationism about truth comes to in the end. We should not aim at describing the nature of truth because there is no such thing. Rather, we should aim at describing the inferential behavior of truth.

Brandom goes much further and claims that the content of *all* our concepts is given by inferential connections [Brandom 2000, p. 61]:[3]

... conceptual content is to be understood in terms of role in reasoning rather than exclusively in terms of representation.

This goes well beyond the commitments of the theory advocated here. It is consistent with everything that was said so far that truth is quite an exceptional concept. It may be, for instance, that the meaning of the mathematical vocabulary is not determined by its inferential role.

At any rate, no claim is made to the effect that the inference rules of *PKF* exhaust the meaning of the concept of truth. It is only claimed that the inference rules of *PKF* give a *partial* articulation of the meaning of the concept of truth. Understanding the inference rules of *PKF* entails having a partial grasp of the meaning of the truth predicate. This is so for two reasons. First, as mentioned in the previous paragraph, the meaning of the concept of truth is inextricably intertwined with the meaning of syntactical concepts, and their meaning may not be determined in a purely inferential manner. In addition, *PKF* (and Kripke's truth theory in general) only looks good until the better theory comes along. We should surely hold open the possibility that some future stronger inferential truth theory may determine the meaning of the concept of truth even further or may determine it in a slightly different way.

It seems to me that inferential deflationism, described in this way, is essentially on the right track. But this does not mean that all philosophical issues that surround it have been completely resolved. Gupta has considered the version of inferential deflationism according to which the meaning of the truth predicate is completely determined by the (restricted) Tarski-biconditionals considered as rules of inference, and he has dismissed it [Gupta 1993, p. 303]. It should be clear by now that this is not the inferential theory that is advocated here. But Gupta's misgivings, if they are justified, apply equally to the version of inferential deflationism that we are presently considering.

According to inferential deflationism, the meaning of the concept of truth is explained in terms of rules of inference (of which axioms are limiting cases). Gupta observes that inferential deflationism requires that the concept of a rule can be explained in a way that does not involve the notion of truth [Gupta 1993, p. 303]. There is the related question of whether a person can follow any rule at all if she does not already possess the concept of truth. So eventually we are led to the fundamental questions concerning rule-following, of which is

---

3. Brandom advocates the pro-sentential theory of truth [Brandom 1994]. Because this theory does not deal with the paradoxes in a satisfactory way, I do not discuss it here.

paramount: What is involved in following a rule (What does it mean to follow a rule)? These are deep philosophical questions indeed. But there is no need to address these questions here. It seems to be a subject of its own. Moreover, it is at least not obviously the case that the concept of truth is involved in explaining what it means to follow a rule. At least at first sight, it appears that one could well imagine someone correctly applying a rule of inference without even possessing the concept of truth. Notice that there is no reason to think that any of this is incompatible with the notion of truth being heavily involved in the notion of a *valid* inference rule.

Thus, truth is a property that either lacks a fixed nature or essence or is a property, the nature of which is forever elusive. Of course in a lax sense, one may say that even if one inferentially articulates the workings of truth in a natural way, one thereby describes aspects of the nature of truth. But this statement is palatable even for the deflationist because a sufficiently light notion of nature is operative here.

In summary, there is a deep, important, and insufficiently recognized sense in which truth is a light notion. This sense is captured by the thesis that truth is a property that cannot be described in terms of unrestricted general laws; there exist only restricted laws of truth. In this sense, truth differs from mathematical and scientific properties and relations (such as "prime," "force," and "mass").

10.3 How Truth Rules Are Used

For many purposes, the full inferential strength of the concept of truth is not required. It appears that our best theory of truth is able to generate more inferences than are needed today in philosophy, at least when we disregard logic and the philosophy of language.

10.3.1 Truth in the Foundations of Mathematics

The only example of use of self-referential truth in philosophical argumentation that can clearly be discerned at the moment is situated in the foundations of mathematics. Feferman has tried to use *KF* to show that if one accepts *PA* and the reflexive uniform notion of truth, then one has to accept the arithmetical part of a theory of mathematical analysis that is known as *predicative analysis*. He explains the motivation behind his work on *KF* in the following way [Feferman 1991, p. 1]:

[Gödel's incompleteness theorems] point to the possibility of systematically generating larger and larger systems whose acceptability is implicit in acceptance of the starting theory. The engines for that purpose are what have come to be called *reflection principles*. These may be iterated into the constructive transfinite, leading to what are called *recursive progressions of theories*. […] [F]or some years I had hoped to give a more realistic and perspicuous finite generation procedure. […] What is presented here [i.e., Feferman's work on *KF* and its variants] is a new and simple notion of the *reflective closure of a schematic theory* which can be applied quite generally.

In the light of the philosophical unsoundness of *KF*, Feferman's argumentation appears philosophically unconvincing. But of course *PKF* can be used to carry out this line of reasoning on a more modest scale.

Roughly speaking, the extra power of analysis over arithmetic springs from the fact that it reasons not just about natural numbers but also about sets of natural numbers. In chapter 5, we saw how the truth predicate allows us to transform sentences into objects. It likewise allows us to turn *formulae* into objects. Extensions of formulae with one free variable are classes. So in a derivative sense, the truth predicate introduces classes into our ontology: The truth predicate allows us to *inflate* a no-class theory to a class theory. At least on the surface, it looks as if the truth predicate introduces a form of realism about classes. What goes for mathematics in this respect also goes for philosophy. For instance, when added to a formalization of the language, including color predicates, the truth predicate inflates these predicates to a kind of entities: Perhaps they are extensions or properties.

Does this tell against the thesis of the insubstantiality of truth? Not really because it can just as well be maintained that the classes (properties) that are introduced by the truth predicate are purely "virtual." Because we only quantify over classes (properties) that are defined by predicates, we can say with a straight face that we are quantifying only over predicates. So it is not at all clear that even strong theories of self-referential truth fail to respect the spirit of deflationism.

How much can be proved about the virtual classes (properties) thus introduced depends on the strength of the truth axioms. In this sense, the situation is *unlike* the situation in mathematical analysis. Subsystems of analysis generally differ from each other with respect to the classes of natural numbers that they postulate. They agree with each other with respect to the proof principles that can be applied to the classes. Theories of self-referential truth agree with each other with respect to the classes they (apparently) postulate: To each formula, there corresponds a class. But they disagree with each other about what proof principles can be applied to the classes thus introduced.

So one can take the fact that truth theories allow us to simulate fragments of analysis to show that truth theories introduce substantial new ontological commitments and are thus inflationary. But the message can also be taken to be that this fact shows that fragments of analysis can be interpreted as carrying no extra commitments over arithmetic and can thus be interpreted in a deflationary way. The latter is in the spirit of Feferman's way of looking at the matter.

10.3.2 Truth in Philosophy

It is not presently clear that, for philosophical purposes that are extrinsic to the theory of truth itself, a truth theory that is as strong as *PKF* is needed. Our investigations in chapter 7 indicated that an effort has to be made to find an epistemological argument for which typed principles of truth that go beyond *DT* are needed. We have found no arguments for which principles of type-free truth are required. So it seems that, at the moment, developing strong systems of self-referential truth is still a rather "pure" enterprise that is of limited interest of the toiling philosophical masses.

An analogy with mathematical practice can be drawn at this point. *ZFC* is generally accepted as a natural, sound, and strong foundational theory. But in ordinary mathematical practice, only a fragment of *ZFC* is needed. In Quinian terms, one might say that *ZFC* is a convenient rounding off of the principles governing sets that are needed in present-day mathematical practice. In a similar vein, we might say that *TC* is a convenient rounding off of the truth principles that are currently needed in philosophy but outside the theory of truth itself.

When it comes to logic and the philosophy of language, the situation is different. The concept of truth seems to be an essential part of theory of meaning, and a theory of meaning must give an account of the meaning of truth. We have to explain the semantics of English, which includes a truth predicate using a truth predicate.

This development involves us in reflexive uses of truth. When we develop a type-free, compositional theory of truth in a natural way, while staying on our guard to maintain philosophical soundness, we are led to systems in the neighborhood of *PKF*.

10.4 A Last Look at Deflationism

The overall structure of the argument for inferential deflationism in this chapter consists of an inference from the proposition that there are no general laws of truth to the thesis that there is no nature of truth. Now it may be suspected that the general inference pattern behind this move is invalid. One might suspect that it is not always the case that if X has a nature, then X is governed by general principles.

One form that this challenge might take is the following. Someone might argue that no general principles can be formulated about ordinary concepts, such as the concept of a chair. Then the general inference pattern would have us conclude from this that the concept of a chair is somehow insubstantial, and this would be an unpalatable result. But it is far from clear that such ordinary concepts are not governed by general principles. The concept of a chair may have vague boundaries. But even so, if for vagueness truth amounts to supervaluation-truth, then "Every chair is self-identical," for instance, would come out true. It would be a true and absolutely general principle about chairs.

A second objection along these lines runs as follows. Some say that because it is impossible to quantify over all sets, no true absolutely general propositions about sets can even be expressed. Yet it would be folly to conclude from this that the notion of set is an insubstantial concept. This objection also does not ring true. First of all, it is a controversial thesis that it is impossible to quantify over all sets. For one thing, as we have seen earlier,[4] one wonders how by the lights of this position itself the thesis could possibly expressed: What does the universal quantifier in "it is impossible to quantify over all sets" range over? Even if this problem can be overcome, the situation is relevantly different from the case of the notion of truth. In the case of the notion of truth, there was no problem in expressing absolutely general laws of truth; it was just that none of them was true.

This takes us to a more principled response to the worry about the structure of the argument for inferential deflationism. The inference from the absence of general principles about truth to the absence of an essence of the concept of truth is to be seen as an instance of inference to the best explanation rather than as an instance of (elliptic) deductive reasoning. It seems that the absence of general laws of truth is best explained by the absence of an essence of truth. Considerations of best explanation are also what lead me to conclude that truth does not have an essence rather than that truth does have a nature, but one that will forever remain elusive.

Let us finally return to the lives and times of Galilei and Newton. Galilei transformed our conception of force. The mathematization of the concept of force was a way of deflating the concept of force. But heated discussions about the nature of force persisted long after his death and continue on to this day. I suspect that for truth, the situation is no different. Tarski's logical analysis of the concept of truth is deflationary in a way that we found hard to express accurately and precisely.

Tarski reflected on the significance of his own theory of truth, but he did not arrive at a clear conclusion.[5] On the one hand, he described his theory of truth as neutral in substantial philosophical debates. On the other hand, he

---

4. Compare chapter 2, section 2.3.
5. Compare supra, section 2.2.

characterized it as a variant of the correspondence theory of truth. Robert Musil, a contemporary of Tarski, sees perhaps more clearly when he explains how a similar difficulty and ambiguity arises when attempts are made to explicate "Geist" [Musil 1978, Erstes Buch, 40]:[6]

> ... diesen fast stündlich wachsenden Leib von Tatsachen und Entdeckungen, aus dem der Geist heute herausblicken muß, wenn er irgendeine Frage genau betrachten will. Dieser Körper wächst dem Inneren davon. Unzählige Auffassungen, Meinungen, ordnende Gedanken aller Zonen und Zeiten, aller Formen gesunder und kranker, wacher und träumender Hirne durchziehen ihn zwar wie Tausende kleiner empfindlicher Nervenstränge, aber der Strahlpunkt, wo sie sich vereinen, fehlt.

The Tarskian turn will not make the discussion about the nature of truth go away. Perhaps this is as it should be. Foundational discussions about the nature of force have in the long run been highly beneficial for the development of theoretical physics: think about how the discussion about *actio in distans* stimulated the development of the field concept. Let us hope that the continuing discussion about the nature of truth will turn out to be as fruitful in the long run.

---

6. "...this almost continuously growing body of facts and discoveries, from within which the Spirit must look outwards, when it wants to consider any question carefully. This body outgrows the interior. Innumerable conceptions, opinions, regulating thoughts from all places and times, all sorts of awake and dreaming brains pass through it like thousands of small sensitive nerve fibers, but the point of focus, where they join, is missing." [my translation]

Bibliography

[Aquinas 1981] Aquinas, Th. *Summa Theologica*. Christian Classics, 1981.

[Armour-Garb & Beall 2005] Armour-Garb, B., & J Beall, J. (eds) *Deflationary Truth*. Open Court Readings in Philosophy, 2005.

[Armstrong 2004] Armstrong, D. *Truth and Truthmakers*. Cambridge University Press, 2004.

[Barwise & Etchemendy 1987] Barwise, J., & Etchemendy, J. *The Liar: An Essay on Truth and Circularity*. CSLI Publications, 1987.

[Beall 2007] Beall, J. C. (ed) *Revenge of the Liar. New Essays on the Paradox*. Oxford University Press, 2007.

[Beebee & Dodd 2005] Beebee, H., & Dodd, J. (eds) *Truthmakers: The Contemporary Debate*. Oxford University Press, 2005.

[Beall & Armour-Garb 2005] Beall, J. C. & Armour-Garb, B. (eds) *Deflationism and Paradox*. Clarendon Press, 2005.

[Bennett 2003] Bennett, J. *A Philosophical Guide to Conditionals*. Oxford University Press, 2003.

[Blackburn & Simmons 1999] Blackburn, S., & Simmons, K. (eds) *Truth*. Oxford University Press, 1999.

[Boolos & Jeffrey 1989] Boolos, G., & Jeffrey, R. *Computability and Logic*. Third Edition. Cambridge University Press, Cambridge, 1989.

[Brandom 1994] Brandom, R. *Making It Explicit*. Harvard University Press, 1994.

[Brandom 2000] Brandom, R. *Articulating Reasons. An Introduction to Inferentialism*. Harvard University Press, 2000.

[Burge 1979] Burge, T. Semantical Paradox. Reprinted in [Martin 1983, pp. 83–117].

[Burgess 1986] Burgess, J. The Truth Is Never Simple. Journal of Symbolic Logic 51(1986), pp. 663–681.

[Cantini 1990] Cantini, A. A Theory of Formal Truth Arithmetically Equivalent to ID_1. Journal of Symbolic Logic 55(1990), pp. 244–259.

[Cantini 1996] Cantini, A. *Logical Frameworks for Truth and Abstraction*. North-Holland, 1996.

[Carnap 1934] Carnap, R. *Logische Syntax der Sprache*. Julius Springer, 1934.

[Cieśliński 2007] Cieśliński, C. Deflationism, Conservativeness and Maximality. Journal of Philosophical Logic 36(2007), pp. 695–705.

[Davidson 1967] Davidson, D. Truth and Meaning. In [Davidson 1984, pp. 17–36].

[Davidson 1973] Davidson, D. Radical Interpretation. In [Davidson 1984, pp. 125–140].

[Davidson 1984] Davidson, D. *Inquiries Into Truth and Interpretation*. Oxford University Press, 1984.

[Davidson 1990] Davidson, D. The Structure and Content of Truth. Journal of Philosophy 87(1990), pp. 279–328.

[Davidson 1996] Davidson, D. The Folly of Trying to Define Truth. Journal of Philosophy 93(1996), pp. 263–278.

[Douven et al. 2010] Douven, I., Horsten, L., & Romeijn, J.-W. Probabilist Anti-Realism. Pacific Philosophical Quarterly 91(2010), pp. 38–63.

[Enderton 1977] Enderton, H. *Elements of Set Theory*. Academic Press, 1977.

[Feferman 1984] Feferman, S. Towards Useful Type-Free Theories, I. Journal of Symbolic Logic 49(1984), pp. 75–111.

[Feferman 1991] Feferman, S. Reflecting on Incompleteness. Journal of Symbolic Logic 56(1991), pp. 1–49.

[Field 1992] Field, H. Critical Notice: Paul Horwich's "Truth." Philosophy of Science 59(1992), pp. 321–330.

[Field 1994] Field, H. Deflationist Views of Meaning and Content. Reprinted in [Blackburn and Simmons 1999, pp. 351–391].

[Field 1999] Field, H. Deflating the Conservativeness Argument. Journal of Philosophy 96(1999), pp. 533–540.

[Field 2005] Field, H. Is the Liar Sentence Both True and False? In [Beall & Armour-Garb 2005, pp. 23–40].

[Field 2007] Field, H. Solving the Paradoxes, Escaping Revenge. In [Beall 2007, pp. 78–144].

[Field 2008] Field, H. *Saving Truth From Paradox*. Oxford University Press, 2008.

[Fine 1975] Fine, K. Vagueness, Truth and Logic. Synthese 30(1975), pp. 265–300.

[Fischer 2008] Fischer, M. *Davidson's semantisches Programm und deflationäre Wahrheitskonzeptionen*. Ontos Verlag, 2008.

[Fischer 2009] Fischer, M. Minimal Truth and Interpretability. Review of Symbolic Logic 2(2009), pp. 799–815.

[Fischer 2010] Fischer, M. Deflationism and Reducibility. In T. Czarnecki, T. Kijana-Placek, O. Doller & J. Wolenski (eds) The Analytical Way. Proceedings of the 6th European Congress of Analytical Philosophy. College Publications, 2010, pp. 357–369.

[Fischer & Horsten in prep.] Fischer, M., & Horsten, L. Truth and Interpretability. In preparation.

[Fitch 1963] Fitch, F. B. A logical analysis of some value concepts. Journal of Symbolic Logic 28(1963), pp. 135–142.

[Franzen 2004] Franzen, T. *Inexhaustibility: A Non-Exhaustive Treatment*. A. K. Peters, 2004.

[Frege 1918] Frege, G. Die Gedanke. Eine logische Untersuchung. (1918) Reprinted in: *Gottlob Frege, Logische Untersuchungen. Einleitung von Günther Patzig*. Vandenhoeck & Ruprecht, 1966, pp. 30–53.

[Friedman & Sheard 1987] Friedman, H., & Sheard, M. Axiomatic Theories of Self-Referential Truth. Annals of Pure and Applied Logic 33(1987), pp. 1–21.

[Fujimoto 2010] Fujimoto, K. Relative Truth Definability of Axiomatic Truth. Bulletin of Symbolic Logic 16(2010), pp. 305–344.

[Gaifman 1992] Gaifman, H. Pointers to Truth. Journal of Philosophy 89(1992), pp. 223–261.

[Galilei 1638] Galilei, G. *Dialogues Concerning Two New Sciences*. (1638) Translated by Henry Crew & Alfonso de Salvio. Northwestern University Press, 1946.

[Goldstern & Judah 1998] Goldstern, M., & Judah, H. *The Incompleteness Phenomenon. A New Course in Mathematical logic*. A. K. Peters, 1998.

[Greenough & Lynch 2006] Greenough, P., & Lynch, M. (eds) *Truth and Realism*. Oxford University Press, 2006.

[Grover 2001] Grover, D. The Prosentential Theory: Further Reflections on Locating Our Interest in Truth. In [Lynch 2001, pp. 505–526].

[Gupta 1993] Gupta, A. A Critique of Deflationism. Reprinted in [Blackburn & Simmons 1999, pp. 282–307].

Bibliography

[Gupta & Belnap 1993] Gupta, A., & Belnap, N. *The Revision Theory of Truth.* MIT Press, 1993.

[Halbach 1994] Halbach, V. A System of Complete and Consistent Truth. Notre Dame Journal of Formal Logic 35(1994), pp. 311–327.

[Halbach 1996] Halbach, V. *Axiomatische Wahrheitstheorien.* Akademie Verlag, 1996.

[Halbach 1999a] Halbach, V. Conservative Theories of Classical Truth. Studia Logica 62(1999), pp. 353–370.

[Halbach 1999b] Halbach, V. Disquotationalism and Infinite Conjunctions. Mind 108(1999), pp. 1–22.

[Halbach 2001] Halbach, V. How Innocent Is Deflationism? Synthese 26(2001), pp. 167–194.

[Halbach 2009] Halbach, V. Reducing Compositional to Disquotational Truth. Review for Symbolic Logic 2(2009), pp. 786–798.

[Halbach 2010] Halbach, V. *Axiomatic Theories of Truth.* Cambridge University Press, 2010.

[Halbach & Horsten 2002a] Halbach, V., & Horsten, L. (eds) *Principles of Truth.* Hänsel-Hohenhausen, 2002.

[Halbach & Horsten 2002b] Halbach, V., & Horsten, L. *Contemporary Methods for Investigating the Concept of Truth. An Introduction.* In [Halbach & Horsten 2002a, pp. 11–35].

[Halbach & Horsten 2005] Halbach, V., & Horsten, L. The Deflationist's Axioms for Truth. In [Beall & Armour-Garb 2005, pp. 203–217].

[Halbach & Horsten 2006] Halbach, V., & Horsten, L. Axiomatizing Kripke's Theory of Truth. Journal of Symbolic Logic 71(2006), pp. 677–712.

[Heidegger 1943] Heidegger, M. Vom Wesen der Wahrheit. Klosterman, 1943.

[Hellman 1985] Hellman, G. Review of (Kripke 1975) and (Gupta and Belnap 1993). Journal of Symbolic Logic 50(1985), pp. 1068–1071.

[Hempel 1958] Hempel, C. The Theoretician's Dilemma. In H. Feigl et al. (eds) *Minnesota Studies in the Philosophy of Science, II.* University of Minnesota Press, 1958, pp. 37–98.

[Horsten 1995] Horsten, L. The Semantical Paradoxes, the Neutrality of Truth, and the Neutrality of the Minimalist Theory of Truth. In P. Cortois (ed) *The Many Problems of Realism.* Tilburg University Press, 1995, pp. 173–187.

[Horsten 2004] Horsten, L. A Note Concerning the Notion of Satisfiability. Logique et Analyse 185-188(2004), pp. 463–468.

[Horsten 2009] Horsten, L. Levity. Mind 118(2009), pp. 555–581.

[Horsten 2010] Horsten, L. On a Necessary Use of Truth in Epistemology. In T. Czarnecki, K. Kijania-Placek, O. Doller & J. Wolenski (eds) *The Analytical Way. Proceedings of the 6th European Congress of Analytic Philosophy.* College Publications, 2010, pp. 371–376.

[Horsten & Leitgeb 2001] Horsten, L., & Leitgeb, H. No Future. Journal of Philosophical Logic 30(2001), pp. 259–265.

[Horsten et al. in prep.] Horsten, L., Leitgeb, H., & Welch, P. Principles for the Revision Theory of Truth. In preparation.

[Horwich 1998] Horwich, P. *Truth.* Second Edition. Clarendon Press, 1998.

[Horwich 1999] Horwich, P. *Meaning.* Oxford University Press, 1999.

[Horwich 2005] Horwich, P. A Minimalist Critique of Tarski on Truth. In [Beall and Armour-Garb 2005, pp. 75–84].

[James 1907] James, W. Pragmatism's Conception of Truth. In [Blackburn & Simmons 1999, pp. 53–68].

[Ketland 1999] Ketland, J. Deflationism and Tarski's Paradise. Mind 108(1999), pp. 69–94.

[Kirkham 1995] Kirkham, R. *Theories of Truth: An Introduction.* MIT Press, 1995.

[Kotlarski et al. 1981] Kotlarski, H., Krajewski, S., & Lachlan, A. Construction of Satisfaction Classes for Nonstandard Models. Canadian Mathematical Bulletin 24(1981), pp. 283–293.

[Kripke 1975] Kripke, S. (1975) Outline of a Theory of Truth. Reprinted in [Martin 1983, pp. 53–81].

[Kripke 1976] Kripke, S. Is There a Problem With Substitutional Quantification? In G. Evans & J. McDowell (eds) *Truth and Meaning. Essays in Semantics.* Oxford University Press, 1976, pp. 325–419.

[Kripke 1980] Kripke, S. *Naming and Necessity.* Harvard University Press, 1980.

[Kripke 1982] Kripke, S. *Wittgenstein on Following a Rule.* Harvard University Press, 1982.

[Leeds 1978] Leeds, S. Theories of Reference and Truth. Erkenntnis 13(1978), pp. 111–129.

[Leitgeb 2005] Leitgeb, H. What Truth Depends on. Journal of Philosophical Logic 34(2005), pp. 155–192.

[Lindström 1997] Lindström, P. *Aspects of Incompleteness.* Springer, 1997.

[Lynch 2001] M. P. Lynch, (ed) *The Nature of Truth. Classical and Contemporary Perspectives.* MIT Press, 2001.

[Martin 1983] Martin, R. (ed) *Recent Essays on Truth and the Liar Paradox.* Oxford University Press, 1984.

[Martin 2009] Martin, T. Field on Truth. Unpublished manuscript.

[Maudlin 2004] Maudlin, T. *Truth and Paradox. Solving the Riddles.* Oxford University Press, 2004.

[Maudlin 2007] Maudlin, T. Reducing Revenge to Discomfort. In [Beall 2007, pp. 184–196].

[McGee 1985] McGee, V. How Truth-Like Can a Predicate Be? A Negative Result. Journal of Philosophical Logic 14(1985), pp. 399–410.

[McGee 1991] McGee, V. *Truth, Vagueness and Paradox. An Essay on the Logic of Truth.* Hackett, 1991.

[McGee 1992] McGee, V. Maximal Consistent Sets of Instances of Tarski's Schema (T). Journal of Philosophical Logic 21(1992), pp. 235–241.

[McGee 2003] McGee, V. In Praise of the Free Lunch: Why Disquotationalists Should Embrace Compositional Semantics. Unpublished manuscript, 2003, 37 pp.

[Montague 1963] Montague, R. Syntactical Treatments of Modality, With Corollaries on Reflection Principles and Finite Axiomatizability. Acta Philosophica Fennica 16(1963), pp. 153–167.

[Musil 1978] Musil, R. *Der Mann ohne Eigenschaften. 1.* Rohwolt, 1978.

[Newton 1687] Newton, I. *Principia Mathematica Philosophiae Naturalis.* Second Edition.

[Niebergall 2000] Niebergall, K. On the Logic of Reducibility: Axioms and Examples. Erkenntnis 53(2000), pp. 27–62.

[Patterson 2002] Patterson, D. Theories of Truth and Convention T. Philosopher's Imprint 2(2002), pp. 1–16.

[Peirce 1978] Peirce, C. S. *Collected Papers* (edited by C. Hartshorne, P. Weiss, & A. Burks). Harvard University Press, 1978.

[Prawitz 1978] Prawitz, D. Proofs and the Meaning and Completeness of the Logical Constants. In J. Hintikka et al. (eds) *Essays in Mathematical and Philosophical Logic.* Reidel, 1978, pp. 25–39.

[Priest 1987] Priest, G. *In Contradiction.* Kluwer, 1987.

[Priest 2005] Priest, G. Spiking the Field-Artillery. In [Beall & Armour-Garb 2005, pp. 41–52].

[Priest & Beall 2004] Priest, G., & Beall, J. C. (eds) *The Law of Non-Contradiction: New Philosophical Essays.* Oxford University Press, 2004.

[Quine 1936] Quine, W. V. O. Truth by Convention. Reprinted in [Quine 1966, pp. 77–106].

[Quine 1946] Quine, W. V. O. Concatenation as a Basis for Arithmetic. Journal of Symbolic Logic 10(1946), pp. 105–114.

[Quine 1961] Quine, W. V. O. The Ways of Paradox. Reprinted in [Quine 1966, pp. 1–18].

Bibliography

[Quine 1966] Quine, W. V. O. *The Ways of Paradox and Other Essays. Revised and Enlarged Edition*. Harvard University Press, 1966.

[Quine 1970] Quine, W. V. O. *Philosophy of Logic*. Prentice Hall, 1970.

[Ramsey 1927] Ramsey, F. Facts and Propositions. In R. Braithwaite (ed) *The Foundations of Mathematics and other Logical Essays*. Kegan Paul, 1931, pp. 138–155.

[Reinhardt 1986] Reinhardt, W. Some Remarks on Extending and Interpreting Theories With a Partial Predicate for Truth. Journal of Philosophical Logic 15(1986), pp. 219-251.

[Rescher 1982] Rescher, N. *The Coherence Theory of Truth*. University of America Press, 1982.

[Restall 1994] Restall, G. *On Logics Without Contraction*. PhD dissertation. University of Queensland, 1994.

[Rogers 1967] Rogers, H. *Theory of Rercursive Functions and Effective Computability*. MIT Press, 1967.

[Shakespeare 1600] Shakespeare, W. *Hamlet*. Edited by E. Braunmuller. Penguin, 2001.

[Shapiro 1991] Shapiro, S. *Foundations Without Foundationalism: A Case for Second-Order Logic*. Clarendon Press, 1991.

[Shapiro 1998] Shapiro, S. Proof and Truth: Through Thick and Thin. Journal of Philosophy 95(1998), pp. 493–521.

[Shapiro 2002] Shapiro, S. Deflation and conservation. In [Halbach & Horsten 2002a, pp. 103–128].

[Sheard 2001] Sheard, M. Weak and Strong Theories of Truth. Studia Logica 68(2001), pp. 89–101.

[Simmons 2007] Simmons, K. Revenge and Context. In [Beall 2007, pp. 345–367].

[Smullyan 1957] Smullyan, R. Languages in Which Self-Reference Is Possible. Journal of Symbolic Logic 22(1957), pp. 55–67.

[Soames 1999] Soames, S. *Understanding Truth*. Oxford University Press, 1999.

[Strawson 1950] Strawson, P. On Referring. Mind 59(1950), pp. 320–344.

[Sundholm 1983] Systems of Deduction. In D. Gabbay & F. Guenthner (eds) *Handbook of Philosophical Logic. Volume 1*. Reidel, 1983, pp. 133–188.

[Tarski 1935] Tarski, A. The Concept of Truth in Formalized Languages In [Tarski 1983, pp. 152–278].

[Tarski 1936] Tarski, A. The Establishment of Scientific Semantics. In [Tarski 1983, pp. 401–408].

[Tarski 1944] Tarski, A. The Semantic Conception of Truth and the Foundations of Semantics. Philosophy and Phenomenological Research 4(1944), pp. 341–375.

[Tarski 1969] Tarski, A. Truth and Proof. Scientific American (June 1969), pp. 63–77.

[Tarski 1983] Tarski, A. *Logic, Semantics, Meta-Mathematics*. Translated by J. H. Woodger. Second, Revised Edition. Hackett, 1983.

[Welch 2001] Welch, P. On Gupta-Belnap Revision Theories of Truth, Kripkean Fixed Points, and the Next Stable Set. Bulletin of Symbolic Logic 7(2001), pp. 345–360.

[Williams 1988] Williams, M. Epistemological Realism and the Basis of Skepticism. Mind 97(1988), pp. 415–439.

[Williamson 1994] Williamson, T. *Vagueness*. Routledge, 1994.

[Williamson 2000] Williamson, T. *Knowledge and Its Limits*. Oxford University Press, 2000.

[Williamson 2006] Williamson, T. Must Do Better. In [Greenough & Lynch 2006, pp. 177–187].

[Wittgenstein 1958] Wittgenstein, L. *Philosophical Investigations*. Blackwell, 1958.

[Wodehouse 1930] Wodehouse, P. G. Jeeves and the Impending Doom. In P. G. Wodehouse. *Very Good, Jeeves*. Vintage, 1995, pp. 11–31.

[Yablo 1982] Yablo, S. Grounding, Dependence, and Paradox. Journal of Philosophical Logic 11(1982), pp. 117–137.

Glossary

$=:$	equality by definition
$\Box$	necessity operator
$\Diamond$	possibility operator
ϵ_0	supremum of the collection $\{\omega, \omega^\omega, \omega^{\omega^\omega}, \ldots\}$
$\exists$	existential quantifier
$\forall \vec{x}$	finite list of quantifiers $\forall x_1, \forall x_2, \ldots$
$\forall$	universal quantifier
$\ulcorner \ldots \urcorner$	gödel code
$\leftrightarrow$	material equivalence
$\mathbb{N}$	natural numbers structure
K	minimal modal logic
$\mathcal{L}^-$	(nonspecific) language without truth predicate
$\mathcal{L}$	formal language
$\mathcal{L}_{PA}$	language of Peano arithmetic
$\mathcal{L}_T$	language of truth
$\mathfrak{M}$	model
$\models$	classical logical consequence relation
$\models_{sk}$	strong Kleene consequence relation
$\neg$	negation
ω_1^{CK}	first nonrecursive ordinal number
$\overline{n}$	standard numeral
$\vec{x}$	list of variables $x_1, x_2, \ldots$
$\phi(n/x)$	result of substituting all free occurrences of x by n
Π_n	equivalent to prenex normal formula with n alternating quantifiers, of which the first one is universal
$\rightarrow$	material implication
$\rightarrowtail$	Field's conditional operator
$\rightleftharpoons$	Field's biconditional operator
Σ_n	equivalent to prenex normal formula with n alternating quantifiers of which the first one is existential
$\vdash$	classical first-order logical derivability

$\vee$	disjunction
$\wedge$	conjunction
$a*b$	concatenation of the sequences a and b
Bew	property of being provable in a formal system
Con	property of consistency
$D(\ldots)$	property of determinate truth
den	denotation relation
K	it is known that
Sat	relation of being true of (satisfaction)
T_1	truth predicate for $\mathcal{L}_T$
tot	property of truth-determinateness
val^+	true atomic arithmetical formula
val^-	false atomic arithmetical formula
T	truth predicate

Author Index

Aquinus, Th., 11
Aristotle, 11
Armour-Garb, B., 6
Armstrong, D., 12

Barwise, J., 57
Beall, J. C., 6, 24, 124
Beebee, H., 12
Belnap, N., 20, 105, 112
Bennett, J., 25
Blackburn, S., 2
Boolos, G., 7, 28, 30, 32
Brandom, R., 92, 147
Burge, T., 56, 58
Burgess, J., 122

Cantini, A., 26, 97, 131, 139, 142
Carnap, R., 143
Cieśliński, 82
Craig, W., 130

Davidson, D., 67, 71, 92
Decock, L., xii
Dodd, J., 12
Douven, I., xii, 14, 91

Enderton, H., 7, 73
Etchemendy, J., 57
Everett, A., xii

Feferman, S., 124, 126, 135, 148, 150
Field, H., 21, 24, 65, 67, 71, 79, 80, 82, 83, 144–146
Fine, K., 25, 72
Fischer, M., xii, 92, 94, 95, 97
Fitch, F., 87
Franzen, T., 10, 32
Frege, G., 17, 65
Friedman, H., 103, 104, 108
Fujimoto, K., 95

Gaifman, H., 57
Galilei, G., 14, 151
Galinon, H., xii, 55
Gödel, K., 7, 22, 27, 28, 31, 32, 34
Goldstern, M., 7, 27–30, 35
Greenough, P., 64
Grover, D., 2
Gupta, A., 20, 60, 61, 105, 112, 147

Halbach, V., xi, 25, 26, 64, 76, 78, 80, 81, 92, 98, 100, 104, 108, 109, 111, 132, 138
Heidegger, M., 15
Hellman, G., 123
Hempel, C., 130
Horsten, L., xi, 41, 74, 79, 111, 115, 132, 138
Horwich, P., 1, 4, 49, 50, 62, 67, 86, 90, 92

James, W., 12
Jeffrey, R., 7, 28, 30, 32
Judah, H., 7, 27–30, 35

Kant, I., 64
Ketland, J., xii, 25, 80, 82
Kirkham, R., 6
Kotlarski, H., 78
Kripke, S., 6, 8, 20, 55, 61, 88, 117, 120, 123, 124, 126, 129, 132, 137, 139, 144, 147

Laughlin, P., xii
Leeds, S., 85
Leibniz, G. W. F., 28, 81
Leitgeb, H., 41, 115, 123
Lindström, P., 94
Linnebo, Ø., xii
Löwenthal, M., xii
Lynch, M., 64

Martin, T., 130
Maudlin, T., 127

McGee, V., 21, 49, 83, 98, 109, 110, 129, 135, 136, 139
Montague, R., 39
Musil, R., 152

Newton, I., 14, 19, 151
Niebergall, K.-G., xii, 94

Patterson, D., 18, 70
Peirce, C. S., 12, 13
Prawitz, D., 143
Priest, G., 24, 25

Quine, W.V.O., 14, 23, 50, 63, 67, 136, 143, 144

Ramsey, F., 15, 63
Reinhardt, W., 126, 128–130, 132, 144
Rescher, N., 12
Restall, G., 137
Rogers, H., 120
Rosser, J., 32
Russell, B., 21, 56

Shakespeare, W., 77
Shapiro, S., 79, 82, 85
Sheard, M., 103, 104, 108, 114, 115
Simmons, K., 57
Smullyan, R., 23
Sneyers, J., xii
Soames, S., 144
Strawson, P., 25, 73
Sundholm, G., 132

Tarski, A., 1, 7, 15, 16, 18–22, 26, 27, 35, 47–49, 53, 55, 57, 60, 69, 71, 74, 144, 151

Urbaniak, J., xii

van Fraassen, B., 123, 139

Welch, P., xii, 115
Weyl, H., 113
Williams, M., 61
Williamson, T., 5, 13, 72, 87, 128
Wittgenstein, L., 16, 61
Wodehouse, P. G., 2

Yablo, S., 123

Zermelo, E., 86, 137

Subject Index

ACA, 100
ACA_1, 113
ACA_{ϵ_0}, 126
ACA_ω, 113
ACA_{ω^ω}, 138
$COND$, 132
$CONEC$, 104
$DIST$, 88
DT, 50
DT_1, 54
$FACT$, 88
FI, 89
FS, 104
IKF, 129
K, 88
KF, 124
NEC, 104
NP, 40
NT, 38
PA, 29
PA^2, 99
PA^T, 37
PKF, 132
PT^-, 96
$PUTB$, 98
$RCOND$, 133
RKF, 130
S_1, 114
SV, 87
SV^*, 89
TC, 71
TC_1, 77
TC_{ϵ_0}, 126
TC_ω, 111
VF, 139
WV, 87
WV^*, 89
ZFC, 62

anti-extension, 117
anti-realist truth theory, 12

axiomatic truth theory, 3, 20

bounded truth predicate, 41

Cantor's theorem, 7
categorical theory, 85
classes
  virtual, 149
closing off, 121
co-necessitation rule
  for truth, 104
coding, 23
coherence theory, 12
completeness
  truth-theoretic, 25
completeness theorem, 34
compositionality intuition, 72
compositional theory of truth, 71
comprehension scheme
  arithmetical, 100
  full, 99
  naive, 137
conceptual reducibility, 94
conditionalization, 132
  restricted, 133
conservativeness, 74
  arithmetical, 75, 82
  generalized, 80
  ideological, 82
  ontological, 82
  over epistemology, 86
  over logic, 81
  over metaphysics, 85
  over science, 85
  second-order, 85
  semantical, 80
consistent, 31
correspondence theory, 11
  Tarski on, 16

Davidson's semantic program, 92
deduction theorem, 18
deflationism, 59
derivability, 34
derivability conditions, 33
determinate truth, 146
diagonal function, 30
diagonal lemma, 30
　extended, 37
　strengthened, 30
　strengthened extended, 37
dialetheism, 6, 24
disjunctive normal form, 41
disquotational intuition, 17, 37, 137
disquotationalism, 50, 97–99
disquotational theory of truth, 50, 63
　proof-theoretic strength, 69

extension, 117

Field-biconditional, 145
first incompleteness theorem, 31
Fitch's argument, 87
formalized modus ponens, 145

global reflection principle, 76
gödel code, 28
gödel number, 28
gödel sentence, 31
groundedness, 123

Hilbert's program, 93

inconsistency, 24
　ω-inconsistency, 109
　diachronic, 107
inferential deflationism, 4, 147
inner logic, 129
iterative conception of sets, 137

Knower paradox, 40
knowledge
　traditional analysis of, 86

least fixed point model, 120
liar paradox, 18
　diagnosis of, 50
　formalized, 38
liar sentence, 36
　strengthened, 58
Löb's lemma, 34
logic
　multivalued, 6
　partial, 5
　second-order, 84
logical consequence, 34
Luxemburger Zirkel, xii

material adequacy condition, 48
mathematical induction, 29
　expressed in one sentence, 63
　second-order, 84
meaning, 91
　inferential theories of, 92
metalanguage, 47
metatheory, 48
Metawissenschaft, 48
minimalism, 4
model
　nice, 51
　minimal, 52
　partial, 118
monotonicity, 119
Montague's theorem, 39

naive theory of truth, 38
name
　quotational, 48
　structural-descriptive, 48
natural deduction, 143
nearly stable truth, 106
necessitation rule
　of modal logic, 39
　for truth, 40, 104
necessity
　operator, 41
　predicate, 41
nonconservativeness phenomenon, 84

objectlanguage, 47

paradox of informal provability, 40
paradox of necessity, 40
Peano arithmetic, 29
　second-order, 99
Pilate's question, 15
positive occurrence, 98
power game, 101, 111, 115
power set, 7
pragmatic theory, 12
predicative analysis, 148
predicative number theory, 113
predicativism, 100
prenex normal form, 41
presupposition, 73
proposition, 67

quantification
　objectual, 88
　over everything, 21, 151
　propositional, 88

redundancy theory of truth, 56
reflexive truth theory, 103
reflexivity axiom, 40

Subject Index

relative interpretability, 94
revision theory of truth, 105
rule-following, 147
rule of assertion, 127
Russell's paradox, 137

satisfaction relation, 74
scheme, 64
second incompleteness theorem, 32
self-reference, 23
  coherence of, 18
semantically closed truth theory, 103
semantic truth theory, 3, 20
semi-classical truth theory, 142
soundness, 24, 31
  arithmetical, 52, 110
stable truth, 106
standard numeral, 28
strengthened liar problem, 124, 144
strong Kleene scheme, 118
strong verificationism, 87
substantial truth theory, 11, 59
substitution function, 43
supervaluation scheme, 123

Tarskian hierarchy, 54
Tarski-biconditionals, 3, 17, 37
Tarski's Angels, xii
  restricted, 50
theory, 9, 32
total, 96
translation
  from object- to metalanguage, 47, 67
true of, 74
truth
  as a disquotational device, 63
  as a logical notion, 65
  as a logico-linguistic notion, 65
  as a logico-mathematical notion, 65
  bearer of, 2
  blind ascriptions, 63
  compositional nature of, 70
  definition of, 19, 48
  essence of, 15, 148
  expressive power of, 64
  function of, 63
    negative, 64
    positive, 63
  laws of, 148
  meaning of, 61
  nature of, 148, 150
  property, 2
  redundancy of, 63
  reflexive, 8
  simplicity of, 62
  uniformity of, 55

truth-definability, 95
truth-determinate, 96
truth-iteration, 8, 53
truthmaker, 12, 96
truth-teller sentence, 122
typed truth theory, 103

undefinability theorem, 35
  strengthened, 36
  strengthened extended, 38
untyped truth theory, 103

vagueness, 72, 97, 139
vicious circle principle, 100

weak verificationism, 87